# Great Britain Travel Guide

# How to have a LUXURY trip to Great Britain on a BUDGET

"This sceptred isle, this earth of majesty, this seat of Mars, this other Eden." William Shakespeare's play "King Richard II.

# The Magical Power of Bargains

Have you ever felt the rush of getting a bargain? And then found good fortune just keeps following you?

Let me give you an example. In 2009, I graduated into the worst global recession for generations. One unemployed day, I saw a suit I knew I could get a job in. The suit was £250. Money I didn't have. Imagine my shock when the next day I saw the exact same suit (in my size) in the window of a second-hand shop (thrift store) for £18! I bought the suit and after three months of interviewing, without a single call back, within a week of owning that £18 suit, I was hired on a salary far above my expectations. That's the powerful psychological effect of getting an incredible deal. It builds a sense of excitement and happiness that literally creates miracles.

I have no doubt that from the towering majesty of Buckingham Palace and the mystical charm of Stonehenge will uplift and inspire you but when you add the bargains from this book to your vacation, not only will you save a ton of money; you are guaranteed to enjoy a truly magical trip to UK.

# Welcome to your guide to a Luxury Trip to UK on a budget!

Welcome to your ultimate guide to experiencing a Luxury Trip to the UK on a budget! In this comprehensive travel manual, we'll show you how to seamlessly blend luxury with budget options, unlocking top-notch accommodations, savoring the finest culinary delights, and indulging in once-in-a-lifetime experiences across the UK—all at a fraction of the typical cost.

Luxury, often associated with first or business class flights, five-star hotels, chauffeur services, exclusive experiences, and exquisite fine dining, can indeed be enjoyed without breaking the bank. This guide is designed to make your journey towards luxury travel in the UK accessible through strategic research and meticulous planning, saving you tens of thousands in the process.

Packed with local insider tips and knowledge, this book aims to debunk any misconceptions surrounding luxury travel. If thoughts like "Money doesn't grow on trees," or "I don't need anything fancy" have crossed your mind, it's time to reconsider. Studies have shown that luxury travel offers more than just material indulgence:

- **Reduced Stress:** Research in the Journal of Travel Research reveals that individuals staying in luxury hotels reported lower stress levels compared to those in standard accommodations.
- **Increased Happiness:** The International Journal of Tourism Research found that luxury travel experiences contribute to heightened happiness and overall life satisfaction. Such experiences can also enhance mental health by providing an escape from daily stressors, fostering relaxation and rejuvenation.
- **Enhanced Creativity:** Engaging in luxury travel experiences has been shown to stimulate creativity and foster more innovative thinking.

While the benefits of luxury travel are evident, you don't have to sacrifice your savings to enjoy them. This guide will demonstrate how you can achieve increased happiness and well-being without depleting your bank account. It's time to embark on a luxurious journey through the UK without compromise—your ultimate guide awaits!

## Who this book is for and why anyone can enjoy luxury travel on a budget

Did you know you can fly on a private jet for $500? Yes, a fully private jet. Complete with flutes of champagne and reclinable creamy leather seats. Your average billionaire spends $20,000 on the exact same flight. You can get it for $500 when you book private jet empty leg flights. This is just one of thousands of ways you can travel luxuriously on a budget. You see there is a big difference between being cheap and frugal.

When our brain hears the word "budget" it hears deprivation, suffering, agony, even depression. But budget travel need not be synonymous with hostels and pack lunches. You can enjoy an incredible and luxurious trip to UK on a budget, just like you can enjoy a private jet flight for 10% of the normal cost when you know how.

Over 20 years of travel has taught me I could have a 20 cent experience that will stir my soul more than a $100 one. Of course, sometimes the reverse is true, my point is, spending money on travel is the best investment you can make but it doesn't have to be at levels set by hotels and attractions with massive ad spends and influencers who are paid small fortunes to get you to buy into something you could have for a fraction of the cost.

This book is for those who love bargains and want to have the cold hard budget busting facts to hand (which is why we've included so many one page charts, which you can use as a quick reference), but otherwise, the book provides plenty of tips to help you shape your own UK experience.

We have designed these travel guides to give you a unique planning tool to experience an unforgettable trip without spending the ascribed tourist budget.

This guide focuses on UK's unbelievable bargains. Of course, there is little value in traveling to UK and not experiencing everything it has to offer. Where possible, we've included super cheap workarounds or listed the experience in the Loved but Costly section.

When it comes to luxury budget travel, it's all about what you know. You can have all the feels without most of the bills. A few days spent planning can save you thousands. Luckily, we've done the planning for you, so you can distill the information in minutes not days, leaving you to focus on what matters: immersing yourself in the sights, sounds and smells of UK, meeting awesome new people and feeling relaxed and happy.

This book reads like a good friend has travelled the length and breadth of UK and brought you back incredible insider tips.

So, grab a cup of tea or coffee, put your feet up and relax; you're about to enter the world of enjoying UK on the Super Cheap. Oh, and don't forget a biscuit. You need energy to plan a trip of a lifetime on a budget.

# Discover the UK

Welcome to the United Kingdom, a land steeped in history, brimming with diverse landscapes, and alive with the vibrant energy of its people. Whether you're drawn to the bustling streets of London, the serene landscapes of the Lake District, or the charming villages of the Cotswolds, the UK has something for every traveler. And guess what? You don't need a royal budget to experience the best of this enchanting kingdom.

In this guide, we're about to embark on a journey together—a journey that will prove you can have a £10,000 trip to the UK for just £1,000. How, you ask? Through a treasure trove of local hacks, insider secrets, and budget-friendly adventures that will open up the UK like never before.

Before we dive into the heart of the UK, let's talk about the art of budgeting. A trip to the UK doesn't have to break the bank, and with a few savvy money-saving strategies blended with budget choices, you can make every pound stretch farther than you ever thought possible.

Forget about the standard hotel experience. We'll show you how to find charming bed and breakfasts, and unique alternatives like staying in an Oxford College or even a castle. Your accommodation will not only be a place to rest but an integral part of your immersive travel experience.

**Savvy Transportation**

Navigating the UK doesn't have to be a drain on your budget. You can save thousands on trains by booking ahead and if you're more spontaneous, buses are available for a fraction of the train costs. You'll be weaving through the charming countryside and cityscapes without worrying about breaking the bank.

## Culinary Adventures on a Budget

Indulge your taste buds without burning a hole in your pocket. We'll guide you to the local markets, hidden eateries, and culinary treasures that will leave you savoring the flavors of the UK without the hefty price tag.

## Embracing the Local Culture

Immerse yourself in the heart and soul of the UK by embracing its rich cultural tapestry. From free museum days to local festivals, you'll discover a wealth of experiences that won't cost you a penny.

The first thing you'll notice is that the Brits have mastered the art of queuing; it's practically a national sport. So, join the orderly lines and embrace the politeness – it's like a cultural dance where everyone knows the steps.

Now, let's talk about tea, shall we? Tea isn't just a beverage here; it's a ceremony, a remedy, and a daily ritual. Don't be surprised if someone offers you a cuppa in times of joy, sorrow, or just because it's 4 o'clock. And speaking of time, the UK has a love affair with history. Every cobblestone seems to whisper tales of kings, queens, and that one eccentric uncle who wore questionable hats. So, wander through the charming streets, soak in the stories, and try not to get lost in the captivating blend of tradition and quirkiness.

Traveling to the UK isn't just a journey; it's a whimsical adventure through a land where manners matter, tea is sacred, and history lives in every corner. And Luxury on a budget in the UK isn't just about pounds and pence; it's about embracing the eccentric, finding the humor in the mundane, and realizing that the true treasures are often hidden in the cobblestone alleys and the whispers of ancient stones. Welcome to the UK, where even the rain has a story to tell, and every visit is a page-turner in the grand novel of British life.

So, pack your bags and grab your brolly (umbrella)– we're delving into the delightful world of traveling to the UK Luxury on a budget style.

# What you need to know before you go

- **Weather Variability:** Be prepared for unpredictable weather. The UK is known for rain, so pack layers, a waterproof jacket, and an umbrella. But don't forget sunglasses—there are sunny days too!
- **Currency:** The currency is the British Pound (£). Credit cards are widely accepted, but it's advisable to carry some cash, especially in rural areas or for small purchases.
- **Public Transportation:** The UK has an extensive public transportation system, including trains and buses. Consider purchasing an Oyster card in London for convenient travel on public transport.
- **Plug Adapters:** The UK uses a different type of electrical outlet (Type G). Ensure you have the right plug adapter to charge your devices.
- **Driving on the Left:** If you plan to rent a car, remember that the UK drives on the left side of the road. Take extra care when crossing streets and familiarize yourself with road signs.
- **Cultural Sensitivity:** The UK is diverse, and it's essential to be culturally sensitive. Respect local customs, queue patiently, and use "please" and "thank you" liberally—it goes a long way.
- **Emergency Services:** The emergency number is 999. Familiarize yourself with this and the local emergency services wherever you go.
- **Tipping Etiquette:** Tipping is customary in restaurants, and it's common to leave around 10-15% of the bill if service is not included. Tipping in pubs is less formal but appreciated.
- **Free Entry to Museums:** Many museums and galleries offer free entry, particularly in London. Take advantage of this to explore the country's rich history and art without breaking the bank.
- **Queuing Culture:** Brits are known for their orderly queuing (standing in line) habits. Respect the queue, and you'll seamlessly blend into the local culture.
- **Healthcare:** If you're from a country without a reciprocal healthcare agreement, consider travel insurance that covers medical expenses. The National Health Service (NHS) provides healthcare for residents but not necessarily for tourists.
- **Countryside Exploration:** Venture beyond the cities to explore the picturesque countryside. From the Lake District to the Cotswolds, the UK offers stunning natural landscapes and charming villages.
- **Language Differences:** While English is the primary language, accents and regional dialects can vary widely. Don't hesitate to ask for clarification if you encounter unfamiliar terms or phrases.
- **Time Zones:** The UK is in Greenwich Mean Time (GMT) during the winter and British Summer Time (BST) during the summer. Be aware of the time difference when planning activities or flights.
- **Pubs and Local Cuisine:** Enjoy the local cuisine, and don't miss the experience of a traditional pub. Pubs are not just for drinks; they often serve delicious meals and offer a cozy atmosphere.

# Some of the UK's Best Bargains

# Sleep in a Castle

The United Kingdom boasts approximately 1,500 castles, a testament to its rich historical tapestry and strategic importance. Originating as medieval defensive fortifications during periods of political turmoil, castles played a vital role in the Norman Conquest's feudal system and in guarding border regions like the Welsh Marches. Evolving beyond mere fortifications, many castles transformed into royal residences, symbols of aristocratic prestige, and enduring icons of cultural heritage. From the tumultuous times of the English Civil War to periods of social hierarchy, these castles stand today as architectural marvels, each narrating a unique story of power, prestige, and historical significance. Staying in a castle can be a unique and memorable experience, and there are ways to do it more affordably. Here are a few options:

YHA St Briavels Castle (Gloucestershire):

*Approximate Cost:* Prices at YHA St Briavels Castle vary, with dormitory beds starting from £20-£30 per night.

Tucked within the historic landscapes of Gloucestershire, YHA St Briavels Castle offers budget-friendly accommodation within the medieval walls of a castle. The hostel experience, complete with shared facilities, adds a communal touch and a dash of adventure to your stay.

Safestay Edinburgh (Edinburgh Castle):

*Approximate Cost:* Dormitory beds at Safestay Edinburgh start from £15-£30 per night.

Although not nestled within Edinburgh Castle itself, Safestay Edinburgh resides in a historic building, providing an affordable lodging option in proximity to this iconic site. Immerse yourself in the city's rich history while relishing the camaraderie of fellow travelers.

Belle Isle Castle (County Fermanagh, Northern Ireland):

*Approximate Cost:* Self-catering accommodation in the converted courtyard at Belle Isle Castle starts from around £50-£80 per night.

Opt for a unique stay at Belle Isle Castle in Northern Ireland. Departing from the traditional hotel format, it offers affordable self-catering apartments within the castle's converted courtyard, allowing you to soak in the charm.

Dalhousie Castle (Edinburgh):

*Approximate Cost:* Prices at Dalhousie Castle can vary, but it's possible to find deals starting from £100-£150 per night.

Providing a touch of luxury, Dalhousie Castle in Edinburgh offers a more upscale experience compared to some budget options. Keep an eye out for competitive rates during specific times of the year, as this castle invites you to indulge in a regal ambiance.

Amberley Castle (West Sussex):
*Approximate Cost:* Prices at Amberley Castle can vary, with occasional deals offering rates around £150-£200 per night.
For those seeking a refined experience, Amberley Castle in West Sussex presents an upscale option. While pricing may lean toward the higher end, be vigilant for promotions or off-peak pricing to maximize your experience in this elegant retreat.

Tips for Budget Castle Stays:

* Look for mid-week or off-season deals, as prices tend to be lower.
* Consider booking directly through the castle's website or contacting them to inquire about special offers.
* Check for last-minute deals or promotions on travel booking platforms.

# Enjoy Michelin Starred Menus

While Michelin-starred restaurants are known for their exceptional cuisine, the prices be high but there are a few Michelin-starred restaurants in the UK that are relatively affordable for a set menu:

**Dabbous, London:**

Nestled in the heart of London, Dabbous offers a culinary journey through Modern European cuisine. With an innovative approach to flavors and presentation, the restaurant has earned a reputation for its contemporary and artistic dishes. The set lunch menu, priced around £35 to £40, invites diners to savor the chef's creations in a stylish and minimalist setting, making Dabbous a destination for those seeking a modern gastronomic experience.

**Galvin La Chapelle, London:**

Embark on a culinary adventure at Galvin La Chapelle, an elegant French restaurant in London. Boasting a Michelin-starred reputation, Galvin La Chapelle presents a set lunch menu starting around £35 to £40, allowing patrons to indulge in the refined flavors of French cuisine. The restaurant's stunning architecture, housed within a former Victorian chapel, adds to the overall ambiance, creating a sophisticated and memorable dining experience.

**Lyle's, London:**

At Lyle's in London, diners can immerse themselves in the essence of Modern British cuisine. Known for its commitment to seasonal and locally sourced ingredients, Lyle's offers a set lunch menu starting around £45 to £50. The culinary creations reflect a contemporary take on British flavors, making it a favorite among those who appreciate inventive and thoughtfully crafted dishes in a welcoming and unpretentious atmosphere.

**Star Inn, Harome:**

Situated in the picturesque village of Harome, the Star Inn is a beacon of Modern British cuisine. The restaurant's set lunch menu, starting around £30 to £40, showcases the culinary prowess of its chefs, emphasizing the use of high-quality, locally-sourced ingredients. With a cozy and inviting ambiance, the Star Inn invites diners to enjoy a taste of the British countryside in a charming and historic setting.

**Moor Hall, Ormskirk:**

Moor Hall in Ormskirk stands as a testament to the artistry of Modern British cuisine. The restaurant, housed in a beautifully restored country manor, offers a set lunch menu starting around £60 to £70. Guests can expect an exquisite culinary experience that harmonizes innovative techniques with the flavors of the region. Moor Hall's dedication to culinary excellence and its idyllic surroundings make it a destination for discerning food enthusiasts.

**Trinity, London:**

Trinity, located in London, is a haven for aficionados of Modern European cuisine. The restaurant's set lunch menu, priced around £35 to £40, features a carefully curated selection of dishes that showcase both creativity and culinary finesse. With a welcoming atmosphere and an emphasis on seasonal ingredients, Trinity offers a delightful dining experience that reflects the richness of European gastronomy.

**Hinds Head, Bray:**

In the charming village of Bray, Hinds Head offers a taste of quintessential British cuisine. With a menu rooted in traditional flavors and culinary heritage, the restaurant presents a set lunch menu starting around £30 to £40. Hinds Head, set in a historic building with a cozy interior, provides a warm and inviting ambiance for guests to enjoy classic British dishes crafted with modern flair.

# Get Spa Deals

The UK's love affair with spa and thermal waters runs deep, tracing its roots back to Roman times when bathing became a cultural norm. Today, this passion endures and has evolved into a modern wellness movement. Brits seek respite from the daily grind, making spas a go-to destination for relaxation and rejuvenation. The allure isn't just about pampering; it's grounded in the belief in the health benefits of thermal waters, with many embracing the therapeutic properties of mineral-rich springs. From historic spa towns like Bath to contemporary wellness retreats, the UK boasts a diverse array of spa destinations, each offering a soothing escape from the hustle and bustle of everyday life. Finding affordable spa deals in the UK is super easy with these two strategies:

**Daily Deal Websites: Check daily deal websites like Groupon, Wowcher, or LivingSocial for discounted spa packages. They often offer deals on treatments, spa days, and overnight stays.**

**Off-Peak Bookings: Many spas offer lower rates during off-peak hours or on weekdays.**

# Stay in a Lighthouse

The United Kingdom has approximately 160 lighthouses, each a stoic guardian standing sentinel along its rugged coasts. These iconic structures, steeped in maritime lore, serve as beacons of safety for seafarers navigating treacherous waters. With origins dating back centuries, these lighthouses have weathered storms and guided countless ships to safety, embodying a maritime legacy etched into the very fabric of the UK's coastal identity. Beyond their practical purpose, these lighthouses are symbols of resilience, their enduring beams casting a light on the nation's maritime history and unwavering commitment to safeguarding those who brave the open sea.

Here are a few lighthouses where you can find accommodation options, along with approximate prices:

- **St. Catherine's Lighthouse, Isle of Wight:**
  - **Description:** Located on the southernmost point of the Isle of Wight, offering self-catering accommodation.
  - **Approximate Prices:** Prices may vary, but self-catering options could range from £100 to £200 per night.
- **Dungeness Lighthouse, Kent:**
  - **Description:** Situated on the unique Dungeness headland, this lighthouse offers self-catering accommodation.
  - **Approximate Prices:** Prices may range from £100 to £200 per night.
- **Trevose Head Lighthouse, Cornwall:**
  - **Description:** Located on the rugged Cornish coast, offering self-catering accommodation.
  - **Approximate Prices:** Prices could range from £100 to £200 per night.
- **Nash Point Lighthouse, Vale of Glamorgan:**
  - **Description:** A working lighthouse with self-catering accommodation along the South Wales coastline.
  - **Approximate Prices:** Prices may range from £100 to £200 per night.
  -

# Explore Storied Pubs

Raise a pint to the beating heart of British social life—the pub. Steeped in history and camaraderie, these iconic establishments have been woven into the fabric of British culture for centuries. From the rustic alehouses of yore to the bustling urban pubs of today, these havens offer more than just drinks—they're living chronicles of community, storytelling, and conviviality. Step into the past where pubs doubled as meeting places for revolutionaries, poets, and thinkers. Explore the evolution from coaching inns to gastro pubs, each pint echoing tales of resilience, celebration, and the simple joy of coming together. Uncover the significance of the local pub, where every nook holds a story and every pour is a nod to the enduring spirit of a nation that knows how to savor life. Here are some iconic literary pubs worth exploring:

**The Eagle (Cambridge, England):**

Steeped in scientific history, The Eagle in Cambridge is where the groundbreaking announcement of the DNA discovery was made by Francis Crick and James Watson, marking a pivotal moment in the world of genetics.

**The Lamb and Flag (London, England):**

With a rich literary connection, The Lamb and Flag in London holds ties to Charles Dickens, who was a regular patron, making it a historic haven for those who appreciate the literary greats.

**The George Inn (London, England):**

Immersed in the pages of Charles Dickens' "Little Dorrit," The George Inn in London is not just a pub; it's a living testament to the words of Dickens, where the ambiance echoes the literary world.

**The Grapes (London, England):**

A haunt favored by Charles Dickens himself, The Grapes in London has earned its place in literature, featuring prominently in his novel "Our Mutual Friend." The pub's historical charm resonates with the echoes of Dickensian London.

**The Crown (Belfast, Northern Ireland):**

In Belfast, The Crown holds more than just pints and conversations. It was a regular haunt for Seamus Heaney, the Nobel Prize-winning poet, infusing the pub with literary significance and poetic inspiration.

**The White Horse (Edinburgh, Scotland):**

Nestled in the heart of Edinburgh, The White Horse is not just a pub but a literary retreat frequented by J.K. Rowling. The magic of the Harry Potter series was, in part, written in the vicinity, making this establishment a pilgrimage for Rowling enthusiasts.

**The Porch House (Stow-on-the-Wold, England):**
With an air of mystery, The Porch House in Stow-on-the-Wold is believed to have hosted J.R.R. Tolkien. This quaint abode is steeped in literary history, providing a glimpse into the world that might have inspired the legendary author.

# Buy Discount Passes

Enter the superhero of your British adventure – the discount passes. From the London Pass to the National Trust Membership, these magical tickets open the doors to a treasure trove of savings of well over £10,000!. You snag priority access, dodge queues like a pro, and unlock exclusive discounts on attractions. It's like having a golden key to the kingdom of savings! So, go ahead, wave your discount wand, and watch as those pounds magically stay in your pocket while you conquer the UK's most iconic spots.

- **English Heritage Membership:**
  - **Description:** Provides access to over 400 historic places in England.
  - **Cost:** £69 for an adult, £48 for seniors, £39 for students.
  - **Starting Benefits:** Free entry to sites, free handbook, and magazine.
  - **Website:** English Heritage Membership
- **National Trust Membership:**
  - **Description:** Grants access to National Trust properties across the UK.
  - **Cost:** £72.60 for an adult, £36.30 for children.
  - **Starting Benefits:** Free entry to sites, members' handbook, and National Trust Magazine.
  - **Savings:** Significant savings for regular visitors.
  - **Website:** National Trust Membership
- **London Pass:**
  - **Description:** Offers access to over 80 attractions in London.
  - **Cost:** 1-day pass starts at £75 for adults, 10-day pass at £229.
  - **Starting Benefits:** Free entry to attractions, skip-the-line privileges, guidebook.
  - **Savings:** Potential savings if visiting multiple attractions.
  - **Website:** London Pass
- **Scottish Heritage Pass:**
  - **Description:** Provides access to over 300 historic properties in Scotland.
  - **Cost:** £49 for an adult, £39 for seniors, £28 for children.
  - **Starting Benefits:** Free entry to sites, free guidebook.
  - **Savings:** Significant savings for those exploring multiple sites.
  - **Website:** Scottish Heritage Pass
- **Royal Historic Palaces Membership:**
  - **Description:** Allows entry to iconic royal palaces in London.
  - **Cost:** £55 for an adult, £27.50 for children.
  - **Starting Benefits:** Free entry to palaces, members' events, and discounts.
  - **Savings:** Substantial savings for frequent visitors.
  - **Website:** Royal Historic Palaces Membership

| Membership | Description | Cost | Starting Benefits | Savings | Website |
|---|---|---|---|---|---|
| **English Heritage** | Provides access to 400+ historic places in England | £69 (adult), £48 (seniors), £39 (students) | Notable attractions include Stonehenge, Haridan's Wall, Dover Castle. | If you visit all, over £3,000! | English Heritage Membership |
| **National Trust** | Grants access to National Trust properties across the UK | £72.60 (adult), £36.30 (children) | Notable attractions include Stonehenge, Cliveden and Giant's Causeway. | Significant savings for regular visitors | National Trust Membership |
| **London Pass** | Offers access to 80+ attractions in London | 1-day pass from £75 (adult), 10-day pass £229 | Free entry to big name attractions, skip-the-line privileges. | Potential savings if visiting multiple big name attractions | London Pass |
| **Scottish Heritage Pass** | Provides access to 300+ historic properties in Scotland | £49 (adult), £39 (seniors), £28 (children) | Notable attractions include Edinburgh Castle and Stirling Castle. | Significant savings for exploring multiple sites | Scottish Heritage Pass |
| **Royal Historic Palaces** | Allows entry to iconic royal palaces in London | £55 (adult), £27.50 (children) | Notable attractions include Tower of London, Hampton Court Palace, Kensington Palace and Banqueting House. | Substantial savings for frequent visitors | Royal Historic Palaces Membership |

Each of these organisations offer family passes for £20 - £40 more, so if you're visiting as a family, you stand to save thousands by purchasing one or more of these passes!

# Museums

Most museums in the UK are free to enter thanks to a commitment to cultural access and inclusivity. Unlike temporary promotions, when the state subsides something it remains cheap or free. Government funding plays a crucial role, supporting these institutions and ensuring that visitors from all backgrounds can explore art, history, and science without financial barriers. If you plan to visit paid museums, you can save a significant amount with these passes:

| Museum Pass | Description | Cost | Benefits | Where to Buy |
| --- | --- | --- | --- | --- |
| National Art Pass | Provides free or discounted entry to hundreds of museums and galleries across the UK. | £73 per year | Free entry to over 240 museums, discounts at museum shops and cafes. | National Art Pass |
| English Heritage Overseas Visitor Pass | Grants access to over 100 historic sites in England. | £45 (9 days), £55 (16 days), £65 (30 days) | Free entry to English Heritage sites, including Stonehenge and Dover Castle. | English Heritage Overseas Visitor Pass |
| Museums Association (MA) Membership | Provides access to numerous museums and galleries in the UK. | £56 per year | Free or discounted entry to participating museums and events, access to professional development opportunities. | Museums Association Membership |

Many museums in the UK offer free guided tours as part of their services to visitors. While the availability of free guided tours may vary depending on the museum and the time of year, here are some notable museums in the UK where you can often find complimentary guided tours:

- **British Museum (London):**
    - The British Museum in London offers free daily eye-opener tours that focus on specific collections or themes. Check the museum's website or inquire at the information desk for the current schedule.
- **National Gallery (London):**
    - The National Gallery provides free guided tours for its collection of European paintings. Tours cover various periods and artists, enhancing your understanding and appreciation of the artworks.
- **National Portrait Gallery (London):**
    - Explore the portraits of famous individuals at the National Portrait Gallery with free guided tours. Themes may include Tudor portraits, contemporary art, and more.
- **Victoria and Albert Museum (London):**
    - The V&A Museum often offers free daily guided tours that highlight different aspects of its vast collection, including art, design, and fashion.
- **Tate Modern and Tate Britain (London):**

- Both Tate Modern and Tate Britain offer free guided tours focusing on specific artists, movements, or themes. Check the museum websites for tour schedules.
- **The National Museum of Scotland (Edinburgh):**
    - The National Museum of Scotland in Edinburgh provides free daily guided tours that explore the diverse collections, including science, technology, and art.
- **The British Library (London):**
    - Discover the treasures of The British Library with free guided tours that showcase rare manuscripts, historical documents, and literary artifacts.
- **Ashmolean Museum (Oxford):**
    - The Ashmolean Museum, located in Oxford, offers free guided tours covering its extensive collection of art and archaeology. Check the museum's website for tour details.
- **The Fitzwilliam Museum (Cambridge):**
    - The Fitzwilliam Museum in Cambridge provides free tours that focus on specific aspects of its collection, such as paintings, sculptures, and decorative arts.
- **National Railway Museum (York):**
    - The National Railway Museum in York offers free guided tours exploring the history of rail travel, including iconic locomotives and railway memorabilia.
- **The National Maritime Museum (London):**
    - Discover maritime history with free guided tours at The National Maritime Museum in Greenwich. Tours cover topics such as naval exploration and navigation.

# City Passes

If you plan to visit a large number of attractions in London, Manchester, Liverpool or York, consider these city passes:

| City Pass | Starting Price | Notable Attractions Included | Recommendation |
|---|---|---|---|
| London Pass | £69 (1 day) | Tower of London, Buckingham Palace, The Shard, etc. | Recommended for extensive London exploration. |
| Manchester Pass | £29 (1 day) | Museum of Science and Industry, Manchester Art Gallery | Recommended for exploring Manchester's culture. |
| Liverpool City Pass | £35 (1 day) | Beatles Story, Liverpool Cathedral, Mersey Ferries | Recommended for Beatles fans and historic sites. |
| York Pass | £47 (1 day) | York Minster, JORVIK Viking Centre, York Castle Museum | Recommended for history enthusiasts in York. |

Note: The starting prices mentioned are for the shortest duration available. Prices may vary depending on the number of days chosen for the pass. Always check the official websites for the most accurate and up-to-date pricing information before making a purchase.

# Visit National Parks

The United Kingdom is home to 15 enchanting National Parks, each a treasure trove of natural wonders waiting to be explored. From the rugged peaks of the Scottish Highlands to the serene beauty of the Broads in East Anglia, these parks are living landscapes that narrate the tale of the UK's diverse ecosystems. Whether you're wandering the mysterious moors of Dartmoor or navigating the breathtaking trails of Snowdonia, these protected spaces invite adventurers to lose themselves in the untamed beauty of the British countryside. With rolling hills, ancient forests, and pristine coastlines, the UK's National Parks are not just destinations; they're immersive journeys into the untamed soul of this island nation. So lace up those hiking boots, breathe in the fresh air, and let the adventure unfold in these natural wonders.

- **Lake District National Park:**
  - **Exploration Tips:**
    - Enjoy free hikes such as the Catbells Walk or Helm Crag.
    - Take advantage of free parking areas for access to scenic viewpoints.
  - **Approximate Prices:**
    - Parking: Varies, but free parking spots are available. Look at parking app Parkopedia.
- **Snowdonia National Park:**
  - **Exploration Tips:**
    - Hike Snowdon via the Llanberis Path, a popular and free route.
    - Explore the beautiful Nant Gwynant Valley without any entrance fees.
- **Peak District National Park:**
  - **Exploration Tips:**
    - Enjoy free walks like the Dovedale Stepping Stones or Mam Tor.
    - Take advantage of free parking areas for trailheads.
- **Brecon Beacons National Park:**
  - **Exploration Tips:**
    - Hike Pen y Fan, the highest peak in South Wales, for free.
    - Explore waterfalls like Sgwd yr Eira without an entrance fee.

# Whiskey Tours

In Scotland, distilleries like Glenfiddich and Glenlivet often offer tours starting around £10-£15 per person. In Ireland, the Jameson Distillery tour in Dublin and the Bushmills Distillery tour in Northern Ireland are commonly priced around £15-£20. For those exploring English whiskey, The Lakes Distillery offers tours starting from approximately £12-£18. Keep in mind that prices may fluctuate based on factors like the type of tour, tasting options, and any promotions or discounts available. It's advisable to check the distilleries' official websites for the most up-to-date pricing information and to explore any special deals that might enhance your affordable whiskey tour experience. Cheers to sipping smartly!

# Coastal Delights

The United Kingdom boasts numerous beautiful beaches that offer stunning views and diverse experiences. Here are some coastal destinations known for their affordability and charm:

**Blackpool, England:**

Indulge in the vibrant charm of Blackpool, an iconic seaside resort boasting a lively promenade, amusement parks, and the world-famous Blackpool Tower. Enjoy the thrills without breaking the bank, as budget-friendly accommodations and a plethora of affordable dining options make this coastal gem accessible to all.

**Tenby, Wales:**

Discover the enchantment of Tenby, a picturesque town offering a quaint harbor, medieval town walls, and golden sandy beaches. Immerse yourself in its medieval charm while enjoying affordable stays in charming B&Bs and guesthouses, complemented by budget-friendly eateries.

**St. Ives, England:**

Escape to the artistic haven of St. Ives, where picturesque beaches, art galleries, and narrow cobbled streets beckon. Despite its popularity, find solace in budget accommodations and relish free coastal walks, proving that this coastal retreat doesn't have to be a splurge.

**Portrush, Northern Ireland:**

Uncover the beauty of Portrush, with its white sandy beaches, vibrant nightlife, and the awe-inspiring Giant's Causeway nearby. Offering reasonably priced accommodations and a diverse range of dining options, Portrush invites you to experience its coastal wonders without breaking the bank.

**Bournemouth, England:**

Bask in the glory of Bournemouth's award-winning beaches, lush gardens, and a lively pier. Embrace the coastal allure with a variety of budget-friendly accommodations and seaside activities that won't dent your wallet.

**Aberystwyth, Wales:**

Experience the Victorian charm of Aberystwyth, featuring a historic promenade, a pier steeped in history, and the scenic Constitution Hill. Enjoy the affordability of guesthouses with stunning views of the Irish Sea, coupled with budget-friendly eateries.

**Whitby, England:**

Embark on a journey to Whitby, where a historic harbor, Gothic Abbey, and sandy beaches await. Revel in reasonably priced accommodations and savor the classic pairing of fish and chips on the charming harbor.

**Scarborough, England:**

Explore the dual bays, medieval castle, and bustling harbor of Scarborough. With a range of budget-friendly accommodation options and affordable seaside entertainment, Scarborough beckons as an accessible coastal escape for all.

# Cheese Rolling

Attending a cheese rolling festival in the UK is a unique and exhilarating experience and its totally free! One of the most famous events is the Cooper's Hill Cheese-Rolling and Wake held in Gloucestershire. Here's a brief guide:

**Event:** Cooper's Hill Cheese-Rolling and Wake

**Location:** Cooper's Hill, near Brockworth, Gloucestershire, England.

**Date:** The event traditionally takes place on the Spring Bank Holiday, which is the last Monday in May.

**Description:**

- Participants chase a wheel of Double Gloucester cheese down a steep hill.
- The hill is so steep that contestants often tumble and roll, adding to the excitement.
- The first person to cross the finish line at the bottom of the hill wins the cheese.

**Tips for Attending:**

- **Footwear:** Wear sturdy shoes with good traction, as the hill is steep and uneven.
- **Clothing:** Dress comfortably and be prepared for the possibility of getting muddy.
- **Safety:** Be cautious if you decide to participate, as the hill can be challenging, and injuries are not uncommon.

# Brewery Tours

There are several options for brewery tours that provide an affordable way to delve into the art and science of beer production.

In South London, The London Beer Factory is a noteworthy choice. Renowned for its diverse craft beers, the brewery typically offers guided tours at a reasonable price, allowing visitors to gain insights into the brewing process without straining their wallets.

Heading to Ellon, Scotland, the BrewDog brewery is a popular destination for those seeking both innovation and affordability. BrewDog provides informative tours at a cost-effective rate, making it an accessible choice for beer enthusiasts keen on exploring their brewing techniques.

In Warwickshire, the Purity Brewing Company in the Midlands is another option with reasonably priced tours. Visitors can expect to learn about the brewery's commitment to sustainability and quality brewing methods without breaking the bank.

In Manchester, the Marble Arch Brewery, located in the city center, offers brewery tours at an affordable cost. Attendees can explore the brewing process and sample a diverse selection of beers without exceeding their budget.

To provide a more concrete idea of the prices, The London Beer Factory tours may range from £10 to £20 per person, while BrewDog tours in Ellon typically fall within the £15 to £25 range. Purity Brewing Company in Warwickshire often offers tours priced around £12 to £18, and Marble Arch Brewery tours in Manchester might be in the £15 to £25 range.

# Factory Tours

Get up-close and personal with the UK's most popular brands with factory tours.

**Brompton Bicycle Factory Tour (London):**

Explore the captivating realm of folding bicycles at the Brompton Bicycle Factory in London. Priced at £30 per person, this guided tour offers a comprehensive journey through the entire manufacturing process. Witness skilled artisans meticulously hand-assembling these iconic bikes and gain valuable insights into the innovative design and engineering that characterize each Brompton.

**Jaguar Land Rover Experience (Solihull):**

For £49 per adult, the Jaguar Land Rover Experience at the Solihull plant provides an immersive exploration of the luxury automotive world. Delve into the behind-the-scenes magic of producing these prestigious vehicles. Marvel at the cutting-edge technology and craftsmanship involved in creating Jaguar and Land Rover models, culminating in a thrilling off-road experience.

**Laphroaig Distillery Tour (Islay, Scotland):**

Whisky aficionados will appreciate the charm of the Laphroaig Distillery on the Isle of Islay. Priced at £10 per person for the standard tour, this experience unfolds the traditional whisky-making process, offering glimpses of malting floors and peat-fired kilns. Conclude your visit with a tasting session, savoring the distinctive flavors of Laphroaig's renowned single malt Scotch whiskies.

**Cadbury World (Birmingham):**

Indulge your sweet tooth with a trip to Cadbury World in Birmingham, where prices start from £12.30 per person. While not a conventional factory tour, this experience provides an interactive journey through the history of chocolate-making and the Cadbury brand. Enjoy immersive exhibits, interactive displays, and even the chance to craft your own personalized chocolate bar.

# Enjoy Free Concerts

**London's Hyde Park Summer Series:**

Indulge in the musical delights of London's Hyde Park Summer Series, an annual event that transforms the iconic park into a haven for music enthusiasts. This free concert series showcases a diverse lineup of top-tier artists across genres, offering unforgettable performances against the backdrop of one of the city's most cherished green spaces. From rock to pop and everything in between, Hyde Park Summer Series delivers world-class entertainment without costing a penny.

**BBC Proms in the Park:**

Immerse yourself in the classical splendor of the BBC Proms in the Park, a highlight of the renowned BBC Proms season. This outdoor extravaganza takes place in parks across the UK, bringing together celebrated orchestras, soloists, and choirs to create a symphonic spectacle. With a festive atmosphere and the chance to enjoy the grandeur of classical music under the stars, BBC Proms in the Park offers a culturally rich and cost-free musical experience for audiences nationwide.

**Notting Hill Carnival:**

Dive into the vibrant rhythms of the Notting Hill Carnival, one of the world's largest street festivals held annually in London. While not exclusively a music festival, the carnival boasts an array of free live performances spanning genres like reggae, soca, calypso, and more. Revel in the infectious energy of the parade and multiple sound systems scattered throughout the streets, showcasing the best of Caribbean and global sounds without an admission fee.

**Southbank Centre's Free Music Weekends:**

For a dose of eclectic musical experiences, head to the Southbank Centre in London during their Free Music Weekends. This cultural hub regularly hosts free live performances spanning various genres, including jazz, world music, and contemporary sounds. With a commitment to accessibility, the Southbank Centre provides a platform for emerging and established artists alike, ensuring that music lovers can enjoy high-quality performances without spending a dime.

**Liverpool International Music Festival (LIMF):**
Celebrate the rich musical heritage of Liverpool at the International Music Festival (LIMF), an annual event featuring an array of free concerts and performances. From pop and rock to electronic and hip-hop, LIMF showcases diverse talent across multiple stages, turning the city into a music lover's paradise. Embrace the spirit of this dynamic festival while enjoying world-class acts without opening your wallet.

# Planning - What to Know

## Money-Saving Tips for Travel in the UK

1. **Book Accommodations wisely:** Look for early booking discounts on hotels or consider alternative accommodations like airbnbs, guesthouses, or vacation rentals. Prices can range from £20-£50 per night in budget-friendly options. Mix and match with some luxury stays for an incredible trip. Last Minute Secret Hotels will often allow you to find a £50 5-star hotel in cities during the weekdays. Apps like Hotwire and Priceline also offer "secret" or unnamed hotels at significantly discounted rates. You book the hotel without knowing its name until after confirmation, but you can often narrow down the location and amenities

2. **Travel During Off-Peak Seasons:** Visit during shoulder seasons or off-peak times to find lower prices on accommodations, flights, and attractions. Off-peak periods often include late fall and early spring, offering reduced rates on various travel expenses.

3. **Use Public Transportation:** Utilize public transportation, such as trains and buses, which can be more cost-effective than renting a car. Travel passes, like the Oyster card in London, offer convenience and savings on public transit.

4. **Explore Free Attractions:** Take advantage of free museums, parks, and landmarks. Many major cities have iconic sites that can be enjoyed without an entrance fee. In London, museums like the British Museum and the Tate Modern offer free entry to their main collections.

5. **Buy Attraction Passes:** Consider purchasing city passes or attraction bundles for discounted entry to multiple sites. The London Pass, for example, provides access to various attractions at a reduced rate compared to individual tickets.

6. **Pack Snacks and Picnic:** Save on dining expenses by packing snacks and enjoying picnics in parks or public spaces. Local markets, such as Borough Market in London, are great for affordable, fresh produce.

7. **Student and Senior Discounts:** If applicable, inquire about student or senior discounts at attractions, transportation, and accommodations. Many attractions offer reduced rates for students and seniors upon presentation of valid identification.

8. **Shop at Local Markets:** Purchase essentials from local markets rather than touristy areas. You can find fresh produce, snacks, and souvenirs at lower prices. Markets like the Manchester Arndale Market offer a variety of affordable options.

9. **Consider City Cards:** Some cities offer tourism cards providing free or discounted entry to attractions and public transportation. Research options for your destination, such as the Edinburgh City Pass, which includes various attractions and transportation.

10. **Walk and Explore On Foot:** Save on transportation costs by walking or cycling around cities. Many attractions are within walking distance in urban areas. Cities like Bath and Oxford are pedestrian-friendly, allowing you to explore at your own pace.

11. **Opt for Free Walking Tours:** Join free walking tours in major cities, where local guides provide insights into the history and culture. Companies like SANDEMANs offer informative and tip-based walking tours in various UK cities.

12. **Use Free Wi-Fi:** Avoid international data charges by connecting to free Wi-Fi available in cafes, libraries, and public spaces. Many cities, including Bristol and Glasgow, offer free Wi-Fi zones for tourists and locals alike.

13. **Budget Airlines and Trains:** Research budget airlines and book train tickets in advance for long-distance travel within the UK. Airlines like easyJet and train services like Avanti West Coast often have discounted fares for early bookings.

14. **Stay Outside City Centers:** Accommodations outside the city center can be more affordable. Use public transportation to reach central attractions. In Edinburgh, for instance, consider staying in areas like Leith or Stockbridge for budget-friendly options.

15. **Bring a Reusable Water Bottle:** Save on bottled water expenses by bringing a reusable water bottle. Most cities have drinking fountains or tap water is safe to drink. Refill stations are widely available in public spaces, including parks and transportation hubs.

16. **Join Loyalty Programs:** Sign up for loyalty programs with airlines, hotels, and transportation services to accumulate points and enjoy discounts. Programs like British Airways Executive Club and hotel chains' loyalty programs offer perks and savings for frequent travelers.

17. **Check for Online Deals:** Look for online deals, promotions, and discount codes for accommodations, attractions, and transportation. Websites like Travelzoo and Groupon often feature discounted offers for various travel-related expenses.

18. **Plan Your Meals:** Research affordable eateries, local markets, and budget-friendly restaurants. Avoid dining in tourist hotspots, and explore neighborhoods like Shoreditch in London or Finnieston in Glasgow for trendy yet affordable dining options.

19. **Use Cashback and Rewards Credit Cards:** Consider using credit cards that offer cashback or travel rewards to earn benefits on your purchases. Cards like the Halifax Clarity Credit Card or American Express Cashback Credit Card can provide cashback benefits and no foreign transaction fees.

20. **Be Flexible:** Stay flexible with your plans. Being open to last-minute deals or spontaneous activities can lead to unexpected savings. Check websites like Lastminute.com for discounted accommodations and experiences for those who are open to spontaneous adventures.

# Hotel Room Costs by Month

| Month | Average Hotel Room Price Range (per night) |
|---|---|
| January | £50 - £120 |
| February | £60 - £130 |
| March | £70 - £140 |
| April | £80 - £160 |
| May | £90 - £180 |
| June | £100 - £200 |
| July | £120 - £220 |
| August | £130 - £230 |
| September | £110 - £200 |
| October | £80 - £160 |
| November | £60 - £130 |
| December | £70 - £150 |

# Birthday freebies

Many UK businesses offer birthday freebies or discounts to customers celebrating their birthdays. While the availability of these offerings can vary, here are some common types of birthday freebies you'll find in the UK:

### Restaurants and Cafes:

Indulge in birthday perks at various restaurants and cafes where you can enjoy complimentary desserts, appetizers, or even an entire meal. Popular chains like Pizza Express, TGI Fridays, and Bella Italia often roll out special offers to make your celebration even more delightful.

### Coffee Shops:

Fuel your birthday with freebies from coffee giants like Starbucks and Costa Coffee by joining their loyalty programs. These establishments may treat you to a complimentary drink or a sweet treat, ensuring your special day begins with a caffeinated boost.

### Beauty and Cosmetics:

Pamper yourself with birthday treats from beauty and cosmetic brands. Sephora, Boots, and The Body Shop are known to offer exclusive discounts, freebies, or special products to celebrate your birthday in style.

### Cinemas:

For movie buffs, some cinema chains extend birthday discounts or even free tickets. Stay updated on promotions by checking with local cinemas or exploring loyalty programs specific to certain chains.

### Bakeries:

Satisfy your sweet tooth with free pastries, cupcakes, or other delectable treats from bakeries and dessert shops on your birthday. Explore local bakeries or check out popular chains like Greggs to sweeten your celebration.

### Ice Cream Shops:

Cool off your birthday with frozen delights from ice cream shops such as Ben & Jerry's or Baskin-Robbins. These establishments may offer birthday discounts or even free scoops, so be sure to inquire about any promotions at your favorite local ice cream spots

# The Seasons

One moment you're basking in the glorious sunshine, plotting a delightful picnic in Hyde Park, and the next, you're caught in a surprise rain shower, desperately seeking shelter with a hastily purchased umbrella that may or may not survive the gusty winds. It's a rollercoaster of meteorological emotions! The Brits are experts at the art of small talk, and our ever-changing weather is the reigning champion of conversation starters. We've got drizzles that can turn into downpours in the blink of an eye, and a fleeting appearance of the sun that sends everyone into a blissful state of Vitamin D appreciation. So, when packing for your UK adventure, think layers, toss in a waterproof jacket just in case, and brace yourself for a weather experience that'll keep you on your toes and give you endless stories to share.

**Spring (March to May):**

- **Weather:** Mild temperatures, occasional rain showers.
  - **What to Pack:**
  - Light layers, including a jacket or sweater.
  - A waterproof jacket or umbrella for unpredictable spring showers.
  - Comfortable walking shoes for exploring blooming gardens and parks.

**Summer (June to August):**

- **Weather:** Warmer temperatures, longer daylight hours.
  - **What to Pack:**
  - Light and breathable clothing, including shorts and T-shirts.
  - Sunscreen, sunglasses, and a hat for sun protection.
  - Comfortable walking shoes for outdoor activities.
  - Swimsuit if you plan to visit beaches or outdoor pools.

**Autumn (September to November):**

- **Weather:** Cooling temperatures, occasional rain.
  - **What to Pack:**
  - Layered clothing, including a medium-weight jacket or sweater.
  - Waterproof jacket or coat for rain.
  - Comfortable shoes suitable for walking through autumn foliage.
  - An umbrella for occasional showers.

**Winter (December to February):**

- **Weather:** Cold temperatures, potential frost and snow.
  - **What to Pack:**
  - Heavy coat, gloves, and a warm hat for chilly temperatures.
  - Layers, including sweaters and thermal clothing.
  - Waterproof and insulated boots, especially if there's a chance of snow.
  - Scarf and earmuffs for additional warmth.
  - Umbrella for rain, as winter can bring both rain and snow.

**General Tips:**

- A power adapter for your electronic devices.
- Comfortable walking shoes suitable for exploring both cities and countryside.
- A small backpack for day trips and carrying essentials.
- Depending on your travel plans, formal attire for special events or upscale restaurants.

# Free Festivals

| Festival Name | All Free | How to Get Cheap Tickets for Paid Parts |
|---|---|---|
| Edinburgh Festival Fringe (Edinburgh) | No | Explore "Half-Price Hut" for discounted tickets on the day of shows |
| Notting Hill Carnival (London) | Yes | - |
| Green Man Festival (Brecon Beacons) | No (Einsteins Garden is free) | Check for early bird or group ticket discounts |
| Manchester International Festival (Manchester) | No | Some events may have lower-priced tickets; check the festival website |
| Delfast Maritime Festival (Belfast) | Yes | - |
| Llangollen International Musical Eisteddfod (Llangollen) | Yes | - |
| Brighton Festival (Brighton) | No (Some events may require tickets) | Look for free outdoor performances and installations |
| Mintfest (Kendal) | Yes | - |
| Freedom Festival (Hull) | Yes | - |
| Cardiff International Food and Drink Festival (Cardiff) | Yes | - |
| Shrewsbury Folk Festival (Shrewsbury) | No (Some fringe events are free) | Explore free fringe events and performances in the town |
| Leeds Waterfront Festival (Leeds) | Yes | - |
| Glasgow Mela (Glasgow) | Yes | - |
| Bristol Harbour Festival (Bristol) | Yes | - |
| Huddersfield Food and Drink Festival (Huddersfield) | Yes | - |
| Reading Water Fest (Reading) | Yes | - |
| Salisbury International Arts Festival (Salisbury) | No (Some events are free) | Check the festival program for free outdoor performances and activities |
| Sheffield Doc/Fest (Sheffield) | Yes (Some screenings are free) | Explore free screenings, talks, and exhibitions |
| Festival of the Sea (Portsmouth) | Yes | - |
| Chester Music Festival (Chester) | No (Some concerts may be free) | Check the festival program for free performances and workshops |

# How to enjoy the major attractions minus the crowds

Avoiding crowds while enjoying major attractions in the United Kingdom requires strategic planning and timing. Here are some tips to help you experience popular sites with fewer people:

**Off-Peak Seasons:**

Optimize your experience by planning visits during off-peak seasons when tourist numbers are at their lowest. Take advantage of the quieter atmosphere during the shoulder seasons, typically spring and autumn in the UK.

**Midweek Visits:**

Maximize your enjoyment by choosing midweek visits to attractions rather than weekends. Mondays and Tuesdays, in particular, tend to offer a less crowded experience compared to the bustling weekends.

**Early Morning or Late Afternoon:**

Enhance your exploration by arriving early in the morning or visiting late in the afternoon. These times allow you to savor attractions during quieter periods, providing a more relaxed and immersive experience.

**Book Timed Entry Tickets:**

Streamline your visit by booking timed entry tickets. Many attractions offer this option, allowing you to select a specific time slot and bypass peak visitor hours, ensuring a more leisurely experience.

**Take Advantage of Member or Early Access Programs:**

Elevate your visit by exploring attractions during early access periods reserved for members or specific ticket holders. Consider joining memberships or programs that provide this privileged access, enhancing your overall enjoyment.

**Plan Around School Holidays:**

Strategize your visit by being mindful of school holiday periods. Attractions often experience higher attendance during school breaks, so plan accordingly to avoid peak times.

# Food and Accommodation

Your two biggest expenses when travelling to UK are accommodation and food. This section is intended to help you cut these costs dramatically without compromising on those luxury feels:

# How to save money on food in the United Kingdom

### Use 'Too Good To Go'

The UK offers plenty of food bargains; if you know where to look. Thankfully the app 'Too Good to Go' is turning visitors into locals by showing them exactly where to find the tastiest deals and simultaneously rescue food that would otherwise be wasted. In the UK you can pick up a $15 buy of baked goods, groceries, breakfast, brunch, lunch or dinner boxes for $2.99. You'll find lots of fish and meat dishes on offer in the UK, which would normally be expensive.

**How it works?** You pay for a magic bag (essentially a bag of what the restaurant or bakery has leftover) on the app and simply pick it up from the bakery or restaurant during the time they've selected. You can find extremely cheap breakfast, lunch, dinner and even groceries this way. Simply download the app and press 'my current location' to find the deals near you in the UK .What's not to love about delicious food thats a quarter of the normal price and helping to drive down food waste?

An oft-quoted parable is 'There is no such thing as cheap food. Either you pay at the cash registry or the doctor's office'. This dismisses the fact that good nutrition is a choice; we all make every-time we eat. Cheap eats are not confined to hotdogs and kebabs. The great thing about using Too Good To Go is you can eat nutritious food cheaply: fruits, vegetables, fish and nut dishes are a fraction of their supermarket cost.

Japan has the longest life expectancy in the world. A national study by the Japanese Ministry of Internal Affairs and Communications revealed that between January and May 2019, a household of two spent on average ¥65,994 a month, that's $10 per person per day on food. You truly don't need to spend a lot to eat nutritious food. That's a marketing gimmick hawkers of overpriced muesli bars want you to believe.

# The best Too Good To Go Providers in the UK

Pret A Manger (Multiple Cities):

Pret A Manger often offers Too Good To Go bags containing a variety of sandwiches, salads, and baked goods.

Costa Coffee (Multiple Cities):

Costa Coffee locations may have Too Good To Go bags with surplus pastries, sandwiches, or snacks.

Tesco (Multiple Cities):

Some Tesco stores participate, offering Too Good To Go bags with a mix of groceries and fresh produce.

Sainsbury's (Multiple Cities):

Sainsbury's is occasionally featured on Too Good To Go, providing bags with surplus groceries.

Morrisons (Multiple Cities):

Morrisons supermarkets have been known to participate, offering Too Good To Go bags with a variety of food items.

Greggs (Multiple Cities):

Greggs, a popular bakery chain, may have Too Good To Go bags containing surplus baked goods.

Yo! Sushi (Multiple Cities):

Yo! Sushi locations sometimes participate, offering Too Good To Go bags with a selection of sushi items.

LEON (London, Manchester, Birmingham, etc.):

LEON, a fast-food chain with a focus on natural and sustainable ingredients, may offer Too Good To Go bags with surplus meals.

Wasabi (London):

Wasabi, a sushi and bento chain, has been known to participate in Too Good To Go, offering bags with surplus items.

Caffe Nero (Multiple Cities):
Caffe Nero locations may participate, offering Too Good To Go bags with surplus pastries and snacks.

## A note on stigma

I can almost hear you saying, I thought this was a guide about luxury. Using apps like Too Good To Go is about scoring top-notch, discounted goodies while doing your part to combat food waste. Some folks might feel a bit iffy about it, maybe due to unfounded stigma or worries about the freshness of the offerings. But let's flip the script—these apps are a win-win! Not only do you snag quality eats at a steal, but you also help the planet by rescuing perfectly good food from the landfill. It's time to break the mold, embrace the eco-friendly vibes, and turn those surplus snacks into a delicious win for your wallet and the environment.

# Must Try British Classics

**The United Kingdom boasts a rich culinary heritage with a variety of iconic dishes. Here are some must-try UK foods with a brief history of each and where to enjoy them:**

### Fish and Chips:

With a history dating back to the 19th century, Fish and Chips emerged during the Industrial Revolution as an affordable and filling meal for the working class. Popularized by street vendors, it became a beloved British dish. To enjoy this classic on a budget, consider chain options like Harry Ramsden's or Fish and Chips Co.

### Full English Breakfast:

The Full English Breakfast, or "fry-up," evolved in the 19th century as a hearty meal designed to fuel a day of labor. Comprising eggs, bacon, sausage, black pudding, tomatoes, mushrooms, and baked beans, it became a weekend indulgence. For an economical version, explore chain establishments like Wetherspoon's or Toby Carvery.

### Roast Beef and Yorkshire Pudding:

Originating in the 18th century, Roast Beef with Yorkshire Pudding was a classic Sunday roast. Yorkshire Pudding, initially served as a filler before the main course to save on expensive meat, has since become a staple. For an affordable option, consider carvery chains like Toby Carvery or Crown Carveries.

### Shepherd's Pie:

Shepherd's Pie, a comforting dish of minced lamb or mutton topped with mashed potatoes, has rural British roots. Originating as a way to use leftover roasted meat, it gained popularity during the Industrial Revolution. To enjoy it on a budget, check out chain pubs like Wetherspoon's.

### Ploughman's Lunch:

The Ploughman's Lunch gained popularity in the mid-20th century, comprising cheese, bread, pickles, and sometimes ham or pâté. Its name reflects its association with rural life. For an affordable version, explore chain pubs such as Greene King or JD Wetherspoon.

### Cornish Pasty:

Originating in Cornwall, the handheld Cornish Pasty filled with meat, potatoes, and vegetables served as a portable meal for tin miners. The distinctive crimped edge served as a practical handle. For an economical option, consider bakery chains like Greggs.

### Bangers and Mash:

Emerging during World War II, Bangers and Mash features sausages served with mashed potatoes and onion gravy. The sausages, colloquially called "bangers," had a high water content, causing them to burst during cooking. For an affordable version, explore traditional British pub chains like Wetherspoon's.

**Black Pudding:**

Black Pudding, a blood sausage made with pork fat and oatmeal, has ancient origins but became a staple of British cuisine. It is a key component of the Full English Breakfast, with regional variations. To experience it on a budget, explore supermarket chains like Tesco or Morrisons.

**Chicken Tikka Masala:**

Though not traditionally British, Chicken Tikka Masala has become an iconic UK dish, believed to have originated in Indian restaurants in Britain. It consists of grilled chicken in a creamy tomato-based curry sauce. For a cost-effective version, consider popular chain curry houses like Wetherspoon's Curry Club or Akbar's.

**Afternoon Tea:**
Afternoon Tea's delightful ritual has been enjoyed since the 1840s when Anna, the Duchess of Bedford, introduced the concept. It typically includes tea, sandwiches, scones with clotted cream and jam, and pastries. For an affordable experience, explore afternoon tea vouchers on Groupon or Wowcher to have the same posh experience without a hefty price tag.

# Food Culture Mistakes to Avoid

Let's chat about some food culture pointers to ensure you're savoring not just the flavors, but also the local customs!

First up, the tipping game. It's a bit of a dance, but generally, leaving 10-15% on the bill is the norm if service isn't included. Pro tip: check the bill for that sneaky service charge; if it's not there, a little extra for table service is always appreciated.

Now, queueing – yes, it's a British thing. Cutting in line is a bit of a no-no, whether you're eyeing that buffet, a coffee fix, or any public space. So, stand in line, chat with your fellow queuers, and embrace the wait.

Don't be shy when it comes to local dishes! Skipping the traditional British delights like fish and chips, a full English breakfast, or a Sunday roast is like missing out on a culinary adventure. Be brave, be bold, and dive into the local flavors.

Picture this: a cozy cafe, a quaint restaurant – quiet spaces where conversation is an art. Keep it down a notch, especially in hushed places. Brits love a serene atmosphere during meals, so let your taste buds do the talking instead.

Now, pubs – the heart of social life! It's a bit of a different scene; ordering and paying happen at the bar, and sometimes, you might need to find your own seat. Pub etiquette 101: grab a pint, soak in the vibe, and enjoy the quintessential British experience.

Please and thank you – these aren't just words; they're magic keys to politeness. Brits appreciate a touch of courtesy, so sprinkle those "pleases" and "thank yous" liberally, especially when dealing with the fantastic folks serving up your scrumptious meals.

# Cheapest Supermarkets

### Aldi:

With a no-frills approach, Aldi has become synonymous with affordability, offering a wide range of products at prices lower than many other supermarkets. The emphasis on cost efficiency allows shoppers to enjoy budget-friendly options without compromising quality.

### Lidl:

Following a model similar to Aldi, Lidl is a discount supermarket chain providing a diverse selection of affordable products. The commitment to keeping prices low has made Lidl a popular choice for budget-conscious consumers seeking quality products without the premium price tag.

### Asda:

As one of the UK's largest supermarket chains, Asda is known for its focus on competitive prices for everyday items. Shoppers at Asda can expect a wide variety of products at affordable rates, making it a go-to destination for cost-effective grocery shopping.

### Morrisons:

Morrisons stands out with its regular promotions and offers, ensuring that shoppers have access to cost-effective options. The supermarket's commitment to providing value makes it an attractive choice for those looking to stretch their budget without sacrificing quality.

### Tesco (Tesco Value Range):

As one of the largest supermarket chains in the UK, Tesco's Value range caters to budget-conscious consumers. The Tesco Value range offers wallet-friendly choices without compromising on the essentials, providing a wide array of affordable options for various needs.

### Sainsbury's (Basics Range):

Sainsbury's, with its Basics range, is dedicated to providing affordable options for essential items. This supermarket chain combines quality with cost-effectiveness, making it an accessible choice for those seeking budget-friendly alternatives without compromising on product standards.

### Iceland:

Known for its frozen food offerings, Iceland is a supermarket that consistently provides budget-friendly options across various product categories. The focus on frozen goods allows customers to access affordable choices while enjoying the convenience of longer shelf life.

**Farmfoods:**

Specializing in frozen foods, Farmfoods is a supermarket that consistently offers competitive prices. With a focus on frozen products, it provides a cost-effective solution for those looking to save on groceries without compromising on quality.

# Cheapest Takeaway Coffees

The cost of takeaway coffees in the United Kingdom can vary based on factors such as the location, size, and type of coffee. As of my last knowledge update in January 2022, here are some places where you can often find relatively affordable takeaway coffees:

**McDonald's:**

Renowned for its quick-service model, McDonald's McCafé is a go-to for competitively priced takeaway coffees. Whether you're in need of a morning pick-me-up or an afternoon caffeine boost, McDonald's offers affordability without compromising on convenience.

**Greggs:**

As a popular bakery chain, Greggs not only satisfies pastry cravings but also provides reasonably priced coffees as part of their menu. The combination of baked goods and pocket-friendly coffee options makes Greggs a favored destination for those seeking quality at an affordable cost.

**Costa Coffee (Express):**

Costa Coffee Express locations, often strategically placed in service stations and convenience stores, may offer more budget-friendly options compared to their full-sized counterparts. These express locations provide a convenient and economical choice for coffee enthusiasts on the go.

**Tesco Café:**

For a cost-effective coffee solution, Tesco supermarkets with in-store cafés are known for providing takeaway coffees at reasonable prices. Shoppers can enjoy the convenience of grabbing a cup of coffee while doing their grocery shopping without breaking the bank.

**Sainsbury's Café:**

Sainsbury's supermarkets with cafés cater to coffee lovers by offering a range of coffees, including takeaway options. The combination of grocery shopping and affordable coffee makes Sainsbury's Café a convenient choice for those looking for both quality and value.

**Asda Café:**

Asda supermarkets with cafés are a great option for affordable takeaway coffees. Shoppers at Asda can enjoy the convenience of grabbing a cup of coffee without straining their budget, making it an accessible choice for a quick caffeine fix.

**Pret A Manger:**

While not the cheapest option, Pret A Manger is renowned for providing good-quality takeaway coffees. The brand's commitment to high-quality ingredients and sustainable practices makes it a favored choice for those willing to invest a bit more for a premium coffee experience.

**IKEA**

Ikea offers free coffee (with a FAMILY CARD). To access the restaurant, you must first go to the IKEA store at Hullenbergweg 2 in south-east UK. From there, take the metro 50 or 54 to station Bullewijk. Its menu includes a 1 euro breakfast, which includes a boiled egg, croissant, jam, and filter coffee.

# Best food trucks and Street vendors

Let's take a stroll through the tantalizing world of street food in the UK, where vibrant markets and culinary delights await in various cities:

### London:

In the bustling metropolis of London, Street Feast takes center stage, with various locations hosting street food markets brimming with diverse vendors. Don't miss the historic Borough Market, a culinary haven offering international cuisines and local specialties that'll satisfy any palate.

### Manchester:

For the foodies in Manchester, Grub Manchester is the go-to destination, hosting food festivals spotlighting independent traders and street food vendors. Venture to Mackie Mayor, a converted market building turned food hall, featuring an array of delightful food options.

### Glasgow:

Glasgow boasts the lively Big Feed, a regular street food market showcasing local vendors and a kaleidoscope of culinary choices. Explore Platform at The Arches, nestled beneath Central Station, where a mix of cuisines tantalizes taste buds.

### Bristol:

St. Nicholas Market in Bristol, one of the city's oldest markets, offers a vibrant street food section with a global flavor palette. On the waterfront, Harbourside Market boasts food stalls focusing on local and sustainable produce.

### Edinburgh:

In the enchanting city of Edinburgh, The Pitt Market is a must-visit, featuring local vendors and live music for a lively atmosphere. During the festival season, Edinburgh Festival Fringe brings forth a plethora of street food stalls offering a delightful variety.

### Leeds:

Inside the Trinity Leeds shopping center, Trinity Kitchen beckons with a rotating selection of street food vendors, ensuring there's always something new to try. Celebrate local talent at the Leeds Street Food Awards, an annual event showcasing the best street food in the city.

**Cardiff:**

Cardiff Street Food Circus is a beloved event that pops up in various locations across the city, showcasing a diverse array of street food vendors. For a mix of tradition and innovation, Cardiff Central Market boasts a historic charm with contemporary food stalls.

**Brighton:**

In the heart of Brighton, the weekly Street Diner market entices food enthusiasts with its diverse and flavorful offerings. For a community-focused experience, Brighton Open Market features a range of street food stalls serving up global cuisines.

# Use delivery services on the cheap

Take advantage of local offers on food delivery services. Most platforms including Uber Eats and Just Eat offer $10 off the first order in UK. Another cost-effective approach is to keep an eye out for promotions and special offers from popular food delivery platforms. Platforms like Just Eat, Deliveroo, and Uber Eats frequently run promotions, discounts, and voucher code campaigns. By staying informed about these promotions, you can save money on delivery fees or even get discounts on your entire order.

.

# Best British Desserts

British desserts have a rich history, and many have become iconic staples of the country's culinary tradition. Here are some classic British desserts along with a glimpse into their histories:

Trifle:

With roots dating back to the 16th century, trifle began as a simple concoction of cream, sugar, rosewater, and alcohol-soaked sponge cake. Evolving over time, this classic dessert transformed into the layered masterpiece we enjoy today, often featuring custard, jelly, fruits, and whipped cream.

Sticky Toffee Pudding:

Originating in the 20th century, sticky toffee pudding owes its creation to the Sharrow Bay Country House Hotel in the Lake District. The rich and moist date sponge is a delectable delight, typically served with a generous drizzle of toffee sauce.

Eton Mess:

A relatively recent creation associated with Eton College, Eton Mess traces its roots to the 19th century. Legend has it that this delightful dessert emerged during a cricket match when a collapsed pavlova resulted in a sweet "mess" enjoyed by the players.

Spotted Dick:

A classic British suet pudding adorned with currants or raisins, Spotted Dick has been tantalizing taste buds since at least the 19th century. The term "dick" likely originated from the word "pudding," and "spotted" playfully refers to the dried fruit within.

Bakewell Tart:

Hailing from the town of Bakewell in Derbyshire, the Bakewell Tart came to be in the 19th century due to a culinary mishap. A cook's misunderstanding led to the accidental layering of almond paste on top of a jam tart, creating this now-beloved dessert.

Victoria Sponge Cake:

A classic British tea-time treat named after Queen Victoria, the Victoria Sponge Cake gained popularity when the Queen enjoyed a simple sponge cake during her afternoon tea. It remains a timeless delight.

Jam Roly-Poly:

Dating back to the 19th century, Jam Roly-Poly is a comforting suet pudding rolled with jam. This nostalgic dessert was a favorite among British schoolchildren, epitomizing traditional fare.

Treacle Tart:

A sweet and sticky dessert made with golden syrup or treacle, Treacle Tart became a hit in the 19th century and is often associated with the charm of British school dinners.

Banoffee Pie:
A more modern creation emerging in the 1970s at The Hungry Monk restaurant in Sussex, Banoffee Pie tantalizes taste buds with its irresistible combination of bananas, toffee, and cream.

# British Beers

British beer boasts a rich and frothy history dating back centuries. From medieval monasteries crafting ales to the rise of the iconic pub culture, beer has been a staple of British life. One of the earliest recorded references to beer in Britain comes from the 8th century, in a text known as the " laws of King Ine." This document mentions regulations related to the selling and pricing of ale. The brewing tradition continued to evolve over the centuries, with various styles emerging. The Industrial Revolution brought mass production, with breweries like Bass pioneering pale ales. The world-famous pub culture solidified during the Victorian era, and the 20th century saw the emergence of beloved beer styles like bitters and porters. In recent years, the craft beer revolution has reinvigorated the scene, with microbreweries adding a modern twist to this timeless British tradition.

### A Guide to British Beers:

#### Bitter:
*Description:* A well-balanced ale with a moderate hop bitterness. Variants include Ordinary, Best, and Extra Special Bitter (ESB).
*Popular Brands:* Fuller's London Pride, Timothy Taylor's Landlord.

#### Mild:
*Description:* A dark, low-alcohol beer with a malty profile. Can be sweet or dry.
*Popular Brands:* Banks's Mild, Black Sheep Ale.

#### Porter:
*Description:* Dark and rich with notes of chocolate and coffee. A historical beer style with a resurgence.
*Popular Brands:* Fuller's London Porter, Titanic Brewery Plum Porter.

#### Stout:
*Description:* A robust, dark beer with flavors of roasted malt and sometimes hints of coffee or chocolate.
*Popular Brands:* Guinness, Samuel Smith's Oatmeal Stout.

#### Pale Ale:
*Description:* Amber-colored with a balance of malt sweetness and hop bitterness. Includes variations like India Pale Ale (IPA).
*Popular Brands:* BrewDog Punk IPA, Adnams Ghost Ship.

#### Barleywine:
*Description:* A strong ale with high alcohol content and a rich, often fruity, malt character.
*Popular Brands:* Fuller's Golden Pride, JW Lees Harvest Ale.

### How to Drink Beer in the UK Cheaply:

#### Visit Local Pubs:
Choose local pubs over tourist-heavy areas. You'll find better prices and a more authentic experience.

#### Happy Hours:
Take advantage of happy hour deals, often available during off-peak times.

#### Real Ale Festivals:

Attend real ale festivals for a variety of choices at reasonable prices. Check local event listings.

Here are some budget-friendly beer tasting options across the United Kingdom:

**BrewDog:**
*Location:* Various cities including London, Edinburgh, Manchester.
*Price:* Check their website for specific locations, but many offer affordable tasting flights.

**Fuller's Brewery:**
*Location:* London.
*Price:* Brewery tours with tastings are reasonably priced. Check their website for current rates.

**Adnams Brewery:**
*Location:* Southwold, Suffolk.
*Price:* Adnams offers brewery tours with tastings at a reasonable cost. Check their website for details.

**Wiper and True Brewery:**
*Location:* Bristol.
*Price:* They often have taproom events with affordable beer flights. Check their events page for details.

**JW Lees Brewery:**
*Location:* Manchester.
*Price:* Brewery tours include tastings and are reasonably priced. Check their website for current rates.

**Timothy Taylor's Brewery:**
*Location:* Keighley, West Yorkshire.
*Price:* Tours with tastings are available at reasonable prices. Check their website for details.

**St Austell Brewery:**
*Location:* Cornwall.
*Price:* Brewery tours with tastings are offered at a reasonable cost. Check their website for current rates.

**Shepherd Neame Brewery:**
*Location:* Faversham, Kent.
*Price:* Brewery tours with tastings are available. Check their website for pricing and availability.

# Wine tastings

The modern English wine industry truly blossomed in the late 20th and early 21st centuries. Historically, the climate posed challenges, but advancements in viticulture techniques and the warming climate have paved the way for success. Sparkling wines, particularly from regions like Sussex and Kent, have garnered international acclaim, rivaling some of the finest. There are lots of options for cheap or even free wine tasting:

### Laithwaite's Wine Tasting Experience:

Laithwaite's Wine Tasting Experience invites enthusiasts to explore various locations, including London, Manchester, and Edinburgh. While prices may vary, their events are often affordable, providing an accessible way for wine lovers to indulge in tastings and expand their palate. For the latest details on pricing and events, checking their website is a wise move.

### Majestic Wine:

With locations nationwide, Majestic Wine offers a broad reach for wine enthusiasts. This wine retailer occasionally hosts free or low-cost wine tastings, providing an excellent opportunity for individuals to discover new flavors. For specific details about upcoming events, interested individuals can visit the Majestic Wine website or inquire at their local store.

### The Wine Society:

Situated in Stevenage, The Wine Society offers tastings as part of its membership benefits. With occasional events organized by The Wine Society, members can explore a diverse selection of wines. Stay informed about their tasting opportunities by checking their website for event details and updates.

### Naked Wines Tastings:

Naked Wines, with various locations, hosts events that may include tastings, offering an engaging experience for wine enthusiasts. To stay in the loop about upcoming events and tastings, individuals can regularly check the Naked Wines website for announcements and details.

### Berry Bros. & Rudd:
Nestled in London, Berry Bros. & Rudd, known for its high-end wines, occasionally extends the opportunity for introductory tastings at reasonable costs. Wine aficionados interested in exploring their offerings can keep an eye on the events page of the Berry Bros. & Rudd website for information on upcoming tastings and experiences.

# Recap on how to save on food

| Cost-Saving Measure | Potential Monthly Savings |
| --- | --- |
| **Pick Up Too Good to Go Bags** | |
| - Groceries and restaurant quality food | £2,000 - £5,000 |
| Bags retail around £2.99 | |
| **Eating Out Strategically:** | |
| - Lunch Specials + pre-theatre set menus | £50 - £100 |
| - Early Bird Dinners | £30 - £60 |
| - Food Markets and Street Food | £30 - £60 |
| **Discounts and Loyalty Programs:** | |
| - Restaurant Discounts (e.g., apps) | £20 - £40 |
| - Supermarket Loyalty Programs | £10 - £20 |
| **Avoiding Touristy Areas:** | |
| - Non-Touristy Restaurants | £30 - £60 |
| - Local Markets | £20 - £40 |
| **BYOB (Bring Your Own Bottle):** | |
| - Buy Alcohol at Supermarkets | £20 - £40 |
| - Choose BYOB Restaurants. Common at India and Asian restaurants | £20 - £40 |
| **Water Refills and Tap Water:** | |
| - Carry a Reusable Water Bottle | £10 - £20 |
| - Request Tap Water in Restaurants | £10 - £20 |
| **Total Potential Monthly Savings:** | **£2,000** |

By mixing and matching food options, you can save thousands on eating delicious food in the UK.

# Itinerary for Seven Days

### Day 1: London

- Morning: Free walking tour to explore landmarks like Westminster Abbey and Big Ben.
- Afternoon: Picnic in St. James's Park or Hyde Park.
- Evening: Affordable West End theater tickets for a show. Use rush tickets or the TKTS app.

### Day 2: London

- Morning: Visit the British Museum (free entry) and explore Bloomsbury.
- Afternoon: Lunch in a local market like Borough Market.
- Evening: Take a stroll along the South Bank and enjoy the views of the Thames.

### Day 3: Edinburgh

- Morning: Travel to Edinburgh (look for megabus options - they are the cheapest).
- Afternoon: Visit the free National Museum of Scotland.
- Evening: Explore the historic Royal Mile and enjoy dinner in a local pub.

### Day 4: Edinburgh

- Morning: Hike up Arthur's Seat for panoramic views.
- Afternoon: Visit the free Scottish National Gallery.
- Evening: Experience live music in a traditional Scottish pub.

### Day 5: Bath

- Morning: Travel to Bath (consider budget-friendly transportation options).
- Afternoon: Explore the Roman Baths (entry fee required) and stroll through the city center.
- Evening: Relax in the Thermae Bath Spa (consider booking discounted evening sessions).

### Day 6: Oxford

- Morning: Visit the Bodleian Library (book a free guided tour) and explore the Radcliffe Camera.
- Afternoon: Have a budget-friendly lunch in a local pub.
- Evening: Take a walk through the historic Oxford University colleges.

### Day 7: Cambridge

- Morning: Travel to Cambridge (book the train in advance or take the megabus).
- Afternoon: Punt on the River Cam or take a self-guided walking tour.
- Evening: Enjoy dinner in one of the city's charming restaurants.

# Month-Long Itinerary

### Week 1: London and Surroundings

### Days 1-3: London

- Explore iconic landmarks, parks, and free museums.
- Indulge in budget-friendly West End shows.
- Enjoy diverse cuisine from street markets.

### Days 4-7: Day Trips from London

- Day trip to Oxford: Explore historic colleges and museums.
- Day trip to Cambridge: Punt on the River Cam and visit universities.
- Day trip to Windsor: Discover Windsor Castle and the charming town.

### Week 2: Edinburgh and Scottish Highlands

### Days 8-11: Edinburgh

- Delve into the city's history on the Royal Mile.
- Hike Arthur's Seat and enjoy panoramic views.
- Experience the lively arts and music scene.

### Days 12-14: Scottish Highlands (Inverness)

- Travel to Inverness by budget-friendly transportation.
- Explore Loch Ness, Urquhart Castle, and the Culloden Battlefield.
- Take a scenic train journey through the Highlands.

### Week 3: Southwest England - Bath and Cornwall

### Days 15-17: Bath

- Visit the Roman Baths and historic architecture.
- Relax in the Thermae Bath Spa.
- Explore the picturesque Cotswolds on a day trip.

### Days 18-21: Cornwall

- Head to Cornwall via budget transportation.
- Discover St. Ives, the Eden Project, and coastal landscapes.
- Enjoy local seafood and relax on beautiful beaches.

### Week 4: Northern England - York and Lake District

### Days 22-24: York

- Wander through York Minster and the Shambles.
- Take a stroll on the medieval city walls.
- Visit the National Railway Museum.

### Days 25-28: Lake District

- Travel to the Lake District by budget-friendly means.
- Explore picturesque villages and hiking trails.
- Enjoy boat rides on Windermere and Coniston Water.

**Day 29-30: Return to London**

- Return to London for final explorations or shopping.
- Reflect on your month-long adventure with a leisurely day.

# Snapshot: How to have a £10,000 Trip to the UK for £1,000

| Day | Location | Accommodation | Transport Hack | Activities |
|-----|----------|---------------|----------------|------------|
| 1-3 | London 🏴 | Boutique hostels. Lastminute secret hotels. | Use Oyster Card for affordable public transport | Free museums, explore parks, Borough Market for meals |
| 4-7 | Day Trips from London 🚂 | | Opt for off-peak train tickets or megabus | Day trips to Oxford, Cambridge, and Windsor |
| 8-14 | Edinburgh & Highlands 🏴 | Budget-friendly guesthouses | Explore Inverness by affordable bus | Edinburgh landmarks, Arthur's Seat, Loch Ness |
| 15-21 | Southwest England Bath & Cornwall 🏴 | guesthouses or budget hotels | Use budget coaches for longer distances | Roman Baths, Cotswolds day trip, explore Cornwall |
| 22-28 | Northern England - York & Lake District 🏴 | Mix of budget hotels and Airbnbs | Consider budget train tickets in advance | York Minster, Lake District hikes, boat rides |
| Last Days | Return to London 🏴 | Indulge in a five-star hotel from £70 with blindbooking | Book a budget bus to the airport for the return journey | Final explorations, shopping |

**Hacks & Tips:**

- **Accommodation:** Mix boutique hostels, budget hotels, and guesthouses.
- **Transport:** Plan and book transportation in advance for discounts.
- **Activities:** Leverage free museum entries and explore local markets.
- **Meals:** Try street food, local markets, and budget-friendly eateries.

**Best Things to Eat:**

- **London:** Street food in Borough Market.
- **Edinburgh:** Haggis and Scotch eggs.
- **Cornwall:** Cornish pasties and fresh seafood.
- **York:** Yorkshire pudding and local ales.
- **Lake District:** Cumberland sausage and sticky toffee pudding.

# How to Enjoy ALLOCATING Money in UK

**'Money's greatest intrinsic value—and this can't be overstated—is its ability to give you control over your time.' - Morgan Housel**

Notice I have titled the chapter how to enjoy allocating money in UK. I'll use saving and allocating interchangeably in the book, but since most people associate saving to feel like a turtleneck, that's too tight, I've chosen to use wealth language. Rich people don't save. They allocate. What's the difference? Saving can feel like something you don't want or wish to do and allocating has your personal will attached to it.

And on that note, it would be helpful if you considered removing the following words and phrase from your vocabulary for planning and enjoying your UK trip:

- Wish

- Want

- Maybe someday

These words are part of poverty language. Language is a dominant source of creation. Use it to your advantage. You don't have to wish, want or say maybe someday to UK. You can enjoy the same things millionaires enjoy in UK without the huge spend.

**'People don't like to be sold-but they love to buy.' - Jeffrey Gitomer.**

Every good salesperson who understands the quote above places obstacles in the way of their clients' buying. Companies create waiting lists, restaurants pay people to queue outside in order to create demand. People reason if something is so in demand, it must be worth having but that's often just marketing. Take this sales maxim 'People don't like to be sold-but they love to buy and flip it on its head to allocate your money in UK on things YOU desire. You love to spend and hate to be sold. That means when something comes your way, it's not 'I can't afford it,' it's 'I don't want it' or maybe 'I don't want it right now'.

Saving money doesn't mean never buying a latte, never taking a taxi, never taking vacations (of course, you bought this book). Only you get to decide on how you spend and on what. Not an advice columnist who thinks you can buy a house if you never eat avocado toast again.

I love what Kate Northrup says about affording something: "If you really wanted it you would figure out a way to get it. If it were that VALUABLE to you, you would make it happen."

I believe if you master the art of allocating money to bargains, it can feel even better than spending it! Bold claim, I know. But here's the truth: Money gives you freedom and options. The more you keep in your account and or invested the more freedom and options you'll have. The principal reason you should save and allocate money is TO BE FREE! Remember, a trip's main purpose is relaxation, rest and enjoyment, aka to feel free.

When you talk to most people about saving money on vacation. They grimace. How awful they proclaim not to go wild on your vacation. If you can't get into a ton of debt enjoying your once-in-a-lifetime vacation, when can you?

When you spend money 'theres's a sudden rush of dopamine which vanishes once the transaction is complete. What happens in the brain when you save money? It increases feelings of security and peace. You don't need to stress life's uncertainties. And having a greater sense of peace can actually help you save more money.' Stressed out people make impulsive financial choices, calm people don't.'

The secret to enjoying saving money on vacation is very simple: never save money from a position of lack. Don't think 'I wish I could afford that'. Choose not to be marketed to. Choose not to consume at a price others set. Don't save money from the flawed premise you don't have enough. Don't waste your time living in the box that society has created, which says saving money on vacation means sacrifice. It doesn't.

Traveling to UK can be an expensive endeavor if you don't approach it with a plan, but you have this book which is packed with tips. The biggest other asset is your perspective.

# How to feel RICH in UK

You don't need millions in your bank to **feel rich**. Feeling rich feels different to every person."Researchers have pooled data on the relationship between money and emotions from more than 1.6 million people across 162 countries and found that **wealthier people feel more positive "self-regard emotions" such as confidence, pride and determination."**

Here are things to see, do and taste in UK, that will have you overflowing with gratitude for your luxury trip to UK.

- Achieving a Michelin Star rating is the most coveted accolade for restaurants but those that obtain a Michelin Star are synonymous with high cost, but in UK there are restaurants with Michelin-stars offering lunch menus for 15 euros or less!If you want to taste the finest seasonal local dishes while dining in pure luxury, visit Ron Blaauw's Gastrobar to indulge in an unforgettable treat. If fine dining isn't your thing, don't worry further on in the guide you will find a range of delicious cheap eats in UK that deserve a Michelin-Star.
- While money can't buy happiness, it can buy cake and isn't that sort of the same thing? Jokes aside, Gail's Bakery has turned cakes and pastries into edible art. Visit to taste the most delicious buttery croissant in London.
- While you might not be staying in a penthouse, you can still enjoy the same views. Visit rooftop bars in UK, like SkyBar to enjoy incredible sunset views for the price of just one drink. And if you want to continue enjoying libations, head over to The Susie's Saloon for a dirt-cheap happy hour, lots of reasonably priced (and delicious) cocktails and cheap delicious snacks.

Those are just some ideas for you to know that visiting UK on a budget doesn't have to feel like sacrifice or constriction. Now let's get into the nuts and bolts of UK on the super cheap.

# How to use this book

Google and TripAdvisor are your on-the-go guides while traveling, a travel guide adds the most value during the planning phase, and if you're without Wi-Fi. Always download the google map for your destination - having an offline map will make using this guide much more comfortable. For ease of use, we've set the book out the way you travel, booking your flights, arriving, how to get around, then on to the money-saving tips. The tips we ordered according to when you need to know the tip to save money, so free tours and combination tickets feature first. We prioritized the rest of the tips by how much money you can save and then by how likely it was that you could find the tip with a google search. Meaning those we think you could find alone are nearer the bottom. I hope you find this layout useful. If you have any ideas about making Super Cheap Insider Guides easier to use, please email me philgattang@gmail.com

**A quick note on How We Source Super Cheap Tips**
We focus entirely on finding the best bargains. We give each of our collaborators $2,000 to hunt down never-before-seen deals. The type you either only know if you're local or by on the ground research. We spend zero on marketing and a little on designing an excellent cover. We do this yearly, which means we just keep finding more amazing ways for you to have the same experience for less.

Now let's get started with juicing the most pleasure from your trip to UK with the least possible money!

# Booking Your Flights

# How to Find Heavily Discounted Private Jet Flights to or from UK

If you're dreaming of travelling to UK on a private jet you can accomplish your dream for a 10th of the cost.

Empty leg flights, also known as empty leg charters or deadhead flights, are flights operated by private jet companies that do not have any passengers on board. These flights occur when a private jet is chartered for a one-way trip, but the jet needs to return to its base or another location without passengers.

Rather than flying empty, private jet companies may offer these empty leg flights for a reduced price to travelers who are flexible and able to fly on short notice. Because the flight is already scheduled and paid for by the original charter, private jet companies are willing to offer these flights at a discounted rate in order to recoup some of the cost.

Empty leg flights can be a cost-effective way to experience the luxury and convenience of private jet travel.

**Taking an empty leg private jet flight from America to UK**

The New York City-UK route is one of the busiest private jet routes in the world, with many private jet operators offering regular flights between the two cities.

**There are several websites that offer empty leg flights for booking. Here are a few:**

JetSuiteX: This website offers discounted, last-minute flights on private jets, including empty leg flights.

PrivateFly: This website allows you to search for empty leg flights by location or date. You can also request a quote for a custom flight if you have specific needs.

Victor: This website offers a variety of private jet services, including empty leg flights.

Sky500: This website offers a variety of private jet services, including empty leg flights.

Air Charter Service: This website allows you to search for empty leg flights by location or date. You can also request a quote for a custom flight if you have specific needs.

Keep in mind that empty leg flights are often available at short notice, so it's a good idea to be flexible with your travel plans if you're looking for a deal. It's also important to do your research and read reviews before booking a flight with any company.

**RECAP: To book an empty leg flight in UK, follow these steps:**

1. Research and identify private jet companies and or brokers that offer empty leg flights departing from UK. You can use the websites mentioned earlier, such as JetSuiteX, PrivateFly, Victor, Sky500, or Air Charter Service, to search for available flights.

2. Check the availability and pricing of empty leg flights that match your travel dates and destination. Empty leg flights are often available at short notice.

3. Contact the private jet company or broker to inquire about booking the empty leg flight. Be sure to provide your travel details, including your preferred departure and arrival times, number of passengers, and any special requests.

4. Confirm your booking and make payment. Private jet companies and brokers typically require full payment upfront, so be prepared to pay for the flight in advance.

5. Arrive at the airport at least 30 minutes before the scheduled departure time.

6. Check in at the private jet terminal and go through any necessary security checks. Unlike commercial airlines, there is typically no long queue or security checks for private jet flights.

7. Board the private jet and settle into your seat. You will have plenty of space to stretch out and relax, as well as access to amenities such as Wi-Fi, entertainment systems, and refreshments.

# How to Find CHEAP FIRST-CLASS Flights to UK

### Upgrade at the airport

Airlines are extremely reluctant to advertise price drops in first or business class tickets so the best way to secure them is actually at the airport when airlines have no choice but to decrease prices dramatically because otherwise they lose money. Ask about upgrading to business or first-class when you check-in. If you check-in online look around the airport for your airlines branded bidding system.

### Use Air-miles

When it comes to accruing air-miles for American citizens **Chase Sapphire Reserve card** ranks top. If you put everything on there and pay it off immediately you will end up getting free flights all the time, aside from taxes.

Get 2-3 chase cards with sign up bonuses, you'll have 200k points in no time and can book with points on multiple airlines when transferring your points to them.

Please note, this is only applicable to those living in the USA. In the Bonus Section we have detailed the best air-mile credit cards for those living in other countries.

### How many miles does it take to fly first class?

New York City to UK could require anywhere from 70,000 to 120,000 frequent flyer miles, depending on the airline and the time of year you plan to travel.

# How to Fly Business Class to UK cheaply

TAP Air Portugal is a popular airline that operates flights from New York City to UK with the cheapest business class options. In low season this route typically started at around $1,000-$1,500 per person for a round-trip ticket.

The average cost for a round-trip flight from New York City to UK typically ranged from around $400 to $1200 for an economy seat, so if travelling business class is important to you, TAP Air Portugal is likely to be the best bang for your buck.

To find the best deals on business class flights to UK, follow these steps:

1. Use travel search engines: Start by searching for flights on popular travel search engines like Google Flights, Kayak, or Skyscanner. These sites allow you to compare prices from different airlines and book the cheapest available business option.
2. Sign up for airline newsletters: Airlines often send out exclusive deals and promotions to their email subscribers. Sign up for TAP Air Portugal's newsletter to receive notifications about special offers and discounts on business class flights.
3. Book in advance: Booking your flight well in advance can help you secure a better deal on business class tickets. Aim to book your flight at least two to three months before your travel date.
4.

# How to ALWAYS Find Super Cheap Flights to UK

If you're just interested in finding the cheapest flight to UK here is here to do it!

**Luck is just an illusion.**

Anyone can find incredible flight deals. If you can be flexible you can save huge amounts of money. In fact, the biggest tip I can give you for finding incredible flight deals is simple: find a flexible job. Don't despair if you can't do that theres still a lot you can do.

**Book your flight to UK on a Tuesday or Wednesday**

Tuesdays and Wednesdays are the cheapest days of the week to fly. You can take a flight to UK on a Tuesday or Wednesday for less than half the price you'd pay on a Thursday Friday, Saturday, Sunday or Monday.

**Start with Google Flights (but NEVER book through them)**

I conduct upwards of 50 flight searches a day for readers. I use google flights first when looking for flights. I put specific departure but broad destination (e.g Europe) and usually find amazing deals.

The great thing about Google Flights is you can search by class. You can pick a specific destination and it will tell you which time is cheapest in which class. Or you can put in dates and you can see which area is cheapest to travel to.

But be aware Google flights does not show the cheapest prices among the flight search engines but it does offer several advantages

1. You can see the cheapest dates for the next 8 weeks. Other search engines will blackout over 70% of the prices.
2. You can put in multiple airports to fly from. Just use a common to separate in the from input.
3. If you're flexible on where you're going Google flights can show you the cheapest destinations.
4. You can set-up price tracking, where Google will email you when prices rise or decline.

Once you have established the cheapest dates to fly go over to skyscanner.net and put those dates in. You will find sky scanner offers the cheapest flights.

**Get Alerts when Prices to UK are Lowest**

Google also has a nice feature which allows you to set up an alert to email you when prices to your destination are at their lowest. So if you don't have fixed dates this feature can save you a fortune.

### Baggage add-ons

It may be cheaper and more convenient to send your luggage separately with a service like sendmybag.com Often the luggage sending fee is cheaper than what the airlines charge to check baggage. Visit Lugless.com or luggagefree.com in addition to sendmybag.com for a quotation.

### Loading times

Anyone who has attempted to find a cheap flight will know the pain of excruciating long loading times. If you encounter this issue use google flights to find the cheapest dates and then go to skyscanner.net for the lowest price.

### Always try to book direct with the airline

Once you have found the cheapest flight go direct to the airlines booking page. This is advantageous because if you need to change your flights or arrange a refund, its much easier to do so, than via a third party booking agent.

That said, sometimes the third party bookers offer cheaper deals than the airline, so you need to make the decision based on how likely you think it is that disruption will impede you making those flights.

### More Fight Tricks and Tips

**www.secretflying.com/usa-deals** offers a range of deals from the USA and other countries. For example you can pick-up a round trip flight non-stop from from the east coast to johannesburg for $350 return on this site

**Scott's cheap flights,** you can select your home airport and get emails on deals but you pay for an annual subscription. A free workaround is to download Hopper and set search alerts for trips/price drops.

### Premium service of Scott's cheap flights.
They sometime have discounted business and first class but in my experience they are few and far between.

**JGOOT.com** has 5 times as many choices as Scott's cheap flights.

**kiwi.com** allows you to be able to do radius searches so you can find cheaper flights to general areas.

### Finding Error Fares

Travel Pirates (www.travelpirates.com) is a gold-mine for finding error deals. Subscribe to their newsletter. I recently found a reader an airfare from Montreal-Brazil for a $200 round trip (mistake fare!). Of course these error fares are always certain dates, but if you can be flexible you can save a lot of money.

### Things you can do that might reduce the fare to UK:

• Use a VPN (if the booker knows you booked one-way, the return fare will go up)
• Buy your ticket in a different currency

## If all else fails...

If you can't find a cheap flight for your dates I can find one for you. I do not charge for this nor do I send affiliate links. I'll send you a screenshot of the best options I find as airlines attach cookies to flight links. To use this free service please review this guide and send me a screenshot of your review - with your flight hacking request. I aim to reply to you within 12 hours. If it's an urgent request mark the email URGENT in the subject line and I will endeavour to reply ASAP.

### A tip for coping with Jet-lag

Jetlag is primarily caused by disruptions to the body's circadian rhythm, which is the internal "biological clock" that regulates many of the body's processes, including sleep-wake cycles. When you travel across multiple time zones, your body's clock is disrupted, leading to symptoms like fatigue, insomnia, and stomach problems.

Eating on your travel destination's time before you travel can help to adjust your body's clock before you arrive, which can help to mitigate the effects of jetlag. This means that if you're traveling to a destination that is several hours ahead of your current time zone, you should try to eat meals at the appropriate times for your destination a few days before you leave. For example, if you're traveling from New York to UK, which is seven hours ahead, you could start eating dinner at 9pm EST (which is 3am UK time) a few days before your trip.

By adjusting your eating schedule before you travel, you can help to shift your body's clock closer to the destination's time zone, which can make it easier to adjust to the new schedule once you arrive.

# Accommodation

Your two biggest expenses when travelling to UK are accommodation and food. This section is intended to help you cut these costs dramatically without compromising on those luxury feels:

# Enjoy the Finest Five-star Hotels for a 10th of the Cost

If you travel during the peak season or during a major event, you can still enjoy the finest hotels in UK for a 10th of the normal cost. With a day pass, you can enjoy all the amenities that the hotel has to offer, including the pool, spa, gym, and included lunches at fine restaurants. This can be a great way to relax and unwind for a day without having to spend money on an overnight stay.

Here are some of the best luxury day passes UK hotels. Prices start at £50.

**The Ritz London, London:**

Experience the epitome of luxury at The Ritz Spa, renowned for its opulent surroundings and world-class treatments. A day pass grants access to exclusive spa facilities, providing a serene escape in the heart of London.

**Claridge's, London:**

Immerse yourself in elegance with a day pass to Claridge's spa facilities and gym. Indulge in a sophisticated atmosphere, unwind in the spa, and maintain your fitness routine in a glamorous setting.

**The Dorchester, London:**

The Dorchester Spa promises a haven of tranquility. With a day pass, revel in the lavish facilities, from the relaxation room to the aromatic steam rooms. Treat yourself to rejuvenating spa treatments for the ultimate pampering experience.

**The Langham, London:**

The Chuan Body + Soul spa at The Langham offers a holistic approach to well-being. A day pass allows you to enjoy the serene ambiance, state-of-the-art facilities, and indulge in spa day packages designed to rejuvenate your body and soul.

**Gleneagles, Perthshire, Scotland:**

Escape to the picturesque landscape of Gleneagles and indulge in a day pass offering access to the spa and leisure facilities. Unwind in the Scottish countryside while enjoying top-notch spa treatments and leisure activities.

**The Balmoral, Edinburgh:**

The Balmoral Spa combines luxury and tradition in the heart of Edinburgh. A day pass invites you to experience the spa's unique blend of contemporary treatments and historic charm, ensuring a day of relaxation and rejuvenation.

**The Principal Grand Central Hotel, Glasgow:**

The Grand Central Spa at The Principal offers a retreat in the vibrant city of Glasgow. With a day pass, enjoy a relaxing escape, including spa treatments and access to modern facilities, allowing you to unwind amidst the energy of the city.

**The Midland, Manchester:**

The Midland Spa in Manchester provides a sanctuary of relaxation. A day pass gives you the opportunity to escape the hustle and bustle, indulge in spa therapies, and experience the rejuvenating ambiance of this historical hotel.

**The Malmaison, Liverpool:**

The Malmaison Spa in Liverpool invites you to a day of urban tranquility. With a day pass, explore the contemporary spa facilities, enjoy tailored spa day packages, and discover a haven of relaxation in the heart of the city.

**The Lowry Hotel, Manchester:**

The Lowry Spa offers a luxurious retreat in Manchester. A day pass provides access to the spa's modern facilities and a range of spa day packages, ensuring a revitalizing experience in this contemporary and stylish hotel.

These luxury hotels present an opportunity to indulge in world-class spa facilities, unwind in opulent surroundings, and enjoy the finest treatments, even if just for a day. Each hotel has its unique charm, making it an ideal destination for those seeking a day of lavish relaxation and pampering.

TOP TIP: AVOID The weekend price hike

Hotel prices skyrocket during weekends in peak season (June, July, August and December). If you can, get out of UK for the weekend you'll save thousands on luxury hotels. For example a room at a popular five-star hotel costs $80 a night during the week when blind-booking. That price goes to $400 a night for Saturday's and Sundays. Amazing nearby weekend trips are featured further on and planning those on the weekends could easily save you a ton of money and make your trip more comfortable by avoiding crowds.

# How to Book a Five-star Hotel consistently on the Cheap in UK

The cheapest four and five-star hotel deals are available when you 'blind book'. Blind booking is a type of discounted hotel booking where the guest doesn't know the name of the hotel until after they've booked and paid for the reservation. This allows hotels to offer lower prices without damaging their brand image or cannibalizing their full-price bookings.

Here are some of the best platforms for blind booking a hotel in UK:

1. Hotwire - This website offers discounted hotel rates for blind booking. You can choose the star rating, neighborhood, and amenities you want, but the actual hotel name will not be revealed until after you've booked.
2. Priceline - Once you've made the reservation, the hotel name and location will be revealed.
3. Secret Escapes - This website offers luxury hotel deals at discounted rates. You can choose the type of hotel you want and the general location, but the hotel name and exact location will be revealed after you book.
4. Lastminute.com - You can select the star rating and general location, but the hotel name and exact location will be revealed after booking. Using the Top Secret hotels you can find a four star hotel from $60 a night in UK - consistently! Most of the hotels featured are in the Grange Group. If in doubt, simply copy and paste the description into Google to find the name before booking.

# Unusual Cheap Places to Stay

The United Kingdom offers a variety of unique and affordable accommodation options for travelers seeking unconventional stays. Here are some unusual and budget-friendly places to consider:

- **Convents and Monasteries:**
    - Some religious institutions offer accommodations to travelers. These stays often provide a peaceful and simple environment. Examples include St. Briavels Castle in Gloucestershire.
- **Farm Stays:**
    - Experience rural life with farm stays. You can find affordable options where you contribute to farm activities or simply enjoy the countryside. Check out websites like Farm Stay UK for options.
- **Camping and Glamping:**
    - Enjoy the great outdoors by camping in designated areas or choosing glamping options with more comfort. Look for sites in national parks or private glamping retreats.
- **Boat Stays:**
    - Stay on a houseboat or narrowboat, especially in canal-rich areas like London's Regent's Canal or the Norfolk Broads. These can provide a unique and budget-friendly experience.
- **Treehouse Accommodations:**
    - Unleash your inner child with a stay in a treehouse. Various locations across the UK offer treehouse rentals, providing a whimsical and budget-friendly escape.
- **University Accommodations:**
    - During academic breaks, universities may offer affordable accommodations in their dormitories. Check university websites for availability.
- **Lighthouse Stays:**
    - Stay in a lighthouse for a unique coastal experience. Examples include staying at The Belle Tout Lighthouse in East Sussex.
- **Shepherd's Huts:**
    - Experience a cozy stay in a shepherd's hut, often found in rural areas. These small, rustic huts offer a charming and budget-friendly retreat.
- **Yurts and Tipis:**
    - Glamp in a yurt or tipi for a unique camping experience with added comfort. Numerous glamping sites provide these options across the UK.
- **Historic Castles and Manor Houses:**
    - Some historic properties offer affordable stays, allowing you to experience the grandeur of a castle or manor without breaking the bank. Examples include YHA St Briavels Castle.
- **Converted Railway Carriages:**
    - Stay in a converted railway carriage for a quirky lodging experience. Several locations, such as The Old Station Allerston in North Yorkshire, offer this type of accommodation.

# Universities renting dorm rooms in summer

Several universities in the United Kingdom offer dorm rooms or student accommodations for short-term rentals during the summer months. These options can provide budget-friendly stays in central locations. Here are a few universities known for offering summer accommodations:

- **University of Edinburgh:**
    - The University of Edinburgh often opens its student residences for summer accommodation. Check their official website for details and availability.
- **University of Oxford:**
    - Some of Oxford University's colleges offer student rooms for summer guests. Explore individual college websites or contact the university for information.
- **University of Cambridge:**
    - Similar to Oxford, Cambridge University's colleges may offer summer accommodations. Check with individual colleges for availability.
- **University of London:**
    - The University of London provides summer accommodations in various colleges across the city. Options range from budget to more upscale residences.
- **University of York:**
    - The University of York offers summer accommodation options in its student residences. Check their official website for details.
- **University of Birmingham:**
    - Birmingham University provides summer stays in selected student accommodations. Details can be found on the university's accommodation website.
- **University of Manchester:**
    - The University of Manchester may offer summer accommodations in student residences. Check their accommodation services for information.
- **University of Bristol:**
    - Bristol University often opens its student residences for short-term summer stays. Visit their accommodation services page for details.
- **University of Glasgow:**
    - The University of Glasgow may offer summer accommodations in student residences. Check with the university for availability.
- **University of Warwick:**
    - Warwick University provides summer accommodation options in its student residences. Check their accommodation services for details.

# Strategies to Book Five-Star Hotels for Two-Star Prices in UK

## Use Time

There are two ways to use time. One is to book in advance. Three months will net you the best deal, especially if your visit coincides with an event. The other is to book on the day of your stay. This is a risky move, but if executed well, you can lay your head in a five-star hotel for a 2-star fee.

Before you travel to UK, check for big events using a simple google search 'What's on in UK', if you find no big events drawing travellers, risk showing up with no accommodation booked (If there are big events on demand exceeds supply and you should avoid using this strategy). If you don't want to risk showing up with no accommodation booked, book a cheap accommodation with free-cancellation.

Before I go into demand-based pricing, take a moment to think about your risk tolerance. By risk, I am not talking about personal safety. No amount of financial savings is worth risking that. What I am talking about is being inconvenienced. Do you deal well with last-minute changes? Can you roll with the punches or do you freak out if something changes? Everyone is different and knowing yourself is the best way to plan a great trip. If you are someone that likes to have everything pre-planned using demand-based pricing to get cheap accommodation will not work for you.

### Demand-based pricing

Be they an Airbnb host or hotel manager; no one wants empty rooms. Most will do anything to make some revenue because they still have the same costs to cover whether the room is occupied or not. That's why you will find many hotels drastically slashing room rates for same-day bookings.

### How to book five-star hotels for a two-star price

You will not be able to find these discounts when the demand exceeds the supply. So if you're visiting during the peak season, or during an event which has drawn many travellers again don't try this.

1. On the day of your stay, visit booking.com (which offers better discounts than Kayak and agoda.com). Hotel
   Tonight individually checks for any last-minute bookings, but they take a big chunk of the action, so the better deals come from booking.com.
2. The best results come from booking between 2 pm and 4 pm when the risk of losing any revenue with no occupancy is most pronounced, so algorithms supporting hotels slash prices. This is when you can find rates that are not within the "lowest publicly visible" rate.
3. To avoid losing customers to other websites, or cheapening the image of their hotel most will only offer the super cheap rates during a two hour window from 2 pm to 4

pm. Two guests will pay 10x difference in price but it's absolutely vital to the hotel that neither knows it.

**Takeaway**: To get the lowest price book on the day of stay between 2 pm and 4 pm and extend your search radius to include further afield hotels with good transport connections.

There are several luxury hotels outside of UK's city center that offer good transport connections to the city, as well as easy access to other nearby attractions. Here are a few options to consider:

1. The Grove: This five-star hotel is located in Hertfordshire, just 18 miles north of UK. It offers a free shuttle bus to and from Watford Junction station, where you can catch a train into UK's Euston station in just 18 minutes. The hotel also has its own golf course, spa, and several dining options.
2. Coworth Park: This luxurious country house hotel is located in Ascot, about 25 miles west of UK. It offers easy access to Heathrow Airport, as well as direct train connections to UK's Waterloo station from nearby Sunningdale station. The hotel has its own polo fields, spa, and Michelin-starred restaurant.
3. Pennyhill Park Hotel and Spa: This five-star hotel is located in Surrey, just 30 miles southwest of UK. It is easily accessible by car or train, with direct connections to UK's Waterloo station from nearby Bagshot station. The hotel has a large spa, several dining options, and is set on 123 acres of landscaped gardens and parkland.
4. Cliveden House: This historic country house hotel is located in Berkshire, about 25 miles west of UK. It is easily accessible by car or train, with direct connections to UK's Paddington station from nearby Taplow station. The hotel has a spa, several dining options, and is set on 376 acres of National Trust gardens and parkland.

These are just a few examples of luxury hotels outside of UK's city center with good transport connections to the city and opportunities for last-minute discounts.

# Priceline Hack to get a Luxury Hotel on the Cheap

Priceline.com has been around since 1997 and is an incredible site for sourcing luxury Hotels on the cheap in UK.

Priceline have a database of the lowest price a hotel will accept for a particular time and date. That amount changes depending on two factors:

1. Demand: More demand high prices.
2. Likelihood of lost revenue: if the room is still available at 3pm the same-day prices will plummet.

Obviously they don't want you to know the lowest price as they make more commission the higher the price you pay.

They offer two good deals to entice you to book with them in UK. And the good news is neither require last-minute booking (though the price will decrease the closer to the date you book).

'Firstly, 'price-breakers'. You blind book from a choice of three highly rated hotels which they name. Pricebreakers, travelers are shown three similar, highly-rated hotels, listed under a single low price.' After you book they reveal the name of the hotel.

Secondly, the 'express deals'. These are the last minute deals. You'll be able to see the name of the hotel before you book.

To find the right luxury hotel for you at a cheap price you should plug in the neighbourhoods you want to stay in, an acceptable rating (4 or 5 stars), and filter by the amenities you want.

You can also get an addition discount for your UK hotel by booking on their dedicated app.

## How to trick travel Algorithms to get the lowest hotel price

Do not believe anyone who says changing your IP address to get cheaper hotels or flights does NOT work. If you don't believe us, download a Tor Network and search for flights and hotels to one destination using your current IP and then the tor network (a tor browser hides your IP address from algorithms. It is commonly used by hackers). You will receive different prices.

The price you see is a decision made by an algorithm that adjusts prices using data points such as past bookings, remaining capacity, average demand and the probability of selling the room or flight later at a higher price. If knows you've searched for the area before ip the prices high. To circumvent this, you can either use a different IP address from a cafe or airport or data from an international sim. I use a sim from Three, which provides free data in many countries around the world. When you search from a new IP address, most of the time, and particularly near booking you will get a lower price. Sometimes if your sim comes from a 'rich' country, say the UK or USA, you will see higher rates as the algorithm has learnt people from these countries pay more. The solution is to book from a local wifi connection - but a different one from the one you originally searched from.

# Cheapest villages for renting affordable Airbnb's

On average, you can expect to pay anywhere from £50 to £150 per night for a standard Airbnb accommodation. However, prices can go higher for larger or more luxurious properties in popular tourist destinations or major cities like London and Edinburgh. Conversely, you might find more budget-friendly options in less touristy areas or during off-peak seasons. These villages provide unique experiences, from coastal tranquility to historic charm, making them excellent choices for an affordable and memorable Airbnb stay in the United Kingdom.

**Alnmouth, Northumberland, England:**

Nestled along the Northumberland coast, Alnmouth is a quaint village adorned with sandy beaches, historic architecture, and an inviting atmosphere. An ideal retreat for those in search of a peaceful coastal getaway, Alnmouth offers scenic walks and traditional charm.

**Luss, Loch Lomond, Scotland:**

Perched on the shores of Loch Lomond, Luss is a picturesque village surrounded by rolling hills and verdant landscapes. Its tranquil setting makes it a perfect haven for nature lovers, serving as a gateway to explore the stunning Loch Lomond National Park.

**Staithes, North Yorkshire, England:**

Steeped in maritime history, Staithes is a charming fishing village characterized by narrow cobbled streets, colorful cottages, and a historic harbor. This destination provides a nostalgic step back in time, appealing to artists, photographers, and those seeking a quiet escape.

**Polperro, Cornwall, England:**

Polperro enchants visitors with its quirky charm—winding streets, white-washed cottages, and a vibrant arts scene. Coastal walks, seafood delights, and a relaxed ambiance make Polperro an ideal coastal getaway on the southern coast of England.

**Plockton, Highlands, Scotland:**

Nestled in the Scottish Highlands, Plockton is an idyllic village boasting palm trees, serene Loch Carron views, and a tranquil ambiance. Known for its mild climate and stunning landscapes, Plockton serves as an excellent base for exploring the breathtaking Scottish Highlands.

**Bibury, Cotswolds, England:**

Regarded as one of the most beautiful villages in the Cotswolds, Bibury charms with its honey-colored stone cottages and a tranquil river. A quintessential English countryside experience awaits those seeking picturesque landscapes and charming rural architecture.

### Robin Hood's Bay, North Yorkshire, England:

Steeped in maritime heritage, Robin Hood's Bay is a historic fishing village featuring narrow alleyways, dramatic cliffs, and a captivating atmosphere. Coastal hikes, fossil hunting, and a charming ambiance transport visitors to another era.

### Culross, Fife, Scotland:

Frozen in time, Culross is a well-preserved 17th-century village adorned with cobbled streets, a palace, and colorful houses. Serving as a living museum, Culross showcases Scottish history, architecture, and culture.

### Porlock, Somerset, England:

Tucked between Exmoor National Park and the Bristol Channel, Porlock is a quaint village offering a peaceful retreat. With access to both coastal and moorland landscapes, Porlock provides an idyllic escape in the heart of Somerset.

### Tobermory, Isle of Mull, Scotland:
Gracing the Isle of Mull, Tobermory is a vibrant harbor town boasting colorful buildings, a whisky distillery, and abundant marine wildlife. Ideal for nature enthusiasts, Tobermory offers whale watching, birdwatching, and the exploration of surrounding islands.

# How to get last-minute discounts on owner rented properties

In addition to Airbnb, you can also find owner rented rooms and apartments on www.vrbo.com or HomeAway or a host of others.

Nearly all owners renting accommodation will happily give renters a "last-minute" discount to avoid the space sitting empty, not earning a dime.

Go to Airbnb or another platform and put in today's date. Once you've found something you like start the negotiating by asking for a 25% reduction. A sample message to an Airbnb host might read:

Dear HOST NAME,

I love your apartment. It looks perfect for me. Unfortunately, I'm on a very tight budget. I hope you won't be offended, but I wanted to ask if you would be amenable to offering me a 25% discount for tonight, tomorrow and the following day? I see that you aren't booked.

I can assure you, I will leave your place exactly the way I found it. I will put bed linen in the washer and ensure everything is clean for the next guest. I would be delighted to bring you a bottle of wine to thank you for any discount that you could offer.

If this sounds okay, please send me a custom offer, and I will book straight away.

YOUR NAME.

In my experience, a polite, genuine message like this, that proposes reciprocity will be successful 80% of the time. Don't ask for more than 25% off, this person still has to pay the bills and will probably say no as your stay will cost them more in bills than they make. Plus starting higher, can offend the owner and do you want to stay somewhere, where you have offended the host?

## In Practice

To use either of these methods, you must travel light. Less stuff means greater mobility, everything is faster and you don't have to check-in or store luggage. If you have a lot of luggage, you're going to have fewer of these opportunities to save on accommodation. Plus travelling light benefits the planet - you're buying, consuming, and transporting less stuff.

## Blind-booking

If your risk tolerance does not allow for last-minute booking, you can use blind-booking. Many hotels not wanting to cheapen their brand with known low-prices, choose to operate a blind booking policy. This is where you book without knowing the name of the hotel you're going to stay in until you've made the payment. This is also sometimes used as a marketing strategy where the hotel is seeking to recover from past issues. I've stayed in plenty of blind book hotels. As long as you choose 4 or 5 star hotels, you will find them to be clean, comfortable and safe. priceline.com, Hot Rate® Hotels and Top Secret Hotels (operated by lastminute.com) offer the best deals.

## Hotels.com Loyalty Program

This is currently the best hotel loyalty program with hotels in UK. The basic premise is you collect 10 nights and get 1 free. hotels.com price match, so if booking.com has a cheaper price you can get hotel.com, to match. If you intend to travel more than ten nights in a year, its a great choice to get the 11th free.

## Don't let time use you.

Rigidity will cost you money. You pay the price you're willing to pay, not the amount it requires a hotel to deliver. Therefore if you're in town for a big event, saving money on accommodation is nearly impossible so in such cases book three months ahead.

### How to trick travel Algorithms to get the lowest hotel price

Do not believe anyone who says changing your IP address to get cheaper hotels or flights does NOT work. If you don't believe us, download a Tor Network and search for flights and hotels to one destination using your current IP and then the tor network (a tor browser hides your IP address from algorithms. It is commonly used by hackers). You will receive different prices.

The price you see is a decision made by an algorithm that adjusts prices using data points such as past bookings, remaining capacity, average demand and the probability of selling the room or flight later at a higher price. If knows you've searched for the area before ip the prices high. To circumvent this, you can either use a different IP address from a cafe or airport or data from an international sim. I use a sim from Three, which provides free data in many countries around the world. When you search from a new IP address, most of the time, and particularly near booking you will get a lower price. Sometimes if your sim comes from a 'rich' country, say the UK or USA, you will see higher rates as the algorithm has learnt people from these countries pay more. The solution is to book from a local wifi connection - but a different one from the one you originally searched from.

# OUR SUPER CHEAP TIPS...

**Here are our specific super cheap tips for enjoying a £10,000 trip to UK for just £1,000.**

## Cheapest route to UK from America

**At the time of writing Norwegian Air Shuttle, WOW Air, TUI Airways, Aer Lingus, Icelandair, and Level are flying to UK from $150 return.**

## How to Find Super Cheap Flights to UK

Luck is just an illusion. Anyone can find incredible flight deals. If you can be flexible you can save huge amounts of money. In fact, the biggest tip I can give you for finding incredible flight deals is simple: find a flexible job. Don't despair if you can't do that theres still a lot you can do.

**Book your flight to UK on a Tuesday or Wednesday**

Tuesdays and Wednesdays are the cheapest days of the week to fly. You can take a flight to UK on a Tuesday or Wednesday for less than half the price you'd pay on a Thursday Friday, Saturday, Sunday or Monday.

**Start with Google Flights (but NEVER book through them)**

I conduct upwards of 50 flight searches a day for readers. I use google flights first when looking for flights. I put specific departure but broad destination (e.g Europe) and usually find amazing deals.

The great thing about Google Flights is you can search by class. You can pick a specific destination and it will tell you which time is cheapest in which class. Or you can put in dates and you can see which area is cheapest to travel to.

But be aware Google flights does not show the cheapest prices among the flight search engines but it does offer several advantages

1. You can see the cheapest dates for the next 8 weeks. Other search engines will blackout over 70% of the prices.

2. You can put in multiple airports to fly from. Just use a common to separate in the from input.
3. If you're flexible on where you're going Google flights can show you the cheapest destinations.
4. You can set-up price tracking, where Google will email you when prices rise or decline.

Once you have established the cheapest dates to fly go over to skyscanner.net and put those dates in. You will find sky scanner offers the cheapest flights.

## Get Alerts when Prices to UK are Lowest

Google also has a nice feature which allows you to set up an alert to email you when prices to your destination are at their lowest. So if you don't have fixed dates this feature can save you a fortune.

### Baggage add-ons

It may be cheaper and more convenient to send your luggage separately with a service like sendmybag.com Often the luggage sending fee is cheaper than what the airlines charge to check baggage. Visit Lugless.com or luggagefree.com in addition to sendmybag.com for a quotation.

### Loading times

Anyone who has attempted to find a cheap flight will know the pain of excruciating long loading times. If you encounter this issue use google flights to find the cheapest dates and then go to skyscanner.net for the lowest price.

### Always try to book direct with the airline

Once you have found the cheapest flight go direct to the airlines booking page. This is advantageous in the current covid cancellation climate, because if you need to change your flights or arrange a refund, its much easier to do so, than via a third party booking agent.

That said, sometimes the third party bookers offer cheaper deals than the airline, so you need to make the decision based on how likely you think it is that disruption will impede you making those flights.

### More flight tricks and tips

**www.secretflying.com/usa-deals** offers a range of deals from the USA and other countries. For example you can pick-up a round trip flight non-stop from from the east coast to johannesburg for $350 return on this site

**Scott's cheap flights,** you can select your home airport and get emails on deals but you pay for an annual subscription. A free workaround is to download Hopper and set search alerts for trips/price drops.

**Premium service of Scott's cheap flights.**
They sometime have discounted business and first class but in my experience they are few and far between.

**JGOOT.com** has 5 times as many choices as Scott's cheap flights.

**kiwi.com** allows you to be able to do radius searches so you can find cheaper flights to general areas.

### Finding Error Fares

Travel Pirates (www.travelpirates.com) is a gold-mine for finding error deals. Subscribe to their newsletter. I recently found a reader an airfare from Montreal-Brazil for a $200 round trip (mistake fare!). Of course these error fares are always certain dates, but if you can be flexible you can save a lot of money.

**Things you can do that might reduce the fare to UK:--**
• Use a VPN (if the booker knows you booked one-way, the return fare will go up)
• Buy your ticket in a different currency

## If all else fails...

If you can't find a cheap flight for your dates I can find one for you. I do not charge for this nor do I send affiliate links. I'll send you a screenshot of the best options I find as airlines attach cookies to flight links. To use this free service please review this guide and send me a screenshot of your review - with your flight hacking request. I aim to reply to you within 12 hours. If it's an urgent request mark the email URGENT in the subject line and I will endeavour to reply ASAP.

# How to Find CHEAP FIRST-CLASS Flights to UK

### Upgrade at the airport
Airlines are extremely reluctant to advertise price drops in first or business class tickets so the best way to secure them is actually at the airport when airlines have no choice but to decrease prices dramatically because otherwise they lose money. Ask about upgrading to business or first-class when you check-in. If you check-in online look around the airport for your airlines branded bidding system. KLM have terminals where you can bid on upgrades.

### Use Air-miles

When it comes to accruing air-miles for American citizens **Chase Sapphire Reserve card** ranks top. If you put everything on there and pay it off immediately you will end up getting free flights all the time, aside from taxes.

Get 2-3 chase cards with sign up bonuses, you'll have 200k points in no time and can book with points on multiple airlines when transferring your points to them.

Please note, this is only applicable to those living in the USA. In the Bonus Section we have detailed the best air-mile credit cards for those living in the UK, Canada, Germany, Austria, UK and Australia.

# Arriving

Here are some major airports in the United Kingdom and budget-friendly ways to travel from each to the city:

- **Heathrow Airport (LHR), London:**
  - **Budget Option:** Take the London Underground (Piccadilly Line) for a cost-effective journey into central London. Alternatively, consider budget coaches or buses.
- **Gatwick Airport (LGW), London:**
  - **Budget Option:** Take the Southern or Thameslink trains for a more affordable connection to central London. National Express and easyBus also offer budget-friendly coach services.
- **Stansted Airport (STN), London:**
  - **Budget Option:** Use Stansted Express trains for a faster but budget-friendly option. National Express coaches and Terravision buses are economical choices.
- **Luton Airport (LTN), London:**
  - **Budget Option:** Opt for Thameslink trains for a cost-effective journey to central London. National Express coaches and Green Line buses also provide budget-friendly options.
- **Manchester Airport (MAN):**
  - **Budget Option:** Take the train from Manchester Airport to Manchester Piccadilly. Alternatively, National Express coaches and local buses are affordable choices.
- **Birmingham Airport (BHX):**
  - **Budget Option:** Use the Air-Rail Link monorail to Birmingham International Railway Station, then take a train to the city center. National Express coaches and local buses are economical alternatives.
- **Edinburgh Airport (EDI):**
  - **Budget Option:** Take the Airlink 100 bus to Edinburgh city center for a cost-effective option. Trams and taxis are also available.
- **Glasgow Airport (GLA):**
  - **Budget Option:** Use the Glasgow Airport Express bus service to the city center. Alternatively, local buses and the Paisley Gilmour Street train station offer affordable connections.
- **Bristol Airport (BRS):**
  - **Budget Option:** Take the Airport Flyer Express Link bus to Bristol Temple Meads railway station. Airport Flyer buses and local buses are also budget-friendly options.
- **Newcastle Airport (NCL):**
- **Budget Option:** Use the Metro light rail system for an affordable journey into Newcastle city center. Taxis and buses are also available.

**Check for any ongoing promotions, discounts, or travel passes that may further reduce transportation costs. Utilizing public transportation and booking in advance can significantly contribute to a budget-friendly journey from the airport to the city. Your budget should be always less than £15 for each transfer per person.**

# How to travel around the United Kingdom cheaply

The privatization of train services in the UK has led to a continuous increase in train ticket prices. Opting for buses tends to be a more economical choice, especially when booked in advance. It's essential to acknowledge that securing seats on frequently traveled train routes can be challenging. On the contrary, choosing a bus ensures a guaranteed seat, making it a reliable and often more cost-effective mode of transportation.

- **Advance Train Tickets:** Book train tickets well in advance to snag the best deals on the extensive rail network. Websites like Trainline and National Rail often offer discounted fares for early birds.

- **Bus Travel:** Opt for budget-friendly coach services like Megabus or National Express for inter-city travel. Booking early can result in incredibly low fares from £1!

**Cheapest bike rentals in e-scooters in the United Kingdom with prices**

**Bike Rentals:**

- **Santander Cycles (London):**
  - *Price:* £2 for a single ride up to 30 minutes, with additional fees for longer rides.
  - *How to Access:* Use the Santander Cycles app or hire directly at docking stations.
- **Nextbike (Various Cities):**
  - *Price:* Prices vary by location, but typical rates start at around £1 per 30 minutes.
  - *How to Access:* Use the Nextbike app to locate and rent bikes.
- **YoBike (Bristol and Southampton):**
  - *Price:* Prices vary, but it's generally around £1 per 20 minutes.
  - *How to Access:* Unlock and pay for bikes using the YoBike app.

**E-Scooters:**

- **Voi (Various Cities):**
  - *Price:* Typically starts at around £1 to unlock and £0.35 per minute of use.
  - *How to Access:* Download the Voi app to locate and unlock e-scooters.
- **Lime (Various Cities):**
  - *Price:* Unlocking fee and a per-minute rate, usually around £1 to unlock and £0.25 to £0.35 per minute.
  - *How to Access:* Use the Lime app to find and unlock e-scooters.
- **Tier (Various Cities):**
  - *Price:* Similar to others, with an unlocking fee and per-minute rate.
  - *How to Access:* Locate and unlock Tier e-scooters through the Tier app.

# Guide to Local Transport in the UK's Major Cities

Navigating the local transport systems in the UK's major cities can be efficient and convenient. Here's a guide to help you make the most of public transportation in key urban areas:

## **1. London:

**a. **London Underground (Tube):**

- The London Underground offers single fare prices starting at £2.40. Opt for an Oyster card to save money on daily or weekly travel.

**b. **Buses:**

- London buses have a flat fare of £1.50 per journey. Use an Oyster card or contactless payments for the best rates.

**c. **Dockless Bikes and E-Scooters:**

- Dockless bikes and e-scooters in London cost approximately £1 to unlock and £0.15 per minute of use.

**d. **Trains and Overground:**

- Overground and suburban trains in London vary in price. Use an Oyster card or contactless payments for convenience.

## **2. Manchester:

**a. **Metrolink Trams:**

- Metrolink tram tickets in Manchester start from £1.40 for a single journey. Save with a Metrolink travelcard or use contactless payments.

**b. **Buses:**

- System One travelcards for buses in Greater Manchester start from £4.50 per day. Alternatively, use contactless payments.

**c. **Free Bus Service:**

- Enjoy free Metroshuttle buses in Manchester for convenient city center travel.

## **3. Birmingham:

**a. **West Midlands Metro:**

- West Midlands Metro tram tickets in Birmingham start from £1.70 for a single journey. Use Swift cards or contactless payments.

**b. **Buses:**

- National Express West Midlands bus fares start from £2.40 for a single journey. Swift cards or contactless payments are convenient.

**c. Local Trains:**

- Local train tickets in Birmingham vary. Opt for advance bookings or use contactless payments for flexibility.

## **4. Edinburgh:

**a. Edinburgh Trams:**

- Edinburgh Trams tickets start from £1.80 for a single journey. Save with tram tickets or use contactless payments.

**b. Buses:**

- Lothian Buses fares in Edinburgh start from £1.70 for a single journey. Use contactless payments for simplicity.

**c. Edinburgh Bike Hire:**

- Edinburgh Bike Hire charges £1.50 per 30 minutes. Register and unlock bikes conveniently with the app.

## **5. Glasgow:

**a. Glasgow Subway:**

- Glasgow Subway fares start from £1.70 for a single journey. Save with subway tickets or use contactless payments.

**b. Buses:**

- First Glasgow bus fares start from £2.20 for a single journey. Conveniently pay with contactless methods.

**c. Cycling:**

- Nextbike cycle hire in Glasgow charges £1 to unlock and £0.10 per minute. Register and rent bikes using the app.

## **6. Liverpool:

**a. Merseyrail:**

- Merseyrail train tickets start from £1.90 for a single journey. Opt for advance bookings or use contactless payments.

**b. Buses:**

- Arriva and Stagecoach bus fares in Liverpool start from £2 for a single journey. Use contactless payments for ease.

**c. CityBike:**

- CityBike in Liverpool charges £0.08 per minute. Register and rent bikes using the app for a convenient ride.

### General Tips:

- **Contactless Payments:**
  - Use contactless payments for flexibility and better rates on public transport. Travelcards or passes can save you money on multiple journeys.
- **Travel Apps:**
  - Download city-specific travel apps for real-time information and potential discounts on public transport.
- **Peak and Off-Peak Travel:**
  - Save money by traveling during off-peak hours when ticket prices are often lower.
- **Tourist Passes:**
  - Invest in city-specific tourist passes for unlimited travel on public transport and additional discounts on attractions, providing overall savings.

# Ferries

- **Dover to Calais (P&O Ferries):**
  - *Price:* Starting from around £45 for a standard car and passengers one way.
  - *Provider:* P&O Ferries
- **Dover to Calais (DFDS):**
  - *Price:* Starting from around £39 for a standard car and passengers one way.
  - *Provider:* DFDS
- **Portsmouth to Le Havre (Brittany Ferries):**
  - *Price:* Starting from around £69 for a standard car and passengers one way.
  - *Provider:* Brittany Ferries
- **Hull to Rotterdam (P&O Ferries):**
  - *Price:* Starting from around £99 for a standard car and passengers one way.
  - *Provider:* P&O Ferries
- **Liverpool to Belfast (Stena Line):**
  - *Price:* Starting from around £99 for a standard car and passengers one way.
  - *Provider:* Stena Line
- **Holyhead to Dublin (Irish Ferries):**
  - *Price:* Starting from around £80 for a standard car and passengers one way.
  - *Provider:* Irish Ferries

# Eurostar

**Planning ahead** is the golden rule for saving on Eurostar tickets. Prices tend to rise as the departure date approaches, so secure your tickets as early as possible. You can easily be sitting next to someone who paid £300 for a ticket you paid £20 for.

The primary Eurostar routes from the UK include:

- **Paris, France:** Eurostar connects London St Pancras International to Gare du Nord in Paris. The journey takes approximately 2 hours and 15 minutes.
- **Brussels, Belgium:** Another major route is from London to Brussels, connecting London St Pancras International to Brussels-Midi/Zuid. The journey time is around 2 hours.

- **Lille, France:** Some Eurostar services make stops in Lille, France, before continuing to Brussels or Paris. Lille is approximately 1 hour from London.
- **Amsterdam, Netherlands:** Eurostar has extended its services to Amsterdam, with trains departing from London St Pancras International and making stops in Brussels and Rotterdam before reaching Amsterdam Centraal. The journey from London to Amsterdam takes around 4 hours.

# Driving

For an affordable car rental in the UK, book in advance through online platforms like Rentalcars.com, Kayak, or Skyscanner, where you can compare rates from major providers. Opt for non-airport locations and explore local agencies like Green Motion or Easirent for potentially lower prices. Additionally, consider economy or compact cars for cost-effectiveness, and check for promotions or discounts on the official websites of international companies such as Hertz, Avis, and Enterprise. Always review the terms and conditions, and if flexibility allows, consider adjusting your pickup and drop-off times for potential savings.

# Free Walking tours

In the UK, there are several organizations that offer free walking tours led by volunteers who are passionate about sharing their knowledge of the local history and culture. Keep in mind that while the tours themselves are typically free, it's customary to tip the guide at the end. Here are some famous free options:

- **Free Tours by Foot (London):**
  - **Location:** London
  - **Details:** Free Tours by Foot offers various walking tours in London, covering popular areas like Westminster, Covent Garden, and the East End. Check their website for schedules and meeting points.
- **Free Walking Tours Edinburgh:**
  - **Location:** Edinburgh
  - **Details:** Discover the historic and picturesque city of Edinburgh with Free Walking Tours Edinburgh. Tours cover the Royal Mile, the Old Town, and other significant landmarks.
- **Free Manchester Walking Tours:**
  - **Location:** Manchester
  - **Details:** Explore the industrial and cultural history of Manchester with Free Manchester Walking Tours. Tours often include visits to iconic sites like Albert Square and the Manchester Town Hall.
- **Free Liverpool Walking Tours:**
  - **Location:** Liverpool
  - **Details:** Learn about Liverpool's maritime history, the Beatles, and more with Free Liverpool Walking Tours. Tours typically start at the Royal Albert Dock.
- **Free Glasgow Walking Tours:**
  - **Location:** Glasgow
  - **Details:** Dive into Glasgow's vibrant culture and architecture with Free Glasgow Walking Tours. Tours may cover George Square, the Glasgow Cathedral, and other notable places.
- **Free Cardiff Walking Tours:**
  - **Location:** Cardiff
  - **Details:** Discover the capital of Wales with Free Cardiff Walking Tours. Explore Cardiff Castle, Bute Park, and the National Museum of Wales during these informative walks.
- **Free Walking Tours Oxford:**
  - **Location:** Oxford
  - **Details:** Immerse yourself in the academic and historical charm of Oxford with Free Walking Tours Oxford. Tours often include visits to famous colleges and landmarks.
- **Free Walking Tours Bath:**
  - **Location:** Bath
  - **Details:** Experience the Roman and Georgian history of Bath with Free Walking Tours Bath. Explore the Royal Crescent, the Circus, and the Roman Baths.

# Most Popular Attractions and how to visit cheaply

## London:

- **The British Museum:**
    - **Tip:** Free entry to the permanent collection. Check the website for special exhibitions and free guided tours.
- **Tower of London:**
    - **Tip:** Visit during off-peak hours for discounted tickets. You can attend Ceremony of the keys for £5 instead of paying the entrance fee.
- **The Houses of Parliament and Big Ben:**
    - **Tip:** View from the outside for free. Take the Thames Clipper river boat for a budget-friendly alternative to get up close and personal.
- **Buckingham Palace:**
    - **Tip:** Witness the Changing of the Guard ceremony for free outside the palace.
- **The Natural History Museum:**
    - **Tip:** Free entry, look at their website to join a free guided tour.
- **The Victoria and Albert Museum:**
    - **Tip:** Free entry, look at their website to join a free guided tour.
- **The Tate Modern:**
    - **Tip:** Free entry, but special exhibitions may require tickets. They also have free guided tours.
- **St. Paul's Cathedral:**
    - **Tip:** Attend a service for free entry, or climb to the dome for panoramic views.
- **The National Gallery:**
    - **Tip:** Free entry to the permanent collection.
- **The Shard:**
    - **Tip:** Enjoy skyline views from the Shard's viewing platform during off-peak hours for discounted rates. Or visit with the London Pass for free entry.

## Edinburgh:

- **Edinburgh Castle:**
    - **Tip:** Visit during off-peak hours for discounted tickets OR with the city pass.
- **The Royal Mile:**
    - **Tip:** Explore the historic street for free, and catch street performances during the Edinburgh Festival.
- **Arthur's Seat:**
    - **Tip:** Hike to the top for panoramic views of Edinburgh.

## Manchester:

- **Old Trafford (Manchester United Stadium):**
- **Tip:** Book a stadium tour for a more affordable way to experience the iconic venue.

## Liverpool:

- **The Beatles Story:**
- **Tip:** Visit the Beatles' childhood homes or explore all the free Beatles-related landmarks.

## Bath:

- **The Roman Baths:**
- **Tip:** Visit the nearby Bath Abbey for free, and visit after 4pm for 50% off tickets to the Roman Baths.

## Oxford:

- **The Bodleian Library and Radcliffe Camera:**
- **Tip:** Explore the exterior and nearby colleges for free.

## Cambridge:

- **The University of Cambridge:**
- **Tip:** Wander through the historic colleges and the Backs for free.

## Stratford-upon-Avon:

- **Shakespeare's Birthplace:**
- **Tip:** Consider the Shakespeare Birthplace Trust's multi-house ticket for better value.

## Stonehenge:

- **Stonehenge:**
- **Tip:** View from outside the fence for free, or visit with a discount pass for free entry. Megabus have cheap bus tickets to stonehenge.

## Lake District:

- **Lake District National Park:**
- **Tip:** Explore the stunning landscapes and walking trails for free.

## Scottish Highlands:

- **Glencoe:**
- **Tip:** Hike the trails for free, enjoying the breathtaking Scottish scenery.

## Cornwall:

- **St. Michael's Mount:**
- **Tip:** Visit Marazion Beach for views of the mount without entry fees.

## Wales:

- **Snowdonia National Park:**
- **Tip:** Hike or drive through the scenic national park for free.

## Northern Ireland:

- **Giant's Causeway:**
- **Tip:** Walk along the coast and witness the natural wonder without entering the visitor center. The National Trust membership includes free access to Giant's Causeway

# Major Attractions and which pass covers entry

| City | Attraction | Discount Pass |
|------|-----------|---------------|
| London | The Shard | The London Pass |
| London | The Cutty Sark | The London Pass |
| London | The Royal Observatory Greenwich | The London Pass |
| Edinburgh | Edinburgh Castle | Explorer Pass (Historic Environment Scotland) |
| Edinburgh | The Royal Mile | Explorer Pass (Historic Environment Scotland) |
| Brighton | Royal Pavilion | Brighton Explorer Pass |
| Warwickshire | Warwick Castle | Check for local promotions |
| Stirling | Stirling Castle | Historic Scotland Explorer Pass |
| Dover | Dover Castle | English Heritage Overseas Visitor Pass |

# London

*Natural History Museum*

London, the dynamic and diverse capital of the United Kingdom! Steeped in rich history and cultural vibrancy, this global metropolis seamlessly blends tradition with modernity. Home to iconic landmarks like the Tower of London, Buckingham Palace, and the historic Tower Bridge, London is a city where centuries-old architecture harmoniously coexists with contemporary marvels like The Shard.

The River Thames gracefully winds through its heart, connecting neighborhoods and offering stunning vistas. London's cultural scene is unrivaled, boasting world-class museums such as the British Museum and the Tate Modern. With a population representing a myriad of cultures, the city's culinary landscape is a delightful mosaic of global flavors. Whether you're exploring the trendy streets of Shoreditch, basking in the royal charm of Kensington, or catching a West End show in the Theatre District, London promises an unforgettable blend of tradition, innovation, and vibrant energy. Get ready to immerse yourself in the kaleidoscope of experiences that this iconic city has to offer!

**Cultural Icons and Architectural Marvels:**

Embrace the architectural splendor of St. Paul's Cathedral, a timeless masterpiece that has witnessed royal celebrations and poignant farewells. Venture to the majestic Buckingham Palace, where the Changing of the Guard ritual unfolds in a regal display of tradition. The Houses of Parliament and Big Ben, standing proudly on the banks of the River Thames, narrate tales of political history.

## Artistic Wonders:

For art enthusiasts, London is a treasure trove. The British Museum houses a vast collection of artifacts spanning civilizations, while the Tate Modern showcases cutting-edge contemporary art. Explore the National Gallery in Trafalgar Square, where masterpieces by Van Gogh, da Vinci, and Monet grace the walls, creating a symphony of artistic brilliance.

## Royal Retreats and Green Oases:

Escape the urban bustle with a visit to the serene Kensington Gardens, surrounding Kensington Palace, a former residence of Queen Victoria. Hyde Park, a sprawling green expanse, offers a tranquil retreat for leisurely strolls and afternoon picnics.

## The West End Extravaganza:

As night falls, immerse yourself in the glittering lights of London's West End. Attend a theatrical spectacle at Covent Garden or catch a world-class production in the legendary theatres of Shaftesbury Avenue, continuing the city's tradition of captivating storytelling.

## Gastronomic Delights and Diverse Districts:

London's culinary scene mirrors its multicultural soul. From the exotic aromas of Brick Lane's curry houses to the delectable treats at Borough Market, each bite tells a story of the city's diverse heritage. Explore the trendy boutiques of Carnaby Street or the vintage charm of Notting Hill, where every street corner unveils a unique facet of London's personality.

## Accommodation:

- **Boutique Hostels or Budget Hotels:**
    - Choose well-reviewed boutique hostels or budget hotels for stylish and comfortable stays at a fraction of the cost.
    - Check platforms like Dayuse, ResortPass, or DayPass to explore five-star hotel day pass options in London.
- **Airbnb:**
    - Explore Airbnb for unique and affordable accommodation options. You might find stylish apartments or private rooms in desirable neighborhoods.

## Transportation:

- **Oyster Card:**
    - Utilize the Oyster Card for cost-effective travel on public transportation. It provides discounted rates on buses, trams, the Tube, DLR, London Overground, and some National Rail services.
- **Walking:**

- London's city center is walkable, allowing you to explore attractions on foot and save on transportation costs.

**Attractions:**

- **Free Museum and Gallery Visits:**
  - Take advantage of free entry to major museums and galleries, including the British Museum, National Gallery, and Tate Modern.
- **Discounted Tickets:**
  - Check for discounted tickets for popular attractions when booked in advance online. This often includes attractions like the Tower of London, St. Paul's Cathedral, and the Shard.
  - **Go to services to get into St. Paul's Cathedral and Westminister Abbey** for free. Both hosts regular services, including daily prayers and Sunday services. Entrance to these religious services is typically free, allowing visitors to experience the grandeur of the cathedral's interior.
  - **2-for-1 National Rail offers.** You can get a 2 for 1 ticket when you have purchased a train ticket. Any train ticket. Visit the Days Out Guide website, choose a participating attraction, download the 2-for-1 voucher, and present it along with a valid National Rail ticket or Travelcard at the attraction to receive the discount. Shows: Some West End theaters in London participate in the Days Out Guide promotion, offering 2-for-1 deals on tickets for selected performances.

**Dining:**

- **Markets and Street Food:**
  - Explore food markets like Borough Market and Camden Market for affordable and delicious eats. Try street food for a taste of diverse cuisines from the too good to go app. Leon has some incredible too good to go bags in London and they have a branch in every part of the city.

**Eat in Ethnic Neighborhoods:**
- **Chinatown:** Explore authentic Chinese eateries with affordable lunch specials and tasting menus.
- **Little Italy:** Check out Italian restaurants in areas like Soho for budget-friendly options.
- **Brick Lane (Bangladeshi/Indian):** Known for its curry houses, offering diverse and reasonably priced options.
- **Lunch Specials at Upscale Restaurants:**
  - Experience luxury dining at a fraction of the cost by opting for lunch specials at upscale restaurants. **Pidgin:** Located in Hackney, Pidgin is a Michelin-starred restaurant with a set menu that changes regularly. It has been praised for its creative and affordable approach to fine dining.

**Entertainment:**

- **Theater Tickets:**
  - Purchase discounted theater tickets from TKTS or attend matinee performances for a more affordable theater experience. You can save thousands on west-end tickets on TKTS or by getting Rush tickets.
- **Free Events:**
  - Keep an eye on free events happening in London, including concerts, festivals, and outdoor performances. Timeout has a great listing.

**Shopping:**

- **Outlet Shopping:**
  - Visit outlet stores like Bicester Village for discounted prices on luxury brands.
- **Charity Shops in Upscale Areas:**
  - Explore charity shops in upscale neighborhoods like Knightsbridge for potential luxury finds at a fraction of the cost.

## Parks and Outdoor Activities:

- **Hyde Park and Royal Parks:**
  - Enjoy the luxurious greenery of Hyde Park and other Royal Parks for free. Consider a picnic or boat ride in Hyde Park.
- **Free Walking Tours:**
  - Join free walking tours to explore neighborhoods and learn about London's history from passionate guides. There's even one for Jack the Ripper!

## Luxury for Less:

- **Afternoon Tea Deals:**
  - Indulge in the quintessential London experience of afternoon tea with deals from various establishments on Wowcher.
- **Hotel Bars:**
  - Experience the luxury of hotel bars without the high cost of accommodation. Enjoy a drink in renowned hotel bars like The American Bar at The Savoy.

## Travel Off-Peak:

- **Off-Peak Travel:**
  - Travel during off-peak times to save on accommodation and transportation costs.
- **Travel Packages:**
  - Look for travel packages that bundle accommodations and activities for additional savings.

By combining these strategies, you can create a memorable and luxurious experience in London while maintaining a budget-friendly approach.

# 20 luxurious experiences to have in London on a budget

Experiencing luxury in London on a budget requires a bit of strategic planning but its very easy when you know how

- **Afternoon Tea at a Historic Venue:**
    - **Luxury Experience:** Afternoon tea at The Ritz or The Dorchester with a discount code. They are available frequently with apps like Honey.
    - **Budget Tip:** If those are booked, opt for afternoon tea at more affordable venues like Bea's of Bloomsbury.
    - **Approximate Saving:** £50-£150 per person.

Introduced by Anna, the Duchess of Bedford, in the 1840s, the concept emerged as a solution to the "sinking feeling" she experienced between lunch and the late evening meal. The duchess began inviting friends to join her for a selection of sandwiches, sweets, and of course, tea, served in the late afternoon. This delightful social ritual soon gained popularity among the aristocracy and, later, the broader society.

- **West End Show:**
    - **Luxury Experience:** Premium seats for a popular West End production.
    - **Budget Tip:** Book discounted tickets for matinee shows or check TKTS for last-minute deals.
    - **Approximate Savings:** £150 per ticket.

The Theatre Royal, Drury Lane, established in 1663, is considered the oldest continuously operating theatre in London. Over the centuries, the West End has been a vibrant center for theatrical innovation and entertainment. In the 19th century, the district underwent a cultural transformation with the construction of iconic theatres like the Lyceum and the Criterion, becoming synonymous with high-quality productions and star-studded performances. The late 19th and early 20th centuries witnessed the rise of influential theatre figures, including Oscar Wilde and George Bernard Shaw, who left an indelible mark on the West End's literary and artistic legacy. The area's resilience during wartime and its ability to adapt to changing societal norms have solidified its reputation as a global theatre capital.

- **Fine Dining at Michelin-Starred Restaurants:**
    - **Luxury Experience:** Dining at a Michelin-starred restaurant like Alain Ducasse at The Dorchester.
    - **Budget Tip:** Explore set lunch menus or early dining offers.
    - **Approximate Price:** £30-£100 per person.
- **River Thames Dinner Cruise:**
    - **Luxury Experience:** Evening dinner cruise with scenic views.
    - **Budget Tip:** Websites like Viator, GetYourGuide, or Klook often feature discounted tickets for dinner cruises.

- Approximate Price: £50-£100 per person.
- **Luxury Hotel Bar Experience:**
  - **Luxury Experience:** Cocktails at The American Bar at The Savoy.
  - **Budget Tip:** Enjoy a drink during happy hour or special promotions.
  - **Approximate Price:** £15-£20 per cocktail.
- **Private Cinema Experience:**
  - **Luxury Experience:** Private screening at The Electric Cinema.
  - **Budget Tip:** Attend screenings during off-peak hours for lower prices.
  - **Approximate Price:** £10-£60 per person.
- **Helicopter Tour of London:**
  - **Luxury Experience:** Private helicopter tour.
  - **Budget Tip:** Opt for group helicopter tours with HeliAir.
  - **Approximate Price:** £30.
- **Spa Day at a Luxury Hotel:**
  - **Luxury Experience:** Spa day at The Bulgari Spa.
  - **Budget Tip:** Check for spa day packages or weekday discounts.
  - **Approximate Price:** £30-£150 per person.
- **Private Art Gallery Viewing:**
  - **Luxury Experience:** Private viewing at The National Gallery.
  - **Budget Tip:** Attend free public talks or events at galleries for exclusive access.
- **Vintage Shopping in Notting Hill:**
  - **Luxury Experience:** Designer vintage shopping in Notting Hill.
  - **Budget Tip:** Explore charity shops and second-hand boutiques for unique finds.
  - **Approximate Price:** Variable based on purchases.
- **Concert at Royal Albert Hall:**
  - **Budget Tip:** Opt for cheaper seats or attend rehearsals for reduced prices.
  - **Approximate Price:** £10-£150 per ticket.
- **Cocktail Masterclass:**
  - **Luxury Experience:** Mixology class at a top cocktail bar.
  - **Budget Tip:** Look for discounted group classes or happy hour deals.
  - **Approximate Price:** £10-£80 per person.
- **Luxury Picnic in Hyde Park:**
  - **Budget Tip:** Create your own picnic with gourmet items from too good to go deli's.
  - **Approximate saving:** £80 per person.
- **VIP Entry to Nightclubs:**
  - **Luxury Experience:** VIP entry and table service. Arriving early can increase your chances of gaining VIP entry, especially if the club has limited space.
  - **Approximate Price:** £50-£100 per person.
- **Yoga or Fitness Class:**
  - **Budget Tip:** Attend group classes or use fitness apps for guided sessions.
  - **Approximate Price:** £10-£80 per person for private sessions.
- **Gourmet Food Tour:**
  - **Luxury Experience:** Private food tour with a local expert.
  - **Approximate Price:** £50-£100 per person for private tours.
- **Rooftop Bar Experience:**
  - **Luxury Experience:** Cocktails at a rooftop bar like Sky Garden.
  - **Budget Tip:** Visit during non-peak hours for more affordable drinks and book your visit before.
  - **Approximate Price:** £15-£20 per cocktail.

# How to experience your first day in London for under £20

Embarking on your first day in the United Kingdom need not strain your budget, as there are numerous affordable and enriching experiences to be had for under £20.

Free Walking Tour:
Consider joining a free walking tour, particularly in major cities like London or Edinburgh. Accompanied by knowledgeable guides, these tours provide valuable insights into local history and landmarks, offering an engaging introduction to your new surroundings.

Visit Parks and Landmarks:
Explore iconic parks such as Hyde Park in London or Arthur's Seat in Edinburgh. Delight in the scenic beauty and take in landmarks like Buckingham Palace or the Edinburgh Castle, often visible without incurring entrance fees.

Picnic Lunch:
Opt for an affordable lunch by grabbing lunch from Leon as a too good to go bag and enjoying a leisurely picnic in one of the city's parks. It's a budget-friendly way to savor the surroundings.

Free Museums and Galleries:
Take advantage of complimentary entry to many museums and galleries.

Local Markets:
Immerse yourself in the vibrant atmosphere of local markets. Borough Market in London or the Grassmarket in Edinburgh provide diverse options for exploration and culinary delights.

Discounted Transport:
Maximize your budget by utilizing public transportation, such as an Oyster card in London or a day pass for buses in other cities. Walking is also a wonderful way to explore city centers at no additional cost.

Discounted Theater Tickets:
For those interested in the arts, check for discounted theater tickets on the day of the performance. Some venues offer last-minute deals, allowing you to enjoy a show without exceeding your budget.

Budget-Friendly Eats:
Indulge in affordable local eateries or explore street food markets. Sampling classic British dishes like fish and chips can be a flavorful experience without breaking the bank.

Public Events:
Stay attuned to local event listings for free or low-cost public events, festivals, or live music performances happening on your first day. This adds a dynamic and cultural touch to your budget-friendly itinerary.

By combining these activities, you can craft a memorable and enriching first day in the London without surpassing your £20 budget. Feel free to tailor these suggestions based on your location and personal preferences. Enjoy your time exploring the United Kingdom!

# RECAP

| Category | Cost | Cost-Saving Measure | Why It Feels Luxurious | Potential Savings |
|---|---|---|---|---|
| Accommodation | £30-£120/ night | Opt for boutique hotels like The Z Hotel or The Hoxton or blind book with last minute | Enjoying stylish and comfortable settings. | £400/night |
| Dining | £15-£30/ meal | Explore affordable eateries like Dishoom for upscale Indian cuisine or Flat Iron Square for diverse options. | Savoring diverse and high-quality cuisines. | £10-£20/ meal |
| Entertainment | £20-£50/ show | Take advantage of discounted theater tickets on the day of the performance, or check out free events at places like the National Gallery or Tate Modern. | Enjoying world-class performances in renowned venues like the West End. | £10-£20/ ticket |
| Transportation | £10-£15/ day | Use an Oyster card for public transportation within the city, and consider walking for short distances. | Experiencing the convenience of London's efficient public transport system. | £5-£10/day |
| Sightseeing | £0-£15/ day | Opt for free walking tours or explore parks like Hyde Park and Greenwich Park. | Discovering the city's iconic landmarks and natural beauty. | £10-£15/ day |

**Total Daily Budget:** £65-£125/day

# Canterbury and southeast England

*Canterbury Catheral*

Canterbury is a city synonymous with literary legends and ecclesiastical grandeur. The iconic Canterbury Cathedral, a UNESCO World Heritage Site, stands as a testament to medieval architecture and the pilgrimage routes of yore. Meander through cobbled streets where Chaucer's pilgrims once trod, and discover the rich tales woven into the city's historic fabric.

**Coastal Splendors and Maritime Mystique:**

Venture beyond the city limits to Southeast England's breathtaking coastline. The White Cliffs of Dover, standing tall against the English Channel, evoke a sense of awe and provide a perfect backdrop for coastal hikes. Explore the charming seaside town of Whitstable, where oyster beds and colorful cottages create a picturesque setting for leisurely strolls along the shore.

### Royal Residences and Garden Retreats:

In the verdant countryside, uncover the stately elegance of Leeds Castle, often referred to as the "loveliest castle in the world." Roam through manicured gardens and reflect on the regal history that permeates its halls. For a botanical retreat, lose yourself in the beauty of Sissinghurst Castle Garden, a masterpiece of design and horticultural artistry.

### Historic Towns and Architectural Gems:

Discover the quaint charm of Rye, a town frozen in time with its cobbled streets and medieval architecture. Marvel at the half-timbered houses of Tenterden and delve into the architectural wonders of Canterbury's Westgate Towers. Each town holds a unique chapter in the story of Southeast England.

### Gastronomic Pleasures and Local Delights:

Indulge your taste buds in the culinary delights of the region. Feast on freshly caught seafood in seaside villages, savor traditional cream teas in historic tearooms, and explore the bustling markets where local producers showcase the best of Kentish produce.

### Vineyard Vistas and Culinary Experiences:

Southeast England's rolling hills are dotted with vineyards producing award-winning wines. Embark on a wine-tasting adventure in the Garden of England, where the terroir imparts unique flavors to each vintage. Pair your wines with locally sourced cheeses and artisanal treats for a truly Kentish experience.

### Accommodation:

- Kipps Canterbury:
    - A well-regarded hostel offering a boutique experience with both dormitory and private room options. Located close to the city center, Kipps Canterbury provides a comfortable stay at a reasonable price.
    - Website: Kipps Canterbury
- The Falstaff in Canterbury:
    - This charming hotel provides a boutique guesthouse experience with stylish rooms and a central location. The Falstaff combines luxury touches with budget-friendly rates.
    - Website: The Falstaff in Canterbury
    -

### Transportation:

### 3. Advance Bus and Train Tickets:

- Book train tickets in advance to secure lower fares for travel between Canterbury and Southeast England destinations.
-

### Canterbury:

## 5. Canterbury Cathedral:

- Explore Canterbury Cathedral, a UNESCO World Heritage Site. Entry fees contribute to the cathedral's maintenance. While some areas may have entry fees, attending a service or exploring the exterior is free.
-
    - **Stroll Along the River Stour:**
    - Enjoy a leisurely walk along the River Stour and take in the picturesque views.

**Dover:**

## 7. White Cliffs of Dover:

- Take a walk along the White Cliffs of Dover for breathtaking coastal scenery. Entry is free.

**Deal:**

## 8. Deal Castle:

- Visit Deal Castle for a historical experience. Entry fees apply, but check for any discounts or buy one of the discount passes to enter for free.

**Margate:**

## 9. Turner Contemporary:

- Explore the Turner Contemporary art gallery in Margate. Entry is free, with occasional paid exhibitions.

**Whitstable:**

## 10. Whitstable Harbour:

- Enjoy the charm of Whitstable Harbour, known for its seafood. Stroll along the beach without spending a penny.

**Luxury on a Budget Tips:**

## 11. Gourmet Picnic:

- Create a gourmet picnic with local produce from markets to enjoy in scenic locations.

- **Lunch Specials:**
    - Experience luxury dining for less by opting for lunch specials at upscale restaurants.
- **Happy Hour at Bars:**
    - Enjoy the luxury of trendy bars during happy hours for discounted drinks.
- **Free Walking Tours:**
    - Join free walking tours to explore cities with knowledgeable local guides.
- **Explore Local Markets:**

- Immerse yourself in local culture by exploring markets for unique finds and affordable meals.
- **Nature Walks:**
  - Take advantage of the natural beauty in the region with free nature walks and hiking trails.
- **Student and Youth Discounts:**
  - If applicable, take advantage of student and youth discounts for attractions and transportation.


## Luxury for Less

### Punting in Canterbury:

Enjoy a budget-friendly punting experience on the River Stour in Canterbury. Shared punts with Punt and Trundler start at £10.


### Stroll through The King's Mile:

Discover the rich blend of history and modernity as you stroll through The King's Mile in Canterbury. The cobblestone streets, adorned with boutique stores, invite you to appreciate local craftsmanship and centuries of cultural evolution. Window shopping becomes a cultural exploration against the backdrop of this charming district.


### Visit White Cliffs of Dover:

Embark on a hike along the White Cliffs of Dover. The chalk cliffs offer breathtaking views of the English Channel, providing an opportunity to connect with nature and relish the coastal beauty without spending a dime.


### Deal Castle Gardens:

Immerse yourself in the tranquil gardens of Deal Castle, where the exterior and grounds are often accessible for free or free with any of the discount passes. This historic site allows you to escape into a serene environment, offering a cost-free retreat.


### Dover Castle Grounds:

Wander through the exterior of Dover Castle, marvelling at its grandeur without incurring an entry fee. The castle grounds provide a splendid setting for a leisurely stroll, blending history and natural beauty.


### Canterbury Tales Visitor Attraction:

Step into the medieval tales of Canterbury at the Canterbury Tales Visitor Attraction. Whether securing discounted tickets or visiting during off-peak hours, this immersive experience promises a cultural journey through the city's storied past.

## Botany Bay Beach:

Relax at Botany Bay Beach in Broadstairs, where sun, sand, and iconic chalk stacks create a picturesque setting. Enjoy the coastal ambiance without breaking the bank for a serene seaside experience.

## Visit Chilham Village:

Discover the timeless allure of Chilham Village as you meander through its medieval square and marvel at the historic architecture. This well-preserved village offers a charming glimpse into the past.

## Leeds Castle Grounds:

Explore the grounds of Leeds Castle, appreciating its historic grandeur without entering areas with entry fees. The exterior and gardens provide a cost-free opportunity to soak in the majesty of this iconic site.

## Sunset at Margate Beach:

Experience a budget-friendly luxury by watching the sunset at Margate Beach. The vibrant colors reflecting on the water create a serene atmosphere, making it an ideal spot for a tranquil evening without extravagant spending.

## Richborough Roman Fort:

Unearth the legacy of the past at the Richborough Roman Fort. While the museum may have an entry fee, explore the fort's exterior and surrounding areas for free, immersing yourself in the historical significance of this Roman site.

## Dine in Canterbury's Independent Cafés:

Indulge in a culinary experience at Canterbury's independent cafés, where gourmet coffee and pastries offer a taste of luxury on a budget. These establishments provide a cozy setting to savor local flavors.

## Free Walking Tours:

Immerse yourself in the history and culture of Canterbury by joining free walking tours led by local guides. Gain insights into the city's rich heritage while exploring landmarks and hidden gems on this budget-friendly cultural excursion.

**Canterbury Westgate Gardens:**

Find tranquility in Canterbury Westgate Gardens, where you can relax amidst nature. Pack a picnic and enjoy the serene surroundings, creating a budget-friendly yet delightful experience.

**Dine at The Goods Shed:**

Dine at The Goods Shed in Canterbury for a luxurious meal without breaking the bank. Indulge in locally sourced, high-quality food in a welcoming atmosphere, showcasing the region's culinary excellence.

**Canterbury Roman Museum:**

Explore the Canterbury Roman Museum and look for discounted admission or combination tickets to make the most of this archaeological journey through the city's Roman past.

**Faversham Market:**

Immerse yourself in the vibrant atmosphere of Faversham Market, sampling local produce and enjoying the charming setting. The market provides an authentic experience, offering a budget-friendly way to engage with the community.

**Deal Pier:**

Take a leisurely stroll along Deal Pier, relishing panoramic views of the sea and coastline. The pier offers a tranquil escape, allowing you to enjoy the coastal beauty without spending money.

**Enjoy a Play at The Marlowe Theatre:**
Experience the cultural richness of Canterbury by attending a play or performance at The Marlowe Theatre. Check for discounted tickets or matinee shows to enjoy a theatrical experience within budget constraints.

# RECAP

| Category | Cost | Cost-Saving Measure | Why It Feels Luxurious | Potential Savings |
|----------|------|---------------------|------------------------|-------------------|
| Accommodation | £70-£100/ night | Choose charming B&Bs like The Falstaff or The Arthouse, or explore budget-friendly options like Premier Inn. | Immersing yourself in historic surroundings with personalized service. | £20-£30/ night |
| Dining | £15-£25/ meal | Opt for local gems like The Old Buttermarket or Café du Soleil for affordable yet exquisite meals. | Savoring regional delicacies and farm-to-table dining experiences. | £10-£15/ meal |
| Entertainment | £10-£30/ show | Attend local performances or festivals, often featuring traditional music or theater. Explore free events at cultural sites such as Canterbury Cathedral. | Enjoying cultural events in historic venues like the Marlowe Theatre. | £5-£15/ show |
| Transportation | £10-£15/ day | Use regional buses or trains for day trips to nearby towns. Walk or cycle through Canterbury for short trips. | Exploring charming villages and scenic landscapes at a leisurely pace. | £5-£10/ day |
| Sightseeing | £0-£12/ day | Take advantage of free walking tours or explore the beautiful Canterbury Westgate Gardens. | Discovering Canterbury's historic architecture and picturesque surroundings. | £8-£12/ day |

## Total Daily Budget: £50-£77/day

# Oxford and Cotswolds

Oxford and the Cotswolds, where the hallowed halls of academia meet the rolling hills of the English countryside.

**Oxford's Scholarly Elegance:**

Our journey begins in Oxford, a city synonymous with academic brilliance and literary enchantment. Navigate the cobblestone streets that have witnessed the footsteps of Nobel laureates and literary giants. The University of Oxford, with its dreaming spires and ancient libraries, stands as a living testament to centuries of intellectual pursuit. Explore the Bodleian Library, where the air is thick with the whispers of knowledge, and stroll through the Christ Church Meadow, an idyllic retreat within the heart of the city.

**Literary Legends and Cultural Gems:**

Delve into the literary wonders that inspired the likes of Lewis Carroll and J.R.R. Tolkien. The Bodleian's Divinity School, a masterpiece of Gothic architecture, served as the backdrop for Hogwarts in the Harry Potter films. Wander through the halls of the Ashmolean Museum, where art and antiquities offer a glimpse into diverse cultures.

**Cotswolds' Timeless Tranquility:**

As we venture into the Cotswolds, prepare to be embraced by a landscape straight out of a storybook. Quaint villages with honey-hued cottages line the rolling hills, creating a picture-perfect scene. Bibury, Bourton-on-the-Water, and Stow-on-the-Wold beckon with their charming market squares and tea houses, inviting you to lose yourself in their timeless allure.

### Stately Homes and Gardens:

Discover the grandeur of Blenheim Palace, a UNESCO World Heritage Site and the birthplace of Sir Winston Churchill. Meander through its manicured gardens and reflect on the historical echoes that resonate within its walls. For a dose of tranquility, explore Hidcote Manor Garden, a masterpiece of arts and crafts design that unfolds in a series of outdoor rooms.

### Culinary Delights and Rural Retreats:

Indulge in the culinary pleasures of the Cotswolds, where traditional pubs offer hearty fare, and farm-to-table dining celebrates the region's bounty. Savor the charm of tearooms serving freshly baked scones, and explore local markets for artisanal treats and handmade crafts.

### Scenic Walks and Country Trails:

Embark on scenic walks along the Cotswold Way, where panoramic views reward your efforts. Traverse ancient woodlands, cross babbling streams, and witness the changing colors of the landscape with each passing season.

### Accommodation:

- **University Accommodations in Oxford:**
  - Stay in university accommodations during non-term times for affordable and unique stays.
- **Charming Guesthouses in the Cotswolds:**
  - Choose charming guesthouses or bed and breakfasts in the Cotswolds for a cozy and budget-friendly experience.
- **Airbnb:**
  - Explore Airbnb for characterful accommodations in both Oxford and the Cotswolds.

### Transportation:

### 4. Megabus, Oxford Tube or X90 Bus:

- Travel between Oxford and London on the Megabus, Oxford Tube or X90 bus for £5 tickets.
  - **Cotswolds by Bus:**
    - Use local buses to explore the Cotswolds villages, providing a cost-effective way to enjoy the picturesque surroundings. Begin your journey from a central

hub like Oxford or Cheltenham, where frequent bus services weave through the rolling hills and idyllic towns. Explore hidden gems like Bourton-on-the-Water, Stow-on-the-Wold, and Bibury, hopping on and off at your leisure. The scenic bus routes offer a leisurely way to savor the beauty of thatched cottages, historic market squares, and lush countryside.

**Oxford:**

### 6. Oxford University Colleges:

- Wander around the courtyards of Oxford University colleges, some of which offer free entry.
- **Radcliffe Camera and Bodleian Library:**
    - Admire the Radcliffe Camera and Bodleian Library, iconic Oxford landmarks. While entry fees may apply, exterior views are free.
- **Botanic Garden:**
    - Explore the Oxford Botanic Garden, one of the oldest in the world, for a tranquil experience. Entry fees are £5.

### Explore Oxford's Collegiate Charms:

Oxford, a city synonymous with academic prestige, boasts an array of stunning colleges that beckon exploration. Several of these historic institutions graciously open their doors to visitors, offering a glimpse into their architectural grandeur and scholarly traditions.

**Christ Church College:**

Step into the hallowed halls of Christ Church College, whose Great Hall inspired Hogwarts in the Harry Potter films. While the college charges an entrance fee for its magnificent cathedral, the Tom Quad and Meadow provide a free and delightful stroll amidst centuries-old architecture and manicured gardens.

**Magdalen College:**

Magdalen College invites visitors to traverse its captivating deer park, meander along the picturesque Addison's Walk, and revel in the serene ambiance of the Botanic Garden—all without an entrance fee. The iconic Magdalen Tower stands tall, welcoming those eager to explore the college's timeless beauty.

**University College (Univ):**

University College, affectionately known as Univ, welcomes visitors to its tranquil Front Quad and charming gardens. While entrance to the college's renowned Chapel may require a fee, the exterior and surrounding spaces offer a serene escape into academic history.

**Exeter College:**

Wander through the atmospheric Turl Street, where Exeter College stands proud. While the college itself is not open to the public, the Turl Street Kitchen provides a cozy spot for a coffee break, and the exterior exudes the architectural charm characteristic of Oxford's colleges.

**St. John's College:**

St. John's College treats visitors to the exquisite St. John's Gardens, free to explore at your leisure. While some areas may require an entrance fee, the Front Quad and Bridge of Sighs provide an enchanting backdrop for a leisurely stroll.

**Merton College:**

Merton College, known for its beautiful gardens and Mob Quad, offers free access to the Fellows' Garden, where you can savor the tranquility of this ancient institution. While certain areas may have admission fees, the exterior spaces provide a glimpse into Merton's historical allure.

- **Free entries:** Some National Trust properties in Oxfordshire, such as Buscot Park and Nuffield Place, are within a reasonable distance from Oxford and offer complimentary entry for National Trust members.

**Cotswolds:**

9. **Bourton-on-the-Water:**

- Enjoy the charm of Bourton-on-the-Water, known as the "Venice of the Cotswolds." Stroll along the river without spending money.

- **Broadway Tower:**
- Hike to Broadway Tower for panoramic views of the Cotswolds. While there's an entry fee for the tower, the surrounding grounds are free to explore.

**Bourton-on-the-Water:**
Explore the picturesque village of Bourton-on-the-Water. Enjoy the Cotswold architecture and stroll along the river.
**Broadway Tower:**
Visit Broadway Tower. While there's an entry fee for the tower, the surrounding park is often free to access.
**Chipping Campden High Street:**
Wander along Chipping Campden's High Street. Admire the historic market town architecture.
**Bibury Arlington Row:**
Admire Bibury's Arlington Row. Walk around this iconic row of cottages for free.
**Sudeley Castle Gardens:**
Explore the gardens of Sudeley Castle. While there's an entry fee for the castle, the gardens are often open to the public.

**Cotswold Lavender Farm:**
Visit the Cotswold Lavender Farm. While there's an entry fee, the vibrant lavender fields provide stunning photo opportunities.

**Stow-on-the-Wold Market Square:**
Discover Stow-on-the-Wold's Market Square. Experience the charm of this market town.

**Cotswold Wildlife Park:**
Enjoy the Cotswold Wildlife Park. While there's an entry fee, it's a great place for animal enthusiasts.

**Hailes Abbey:**
Explore the ruins of Hailes Abbey. While there's an entry fee for the abbey, the surrounding fields are often free to explore.

**Lower Slaughter:**
Visit the quaint village of Lower Slaughter. Stroll along the River Eye and take in the idyllic scenery.

11. **Luxury on a Budget Tips:**

- Create a gourmet picnic with local delicacies and enjoy it in Oxford's University Parks.

- **Lunch at Local Pubs:**
  - Experience the charm of local pubs in the Cotswolds for affordable yet delicious meals.
- **Punting in Oxford:**
  - Enjoy a budget-friendly punt along the Cherwell River in Oxford, taking in the scenic surroundings.
- **Happy Hour at Oxford Bars:**
  - Explore Oxford's bars during happy hours for discounted drinks.
- **Explore Local Markets:**
  - Immerse yourself in the local atmosphere by exploring markets in Oxford and Cotswolds.
- **Nature Walks in the Cotswolds:**
  - Take advantage of the scenic walks and trails in the Cotswolds for a luxury nature experience.
- **Visit Free Attractions:**
  - Explore free attractions in the Cotswolds, including charming villages and natural landscapes.
  -

By combining these strategies, you can savor the luxury of Oxford and the Cotswolds while maintaining a budget-friendly approach. Adjustments can be made based on your preferences and the unique experiences each location offers.

**Oxford:**

**Explore Oxford University Colleges:**
Wander through the grounds of various Oxford University colleges. While entry to some areas may have fees, exploring the exteriors is often free.

**Punting on the Cherwell:**
Enjoy a budget-friendly punt on the Cherwell River. Shared punts are more affordable than private ones.

**Visit the Bodleian Library:**

Explore the Bodleian Library's exterior. While there's an entry fee for tours, the exterior is an architectural marvel.

**Botanic Garden:**

Relax in the Oxford Botanic Garden. While there's an entry fee, it's a serene spot for a budget-friendly stroll.

**Radcliffe Camera and Radcliffe Square:**

Marvel at the Radcliffe Camera and Radcliffe Square. Enjoy the architecture and historical significance for free.

**Ashmolean Museum:**

Visit the Ashmolean Museum. Look for discounted admission or explore the free exhibits.

**Oxford Covered Market:**

Immerse yourself in the Oxford Covered Market. While shopping may incur costs, browsing and sampling local products can be budget-friendly.

**Christ Church Meadows:**

Stroll through Christ Church Meadows. Enjoy the riverside views and green spaces for free.

**Oxford Castle Mound:**

Climb to the top of Oxford Castle Mound. While there's an entry fee for the castle, the mound offers panoramic views for free.

**Morse, Lewis, and Endeavour Tour:**

Take a self-guided Morse, Lewis, and Endeavour tour. Visit locations featured in the TV series for free.

| Category | Cost | Cost-Saving Measure | Why It Feels Luxurious |
|---|---|---|---|
| Accommodation | £20-£120/ night | Boutique guesthouses like The Old Parsonage or budget-friendly options like YHA Oxford Hostel. | Immerse in the historic charm of Oxford or a cozy Cotswolds cottage. |
| Dining | £15-£30/meal | Opt for local favorites like The Nosebag in Oxford or traditional pubs in the Cotswolds for affordable meals. | Savor gourmet meals with local flavors and ambiance. |
| Entertainment | £10-£25/ show | Attend student performances at Oxford's theaters or explore free events at colleges and museums. | Enjoy cultural events in the scholarly setting of Oxford or the picturesque Cotswolds. |
| Transportation | £10-£15/day | Utilize local buses or explore Oxford and the Cotswolds on foot or by bike. Consider day passes for trains. | Discover quaint villages and rolling hills at a leisurely pace. |
| Sightseeing | £0-£15/day | Explore historic colleges in Oxford and stroll through picturesque villages in the Cotswolds. | Immerse in Oxford's academic history or the timeless beauty of the Cotswolds. |

**Total Daily Budget:** £40-£205

# Bristol, Bath and Somerset

*Royal Crescent*

Bristol and Bath is where urban energy collides with regal elegance, and the picturesque landscapes of Somerset unveil a tranquil countryside escape.

### Bristol's Maritime Marvels:

Our expedition begins in Bristol, a city steeped in maritime history and modern creativity. Wander through the historic harborside, where the SS Great Britain, a testament to Victorian engineering, proudly graces the docks. Bristol's street art scene, led by the elusive Banksy, adds a contemporary flair to the city's cultural mosaic. Explore the vibrant Stokes Croft neighborhood, where colorful murals and eclectic boutiques define the urban vibe.

### Bath's Regal Resplendence:

Venturing to Bath, immerse yourself in the city's regal allure. The Roman Baths, a marvel of ancient engineering, invite you to step back in time. Saunter along the grandeur of the Royal Crescent and the Circus, architectural gems that stand as symbols of Georgian elegance. Bath Abbey's spires punctuate the skyline, offering a spiritual haven amidst architectural splendor.

### Somerset's Countryside Tranquility:

As we escape the urban bustle, Somerset's countryside unfolds like a patchwork quilt of greenery. The Mendip Hills, with their panoramic views, provide a backdrop for scenic walks and contemplative moments. Explore the mystical beauty of Cheddar Gorge, where limestone cliffs rise dramatically, and the charming town of Wells enchants with its cathedral and medieval charm.

### Stately Homes and Gardens:

Discover the opulence of Longleat House, where Elizabethan grandeur meets modern safari adventures. Stroll through the idyllic grounds of Hestercombe Gardens, a masterpiece of landscape design that spans three centuries. Somerset's stately homes offer glimpses into bygone eras, each with its own tales of aristocratic splendor.

### Gastronomic Delights and Artisanal Markets:

Indulge your taste buds in Bristol's vibrant food scene, where street food markets and harborside eateries serve up culinary delights. Bath's Sally Lunn's Historic Eating House beckons with its famous buns, while Somerset's farmers' markets showcase the region's artisanal cheeses, ciders, and fresh produce.

### Hot Springs and Wellness Retreats:

Unwind in the healing waters of Bath's Thermae Bath Spa, a modern-day sanctuary that pays homage to the city's ancient Roman roots. Somerset's rural retreats offer wellness experiences amidst the tranquility of nature, providing a perfect balance to your journey.

### Accommodation:

- Stay at popular boutique hostels in Bristol, such as "The Bristol Wing" or "Rock n Bowl Hostel," known for their trendy and budget-friendly accommodations. These hostels often offer stylish dormitories and communal spaces, providing a vibrant and social atmosphere. Look for deals and discounts for the cheapest stays in Bristol.
- Opt for budget-friendly guesthouses in Bath, like "Brooks Guesthouse" or "Oldfields House," which offer a cozy and comfortable stay without straining your budget. These guesthouses are known for their welcoming atmosphere and often include amenities such as free Wi-Fi and complimentary breakfast. Find the best deals for the most affordable stays in Bath

### Transportation:

### 4. Train Travel:

- Use trains for travel between Bristol, Bath, and Somerset. Booking in advance will secure lower fares.

- **Local Buses:**
  - Utilize local buses for short-distance travel within Bristol, Bath, and Somerset.

## Bristol:

### 6. Clifton Suspension Bridge:

- Admire the Clifton Suspension Bridge, an iconic Bristol landmark. Walk across the bridge for free or take a guided tour for a small fee.
- **Bristol Harbourside:**
  - Explore Bristol Harbourside, lined with cafes and shops. Enjoy the atmosphere without spending money.
- **Street Art Tour in Stokes Croft:**
  - Take a self-guided street art tour in Stokes Croft, known for its vibrant murals.

## Bath:

### 9. Roman Baths:

- Visit the Roman Baths in Bath. While entry fees apply, consider taking advantage of late afternoon or early evening discounts.

- **Royal Crescent and The Circus:**
  - Stroll around the Royal Crescent and The Circus, iconic architectural landmarks in Bath. Exterior views are free.

## Somerset:

### 11. Cheddar Gorge:

- Explore Cheddar Gorge. While there's an entry fee for some attractions, hiking and enjoying the stunning landscapes are free.

- **Wells Cathedral:**
  - Visit Wells Cathedral in Somerset. While there's a suggested donation, entry is generally affordable.

## Luxury on a Budget Tips:

### 13. Thermal Bath Spa in Bath:

- Experience the Thermae Bath Spa in Bath. Opt for weekday or twilight sessions for significantly reduced prices.

- **Culinary Exploration:**
  - Indulge in luxury dining experiences at local restaurants during lunch or early evening for more affordable menus.
- **Happy Hour in Bristol:**
  - Explore Bristol's bars during happy hours for discounted drinks.
- **Discounted Attraction Tickets:**

- Look for discounted tickets or combination passes for attractions in Bristol, Bath, and Somerset.
- **Off-Peak Travel:**
  - Plan your visit during off-peak times for lower accommodation and transportation costs.
- **Local Markets:**
  - Immerse yourself in local markets in Bristol and Bath for gourmet treats and unique finds.
- **Nature Walks in Somerset:**
  - Take advantage of nature walks and trails in Somerset for a luxurious natural experience.
- **Student and Youth Discounts:**
  - If applicable, leverage student and youth discounts for attractions and transportation.

## Bristol:

### Harbourside Walk:
Take a leisurely walk along Bristol's Harbourside. Enjoy the vibrant atmosphere and historic docks for free.

### Clifton Suspension Bridge Viewpoint:
Admire the Clifton Suspension Bridge from the Clifton Observatory. While there's an entry fee, the viewpoint offers stunning panoramic views.

### Street Art in Stokes Croft:
Explore the street art in Stokes Croft. Witness the vibrant graffiti scene for free.

### SS Great Britain:
Visit the SS Great Britain. Look for discounted admission or explore the exterior and dock area for free.

### Bristol Museum and Art Gallery:
Explore the Bristol Museum and Art Gallery. While there's an entry fee for some exhibitions, general admission is often free.

## Bath:

### Royal Crescent Gardens:
Relax in the Royal Crescent Gardens. Enjoy the greenery and iconic Georgian architecture for free.

### Bath Abbey Interior:
Attend a service at Bath Abbey or explore the interior. While there may be entry fees for tours, attending a service is often free.

### Roman Baths Terrace:
Visit the Roman Baths Terrace. While there's an entry fee for the main attractions, the terrace is often accessible for free.

### Thermae Bath Spa Rooftop Pool:
Experience the rooftop pool at Thermae Bath Spa. Book a twilight session for a more budget-friendly option.

### Pulteney Bridge and Weir:
Stroll across Pulteney Bridge and enjoy the views of Pulteney Weir. It's a picturesque spot for free.

## Somerset:

### Cheddar Gorge Walk:
Embark on a walk through Cheddar Gorge. While some activities may have fees, walking through the gorge is free.

### Wells Cathedral Grounds:
Explore the grounds of Wells Cathedral. While there may be fees for specific areas, the exterior and surrounding area are often free.

### Glastonbury Tor Hike:
Hike up Glastonbury Tor. While there may be donations requested, the panoramic views are worth the climb.

### Barrington Court Gardens:
Visit the gardens of Barrington Court. While there's an entry fee for the manor, the gardens are often free to access.

### Kilver Court Gardens:
Explore Kilver Court Gardens. While there may be an entry fee, it's a beautiful setting for a leisurely stroll.

## Luxurious Dining:

### Dine at The Ivy in Clifton, Bristol:
Enjoy a luxurious meal at The Ivy Clifton Brasserie. Prices may range from £20-£40 per person.

### Sotto Sotto in Bath:
Indulge in Italian cuisine at Sotto Sotto in Bath. Prices may range from £20-£40 per person.

## Local Delicacies:

### Try Bristol's Craft Beers:
Sample local craft beers in Bristol. Prices vary, but enjoying a local pint can be a budget-friendly experience.

### Bath Bun in Bath:
Try the famous Bath Bun. Prices range from £2-£5, and it's a delightful local treat.

### Cheddar Cheese Tasting:
Experience Cheddar cheese tasting in Somerset. Prices depend on the venue, but it's a delicious and quintessentially Somerset experience.

| Aspect | Cost | Cost-Saving Measure | Why It Feels Luxurious | Potential Savings |
|---|---|---|---|---|
| Accommodation | £20-£110/ night | Opt for boutique guesthouses like Brooks Guesthouse in Bristol or budget-friendly options like YHA Bath Hostel. | Immerse in Bristol's vibrant atmosphere or unwind in historic Bath. | £20-£40/ night |
| Dining | £15-£25/ meal | Explore local eateries like The Ox in Bristol or traditional pubs in Bath for affordable yet exquisite meals. | Savor diverse and gourmet dishes with regional flavors. | £10-£15/ meal |
| Entertainment | £10-£30/ show | Attend live music events at Bristol's iconic venues or explore free festivals and events in Bath. | Enjoy cultural richness in Bristol's music scene or Bath's historic setting. | £5-£20/ show |
| Transportation | £10-£15/ day | Utilize local buses or explore Bristol, Bath, and Somerset on foot or by bike. Consider day passes for trains. | Discover picturesque landscapes and historic sites at your own pace. | £5-£10/ day |
| Sightseeing | £0-£12/day | Visit free attractions like Bristol's Clifton Suspension Bridge or stroll through Bath's Royal Victoria Park. | Immerse in Bristol's modern vibe or Bath's Roman and Georgian heritage. | £8-£12/ day |
| Total Daily Budget | | | | £50-£87/ day |

# Hampshire, Wiltshire and Dorset

*Jurassic Coast*

### Historical Echoes in Hampshire:

Hampshire, a county steeped in history and dotted with landmarks that whisper tales of centuries past. Explore the medieval majesty of Winchester Cathedral, where echoes of Saxon kings and queens resonate. Wander through the historic dockyards of Portsmouth, home to the iconic HMS Victory and the Mary Rose. Southampton's medieval walls and Tudor House Museum add layers to the county's rich heritage.

### Wiltshire's Timeless Landscapes:

Venturing into Wiltshire, prepare to be enchanted by its timeless landscapes. The prehistoric marvel of Stonehenge stands as a silent witness to ancient mysteries, while the medieval spire of Salisbury Cathedral graces the horizon. Immerse yourself in the ethereal beauty of the Avebury Stone Circle, a vast Neolithic monument surrounded by rolling hills and charming villages.

### Dorset's Coastal Charms:

As we descend to the coastal allure of Dorset, golden beaches and rugged cliffs await. The Jurassic Coast, a UNESCO World Heritage Site, unfolds like a geological storybook, with Durdle Door and Old Harry Rocks adding drama to the panoramic views. Explore the quaint charm of Lyme Regis, a coastal town where fossil hunting and ice cream indulgence go hand in hand.

## Stately Homes and Gardens:

Discover the grandeur of Highclere Castle in Hampshire, famously known as the setting for "Downton Abbey." In Wiltshire, Bowood House and Gardens invite you to stroll through impeccably manicured landscapes and marvel at the Georgian splendor. Dorset's Athelhampton House, with its Tudor architecture and enchanting gardens, offers a glimpse into the county's historic elegance.

## Gastronomic Pleasures and Farmers' Markets:

Indulge in the culinary delights of the region, where Hampshire's local produce shines in traditional dishes. Wiltshire's market towns, like Devizes and Marlborough, offer a taste of artisanal delights, while Dorset's seafood and farm-fresh offerings showcase the best of coastal and countryside cuisine.

## Wellness Retreats and Countryside Walks:

Unwind in the tranquility of Hampshire's New Forest, where ancient woodlands and heathlands provide a serene backdrop for leisurely walks. Wiltshire's countryside trails, such as the Kennet and Avon Canal, offer scenic routes amidst nature's embrace. Dorset's coastal paths invite you to breathe in the sea air and revel in the beauty of the English Channel.

## Accommodation:

- **Historic Inns in Hampshire:**
  - Stay in historic inns or charming bed and breakfasts in Hampshire for a unique and budget-friendly experience.
- **Countryside Retreats in Wiltshire:**
  - Choose countryside retreats or farm stays in Wiltshire for a tranquil and affordable stay.
- **Coastal Airbnb in Dorset:**
  - Explore coastal Airbnb options in Dorset for scenic and affordable accommodations.

## Transportation:

4. **Bus Travel:**

- Utilize Buses for travel between Hampshire, Wiltshire, and Dorset. Booking in advance can secure lower fares.
  - **Local Buses:**
  - Use local buses for short-distance travel within each county.

**Hampshire:**

## 6. Winchester Cathedral:

- Visit Winchester Cathedral. While entry fees apply, you can attend a service for free or explore the exterior.

    - **New Forest National Park:**
    - Explore New Forest National Park. Entrance to the park is free, and you can enjoy walks, picnics, and wildlife spotting.

**Wiltshire:**

## 8. Stonehenge:

- Visit Stonehenge. While there's an entry fee, booking in advance online can save you money.

    - **Salisbury Cathedral Close:**
    - Stroll around Salisbury Cathedral Close. While there's an entry fee for the cathedral, the close is free to wander.

**Dorset:**

## 10. Jurassic Coast:

- Explore the Jurassic Coast. Walk along the coastline, admire natural landmarks, and visit spots like Durdle Door for free.

    - **Corfe Castle:**
    - Visit Corfe Castle. While there's an entry fee, the exterior views from the village are impressive and free.

**Luxury on a Budget Tips:**

## 12. High Tea in Winchester:

- Experience high tea at one of Winchester's charming tea rooms. Opt for afternoon tea deals for affordability.

- **Countryside Pub Lunch in Wiltshire:**
    - Enjoy a countryside pub lunch in Wiltshire for an authentic and affordable dining experience.
- **Happy Hour by the Coast in Dorset:**
    - Explore Dorset's coastal bars during happy hours for discounted drinks with a view.
- **Discounted Attraction Tickets:**
    - Look for discounted tickets or combination passes for attractions in Hampshire, Wiltshire, and Dorset.
- **Off-Peak Travel:**
    - Plan your visit during off-peak times for lower accommodation and transportation costs.

- **Local Markets:**
  - Immerse yourself in local markets in each county for fresh produce, artisanal goods, and unique finds.
- **Nature Walks in Hampshire:**
  - Take advantage of nature walks and trails in Hampshire, especially in the New Forest.
- **Student and Youth Discounts:**
  - If applicable, leverage student and youth discounts for attractions and transportation.

**Approximate Prices:**

- **Accommodation:** £50-£100 per night (varies based on type and location)
- **Train Travel:** £15-£30 for short-distance journeys
- **Attraction Entry:** £10-£25 per attraction
- **Dining:** £15-£30 per person for mid-range dining

These are approximate prices and can vary based on specific circumstances and promotions available at the time of booking. Always check for discounts, promotions, and seasonal offers to enhance your experience while staying within your budget.

**Hampshire:**

**New Forest National Park:**
Explore the New Forest National Park. Enjoy free walks and hikes through this picturesque area.

**Winchester Cathedral Grounds:**
Wander through the grounds of Winchester Cathedral. While there may be entry fees for certain areas, the exterior and grounds are often free.

**Southampton Old Town:**
Discover the historic Old Town of Southampton. Stroll through medieval streets and enjoy the architecture.

**Jane Austen's House Museum:**
Visit Jane Austen's House Museum. Look for discounted admission or explore the exterior for free.

**Beaulieu Palace House Gardens:**
Explore the gardens of Beaulieu Palace House. While there's an entry fee for the house, the gardens may be accessible for free.

**Wiltshire:**

**Stonehenge Landscape:**
Walk around the Stonehenge landscape. While there's an entry fee for the monument, the surrounding area can be enjoyed for free.

**Salisbury Cathedral Close:**
Explore the Close of Salisbury Cathedral. While there may be fees for specific areas, the exterior and grounds are often free.

**Lacock Village:**
Wander through Lacock Village. Enjoy the preserved medieval architecture, and entry to some areas is free.

**Old Sarum:**
Visit Old Sarum. While there's an entry fee for certain areas, the panoramic views from the hill are often free.

**Wilton House Gardens:**

Explore the gardens of Wilton House. While there's an entry fee for the house, the gardens may be accessible for free.

**Dorset:**

### Durdle Door and Lulworth Cove:
Visit Durdle Door and Lulworth Cove. While there may be parking fees, exploring the natural wonders is free.

### Corfe Castle Village:
Discover Corfe Castle Village. Stroll through the charming village and admire the castle from the exterior.

### Jurassic Coast Walk:
Hike along the Jurassic Coast. Enjoy the stunning coastline and rock formations for free.

### Sherborne Abbey Grounds:
Wander through the grounds of Sherborne Abbey. While there may be fees for specific areas, the exterior is often free.

### Abbotsbury Subtropical Gardens:
Explore Abbotsbury Subtropical Gardens. While there's an entry fee, it's a lush and beautiful setting.

**Luxurious Dining:**

### The Pig Hotel in Brockenhurst, Hampshire:
Indulge in dining at The Pig Hotel. Prices may range from £30-£60 per person.

### The Old Mill in Salisbury, Wiltshire:
Enjoy a meal at The Old Mill in Salisbury. Prices may range from £20-£40 per person.

**Local Delicacies:**

### Cream Tea in Dorset:
Experience a traditional cream tea in Dorset. Prices range from £5-£10 per person.

### Wiltshire Ham:
Try Wiltshire Ham, a local specialty. Prices vary based on the venue but are generally affordable.

### Seafood in Hampshire:
Indulge in fresh seafood in Hampshire. Prices vary depending on the restaurant and the chosen dishes.

| RECAP | Cost | Cost-Saving Measure | Why It Feels Luxurious | Potential Savings |
|---|---|---|---|---|
| Accommodation | £20-£110/ night | Consider charming guesthouses like The King's Head in Wiltshire or budget-friendly options like YHA New Forest Hostel. | Experience local character and hospitality in Hampshire or amid New Forest's natural beauty. | £20-£40/ night |
| Dining | £15-£25/ meal | Opt for local gems like The Greyhound in Hampshire or traditional pubs in Wiltshire for affordable yet delightful meals. | Savor regional dishes in a cozy and authentic atmosphere. | £10-£15/ meal |
| Entertainment | £10-£30/ show | Attend local performances or explore free festivals in Dorset. Visit cultural venues like Salisbury Cathedral in Wiltshire. | Enjoy cultural richness in historic settings or amid Dorset's vibrant events. | £5-£20/ show |
| Transportation | £10-£15/ day | Utilize local buses or explore the scenic landscapes on foot in Hampshire, Wiltshire, and Dorset. Consider day passes for trains. | Discover picturesque countryside and historic sites at a leisurely pace. | £5-£10/ day |
| Sightseeing | £0-£12/ day | Visit free attractions like Winchester Cathedral in Hampshire or stroll through the charming streets of Salisbury in Wiltshire. | Immerse in local history and architecture in Hampshire and Wiltshire. | £8-£12/ day |
| Total Daily Budget | | | | £50-£87/ day |

# Devon, Cornwall and the Isle of scilly

*Mount-edgcumbe-house*

Devon is a county blessed with picturesque coastlines and tales of seafaring glory. Explore the maritime charm of Plymouth, where the Mayflower Steps mark the departure point of the Pilgrims. Meander through the historic port of Dartmouth, with its medieval streets and naval history. The Jurassic Coast, a UNESCO World Heritage Site, showcases ancient cliffs, fossil-rich beaches, and the iconic Durdle Door.

## Cornwall's Rugged Landscapes:

Venturing into Cornwall, be prepared for rugged landscapes that have inspired poets and artists for centuries. Discover the windswept drama of Land's End, where towering cliffs meet the Atlantic Ocean. Marvel at the fairytale allure of Tintagel Castle, linked to the legend of King Arthur. Stroll through the charming fishing villages of St Ives and Port Isaac, where cobbled streets and seaside cottages create a postcard-perfect scene.

## Isles of Scilly's Tranquil Bliss:

As we sail toward the Isles of Scilly, prepare to be enveloped in serene tranquility. This archipelago of islands, scattered off the Cornish coast, offers a retreat into natural beauty. Explore Tresco Abbey Garden, a subtropical paradise with exotic blooms. Wander through St. Mary's, the largest island, where white-sand beaches and turquoise waters invite peaceful contemplation.

## Stately Homes and Gardens:

Discover the grandeur of Powderham Castle in Devon, a historic seat that overlooks the Exe Estuary. Cornwall's Lanhydrock House, a Victorian mansion with extensive gardens, allows you to step back in time. In the Isles of Scilly, the Abbey Garden on Tresco Island showcases a diverse collection of plants from around the world, creating a botanical haven.

## Gastronomic Pleasures and Coastal Cuisine:

Indulge in the gastronomic delights of the region, where Devon's cream teas, Cornwall's pasties, and Scilly's fresh seafood become culinary highlights. Savor the flavors of local produce in farmers' markets, and enjoy traditional pub fare with sea views that stretch to the horizon.

## Coastal Walks and Island Exploration:

Embark on coastal walks along Devon's South West Coast Path, with its breathtaking vistas of cliffs and coves. Explore Cornwall's coastal trails, such as the rugged beauty of the Lizard Peninsula. On the Isles of Scilly, each island offers its own unique charm, best explored by boat or on foot, revealing hidden coves and panoramic viewpoints.

## Accommodation:

- *Luxury on a Budget:* Consider boutique bed and breakfasts like "The Old Rectory" in Exmoor or "The Great Grubb Bed & Breakfast" in Totnes. These charming accommodations offer a touch of luxury without the high price tag.

## Dining:

- *Affordable Indulgence:* Experience gourmet dining at a reasonable cost by visiting local gems like "Riverford Field Kitchen" in Buckfastleigh, known for its farm-to-table ethos and seasonal menus.

## Entertainment:

- *Cultural Experiences:* Take advantage of free cultural events and festivals. Explore historic sites such as Dartmoor National Park or attend local events in towns like Totnes, combining luxury scenery with cultural enrichment.

## Transportation:

- *Scenic Journeys:* Opt for scenic train routes, like the Riviera Line, providing breathtaking views of the coastline. Consider purchasing a Devon Explorer Pass for unlimited bus and train travel within the region.

**Cornwall:**

**Accommodation:**

- *Seaside Charm:* Stay in coastal towns like St Ives or Falmouth and choose guesthouses like "The Gannet Inn" or "Greenbank Hotel" for a luxurious feel with proximity to the beach.

**Dining:**

- *Seafood Delights:* Enjoy fresh seafood at affordable prices in local establishments like "The Shack" in Falmouth or "The Seafood Restaurant" in Padstow, owned by celebrity chef Rick Stein.

**Entertainment:**

- *Coastal Walks:* Embark on scenic coastal walks such as the South West Coast Path, offering stunning views of the Atlantic. Nature's entertainment is both budget-friendly and luxurious.

**Transportation:**

- *Explore by Bus:* Make use of the extensive bus network, including the Atlantic Coaster route, to explore coastal towns and villages without the need for a car.

**Isles of Scilly:**

**Accommodation:**

- *Quaint Guesthouses:* Choose guesthouses like "Colossus" on St Mary's or "Tregarthen's Hotel" on St Mary's for a cozy yet affordable stay on the Isles of Scilly.

**Dining:**

- *Local Flavors:* Indulge in local flavors at places like "Juliet's Garden" on St Mary's, offering a blend of Scillonian and Mediterranean cuisine in a picturesque setting.

**Entertainment:**

- *Island Exploration:* The Isles of Scilly offer unique landscapes. Explore Tresco Abbey Gardens or take a boat trip to spot seals and seabirds, combining nature's wonders with budget-friendly activities.

**Transportation:**

- *Inter-Island Boats:* Utilize the inter-island boats for a cost-effective way to explore the different islands. Enjoy the scenic boat rides between St Mary's, Tresco, and other isles.

# Activities

## Devon:

### Dartmoor National Park:
Explore Dartmoor National Park. Enjoy free walks amidst the rugged landscapes.

### Exeter Cathedral Green:
Stroll through Exeter Cathedral Green. While there may be entry fees for certain areas, the exterior is often free to explore.

### Jurassic Coast Beaches:
Visit the beaches along the Jurassic Coast. Enjoy the stunning coastal scenery, and many beaches are free to access.

### Powderham Castle Grounds:
Wander through the grounds of Powderham Castle. While there's an entry fee for the castle, the exterior and gardens may be accessible for free.

### River Exe Estuary:
Take a walk along the River Exe Estuary. Enjoy the scenic views and birdwatching opportunities for free.

## Cornwall:

### St. Michael's Mount Causeway:
Walk along the causeway to St. Michael's Mount. While there's an entry fee for the castle, the exterior and causeway are often free.

### Porthcurno Beach:
Relax at Porthcurno Beach. Enjoy the golden sands and turquoise waters, and access is generally free.

### Tintagel Castle Coastline:
Explore the coastline near Tintagel Castle. While there's an entry fee for the castle, the coastal paths offer breathtaking views for free.

### The Lost Gardens of Heligan:
Wander through The Lost Gardens of Heligan. While there's an entry fee, it's a lush and beautiful setting.

### Fowey Estuary Walk:
Take a walk along the Fowey Estuary. Enjoy the picturesque views of the river and surroundings for free.

## Isles of Scilly:

### St. Mary's:
Explore St. Mary's, the largest of the Isles of Scilly. Walk around the town and enjoy the peaceful atmosphere.

### Tresco Abbey Gardens:
Visit Tresco Abbey Gardens. While there's an entry fee, it's a unique and beautifully landscaped garden.

### St. Martin's Daymark:
Hike to the St. Martin's Daymark. Enjoy panoramic views of the islands for free.

### Bryher's Hell Bay:
Relax at Hell Bay on Bryher. Access to some beaches may be free, and the scenery is stunning.

### Island Hopping:

Take advantage of budget-friendly inter-island transportation options to explore various isles.

## Luxurious Dining:

### The Elephant Restaurant in Torquay, Devon:
Indulge in dining at The Elephant. Prices may range from £30-£60 per person.

### The Seafood Restaurant in Padstow, Cornwall:
Enjoy a meal at The Seafood Restaurant. Prices may range from £40-£80 per person.

## Local Delicacies:

### Devon Cream Tea:
Experience a traditional Devon cream tea. Prices range from £5-£10 per person.

### Cornish Pasty:
Try a Cornish pasty, a local specialty. Prices vary but are generally affordable.

### Isles of Scilly Seafood:
Indulge in fresh seafood on the Isles of Scilly. Prices vary based on the restaurant and chosen dishes.

# Cambridge and East Anglia

*Punting*

Cambridge is a city synonymous with academic excellence and timeless beauty. Stroll through the venerable halls of the University of Cambridge, where luminaries like Newton and Darwin once sought knowledge. Punt along the River Cam, where the iconic Backs showcase the architectural grandeur of the university's colleges. Explore the historic Cambridge Market Square and savor the intellectual atmosphere that permeates the city.

**Historic Landmarks and Cultural Gems:**

Delve into the historic landmarks of Cambridge, from the awe-inspiring King's College Chapel to the medieval allure of St John's College. Immerse yourself in the Fitzwilliam Museum's rich collection of art and artifacts. Venture beyond the city to Anglesey Abbey, a Jacobean-style house surrounded by stunning gardens that change with the seasons.

**East Anglia's Countryside Retreats:**

As we venture into East Anglia, be prepared for vast landscapes and picturesque countryside. Discover the quintessential charm of Suffolk's medieval villages, such as Lavenham, with its timber-framed cottages. Norfolk's Broads, a network of serene waterways, offer opportunities for boat trips and birdwatching. Explore the grandeur of Ely Cathedral, perched atop an island in the Fens.

**Stately Homes and Gardens:**

Uncover the elegance of Wimpole Estate, a grand mansion surrounded by parkland in Cambridgeshire. Visit the splendid gardens of Anglesey Abbey, where the Winter Garden and Dahlia Garden are highlights. In East Anglia, explore the historic Holkham Hall in Norfolk, a Palladian mansion set amidst a vast estate.

**Gastronomic Pleasures and Local Markets:**

Indulge in the gastronomic delights of Cambridge's culinary scene, where traditional pubs and riverside eateries offer a taste of local flavors. East Anglia's farmers' markets showcase the region's bounty, from Norfolk's famous strawberries to Suffolk's renowned cheeses. Explore the foodie havens of Bury St Edmunds and Norwich for a culinary journey through the heart of East Anglia.

**Countryside Walks and Nature Reserves:**

Embark on countryside walks through the Cambridgeshire Fens, where vast fields and gentle rivers create a serene backdrop. Explore the nature reserves of East Anglia, including RSPB Minsmere, a haven for birdwatchers. The coastal paths of Norfolk and Suffolk unveil panoramic views of the North Sea and unspoiled beaches.

**Accommodation:**

- **Cambridge Colleges Accommodation:**
    - Stay in Cambridge Colleges during vacation periods for a unique and budget-friendly experience. Examples include Christ's College or Sidney Sussex College.
- **Boutique B&Bs in East Anglia:**
    - Choose boutique bed and breakfasts in East Anglia, such as The Great House in Lavenham or The Crown & Castle in Orford.
- **Charming Guesthouses in Cambridge:**
    - Explore charming guesthouses in Cambridge, like Worth House or The Earl of Derby.
- **Isle of Scilly Campsite:**
    - For a budget option on the Isle of Scilly, consider camping at one of the campsites like Garrison Campsite on St. Mary's.

**Transportation:**

5. **Trains and Buses:**

- Utilize trains and buses for travel between Cambridge and East Anglia. Booking in advance can secure lower fares.

**Cambridge:**

6. **King's College Chapel:**

- Admire King's College Chapel in Cambridge. While entry fees apply, the exterior and grounds are free to explore.
    - **Punting on the River Cam:**

- Experience punting on the River Cam. Shared punting tours are more affordable than private ones.

**East Anglia:**

**8. Lavenham, Suffolk:**

- Explore the medieval village of Lavenham in Suffolk. Walk around the charming streets and visit the Guildhall.
  - **Norwich Cathedral:**
    - Visit Norwich Cathedral in Norfolk. While there's a suggested donation, entry is generally affordable.

**Isle of Scilly:**

**10. Tresco Abbey Garden:**

- Explore Tresco Abbey Garden on the Isles of Scilly. While there's an entry fee, the unique flora is worth the visit.

  - **St. Martin's Vineyard:**
    - Visit St. Martin's Vineyard on the Isles of Scilly. Enjoy wine tasting and scenic views.

**Luxury on a Budget Tips:**

**12. Gourmet Picnic in Cambridge:**

- Create a gourmet picnic with local treats and enjoy it in one of Cambridge's beautiful parks.

- **Traditional Pub Lunch in East Anglia:**
  - Experience a traditional pub lunch in East Anglia for an authentic and affordable dining experience.
- **Happy Hour by the River in Cambridge:**
  - Explore Cambridge's riverside bars during happy hours for discounted drinks with scenic views.
- **Discounted Attraction Tickets:**
  - Look for discounted tickets or combination passes for attractions in Cambridge and East Anglia.
- **Off-Peak Travel:**
  - Plan your visit during off-peak times for lower accommodation and transportation costs.
- **Local Markets in East Anglia:**
  - Immerse yourself in local markets in East Anglia for fresh produce, handmade crafts, and unique finds.
- **Nature Walks in East Anglia:**
  - Take advantage of nature walks and trails in East Anglia, such as the Norfolk Coast Path.
- **Student and Youth Discounts:**
  - If applicable, leverage student and youth discounts for attractions and transportation.

**Approximate Prices:**

- **Accommodation:** £50-£100 per night (varies based on type and location)
- **Train Travel:** £15-£30 for short-distance journeys
- **Attraction Entry:** £10-£25 per attraction
- **Dining:** £15-£30 per person for mid-range dining

## Cambridge:

### King's College Chapel Grounds:
Stroll through the grounds of King's College Chapel. While there may be entry fees for certain areas, the exterior is often free.
### Punting on the River Cam:
Enjoy a budget-friendly punt on the River Cam. Shared punts are more affordable than private ones.
### Fitzwilliam Museum:
Explore the Fitzwilliam Museum. While there's an entry fee for special exhibitions, general admission is often free.
### Botanic Garden:
Relax in the Cambridge University Botanic Garden. While there's an entry fee, it's a peaceful setting for a budget-friendly visit.
### Bridge of Sighs:
Admire the Bridge of Sighs. While access to some areas may have fees, enjoying the exterior is free.

## East Anglia:

### Norwich Cathedral Close:
Stroll through the Close of Norwich Cathedral. While there may be entry fees for specific areas, the exterior is often free.
### Blickling Estate Gardens:
Wander through the gardens of Blickling Estate. While there's an entry fee for the house, the gardens may be accessible for free.
### Flatford Mill (Constable Country):
Explore Flatford Mill in Dedham Vale. While there's an entry fee for the mill, the surrounding landscapes inspired artist John Constable and can be enjoyed for free.
### Southwold Pier:
Walk along Southwold Pier. While there may be fees for certain attractions, strolling along the pier is often free.
### Walsingham Abbey Grounds:
Visit the grounds of Walsingham Abbey. While there's an entry fee for the abbey, the gardens may be accessible for free.
## Luxurious Dining:

### Midsummer House in Cambridge:
Indulge in dining at Midsummer House. Prices may range from £80-£150 per person.
### Roger Hickman's Restaurant in Norwich:

Enjoy a meal at Roger Hickman's Restaurant. Prices may range from £40-£80 per person.

## Local Delicacies:

### Cambridge Cream Cake:

Try a Cambridge Cream Cake, a local specialty. Prices range from £2-£5, and it's a delightful treat.

### Norfolk Ale Tasting:

Experience Norfolk ale tasting. Prices vary based on the venue but are generally affordable.

### Cambridge Farmers' Market:

Immerse yourself in the Cambridge Farmers' Market. Sample local produce and artisanal products.

### Wells-next-the-Sea Seafood:

Indulge in fresh seafood In Wells-next-the-Sea. Prices vary based on the restaurant and chosen dishes.

## Countryside Escapes:

### Walks in the Norfolk Broads:

Enjoy walks in the Norfolk Broads. The flat landscapes offer scenic views and are often free to explore.

### Cycling in Cambridge Fens:

Explore the Cambridge Fens by cycling. Renting a bike is an affordable way to discover the countryside.

### Ely Cathedral Grounds:

Stroll through the grounds of Ely Cathedral. While there may be entry fees for specific areas, the exterior is often free.

### Holkham Beach:

Relax at Holkham Beach. Enjoy the expansive sandy beach, and access is free.

| RECAP | Cost | Cost-Saving Measure | Why It Feels Luxurious | Potential Savings |
|---|---|---|---|---|
| Accommodation | £30-£110/ night | Consider boutique guesthouses like The Gonville Hotel in Cambridge or budget-friendly options like YHA Cambridge Hostel. | Immerse in Cambridge's academic charm or amid the natural beauty of East Anglia. | £20-£40/ night |
| Dining | £15-£25/ meal | Opt for local favorites like Fitzbillies in Cambridge or traditional pubs in East Anglia for affordable yet delightful meals. | Savor regional flavors in a charming and historic setting. | £10-£15/ meal |
| Entertainment | £10-£30/ show | Attend student performances in Cambridge or explore free events and festivals in East Anglia. | Experience cultural richness in academic Cambridge or amid East Anglia's vibrant events. | £5-£20/ show |
| Transportation | £10-£15/ day | Utilize local buses or explore Cambridge and East Anglia on foot or by bike. Consider day passes for trains. | Discover picturesque landscapes and historic sites at a leisurely pace. | £5-£10/ day |
| Sightseeing | £0-£12/ day | Visit free attractions like the Fitzwilliam Museum in Cambridge or explore the Norfolk Broads in East Anglia. | Immerse in academic history or the natural beauty of East Anglia. | £8-£12/ day |
| Total Daily Budget | | | | £50-£87/ day |

# Birmingham and Midlands

Birmingham, a city that has seamlessly blended its industrial roots with a modern, cosmopolitan charm. Marvel at the futuristic design of the Library of Birmingham and the iconic Selfridges building at the Bullring. Stroll along the rejuvenated canalside in Brindleyplace, where waterside cafes and cultural venues create a lively atmosphere. Dive into the city's rich industrial past at the Birmingham Museum and Art Gallery, where the Pre-Raphaelite art collection captivates.

**Cultural Hotspots and Modern Landmarks:**

Discover cultural hotspots like the Symphony Hall, a world-class concert venue, and the Repertory Theatre, a hub for innovative performances. The Custard Factory in Digbeth, a creative and digital business workspace, exemplifies Birmingham's commitment to fostering artistic endeavors. For a taste of the city's industrial heritage, explore the Black Country Living Museum, an immersive experience into 19th-century life.

**Midlands' Historic Landscapes:**

Venturing into the Midlands, encounter a tapestry of historic landscapes and charming towns. Stratford-upon-Avon, birthplace of Shakespeare, invites you to explore Tudor-style streets and the renowned Royal Shakespeare Theatre. The atmospheric Warwick Castle perched on the River Avon offers a glimpse into medieval grandeur. The Ironbridge Gorge, a UNESCO World Heritage Site, is a testament to the region's pivotal role in the Industrial Revolution.

## Stately Homes and Gardens:

Uncover the splendor of Midlands' stately homes, from Warwick Castle's medieval fortress to Blenheim Palace's Baroque magnificence. In Birmingham, the Aston Hall and Winterbourne House and Garden provide glimpses into the city's historic opulence. Explore the gardens of Baddesley Clinton, a moated manor house, for a tranquil retreat.

## Gastronomic Adventures and Cultural Diversity:

Indulge in Birmingham's diverse culinary scene, from the aromatic spices of the Balti Triangle to the trendy eateries along the canals. Digbeth Dining Club, a street food haven, showcases the city's gastronomic innovation. The Midlands' market towns, like Stratford-upon-Avon and Leamington Spa, offer a blend of traditional pubs, artisanal cafes, and global cuisines.

## Canal Walks and Nature Escapes:

Embark on leisurely canal walks in Birmingham, where the network of waterways provides a scenic escape. In the Midlands, Cannock Chase, an Area of Outstanding Natural Beauty, invites you to explore woodlands and heathlands. The Peak District, just a stone's throw away, offers hiking trails with panoramic views.

## Accommodation:

- **Boutique Hotels in Birmingham:**
    - Stay in boutique hotels in Birmingham, such as Hotel du Vin & Bistro Birmingham or Malmaison Birmingham.
- **Historic Inns in the Midlands:**
    - Choose historic inns or charming bed and breakfasts in the Midlands, like The Castle Hotel in Shropshire or The George Hotel in Lichfield.

## Transportation:

### 3. Trains and Buses:

- Utilize trains and buses for travel within the Midlands. Booking in advance can secure lower fares.

## Birmingham:

### 4. Birmingham Museum and Art Gallery:

- Explore the Birmingham Museum and Art Gallery. While entry fees apply to some exhibitions, the general entrance is often free.
    - **Jewellery Quarter:**

- Stroll through Birmingham's Jewellery Quarter. Explore independent shops and the Museum of the Jewellery Quarter.

**Midlands:**

6. **Stratford-upon-Avon:**

- Visit Stratford-upon-Avon. Enjoy a walk along the River Avon and explore the birthplace of William Shakespeare.
  - **Ironbridge Gorge:**
  - Explore Ironbridge Gorge in Shropshire. While some museums have entry fees, the gorge and river are free to enjoy.

**Paid Attractions and how to save money**

**Cadbury World:**

Cadbury World, a chocolate-themed visitor center, is among Birmingham's popular paid attractions. To save money, consider booking tickets online in advance, as online prices are often discounted. Additionally, look for promotional offers or family packages that may provide further savings. Keep an eye on seasonal promotions or group discounts if you're traveling with others.

**Birmingham Sea Life Centre:**

The Birmingham Sea Life Centre is a beloved aquatic attraction. Save on admission by purchasing tickets online before your visit. Combo tickets, which include entry to multiple Merlin Entertainments attractions, may offer additional value. Consider visiting during off-peak hours or on weekdays, as ticket prices can vary based on the time of day and day of the week.

**Thinktank, Birmingham Science Museum:**

Thinktank, the Birmingham Science Museum, is a fantastic educational destination. To save on admission, check for discounts available to students, seniors, or families. Many museums offer reduced prices for visitors who book tickets in advance online. Additionally, explore membership options, as frequent visitors may find annual passes or memberships cost-effective.

**The Birmingham Museum and Art Gallery (BMAG):**

The Birmingham Museum and Art Gallery is a cultural gem. Check the museum's website for information on free entry days or discounted admission periods. Some museums offer reduced prices for evening visits, providing a budget-friendly option. Consider becoming a member if you plan to visit multiple times, as memberships often come with perks like free or discounted entry.

**The Birmingham Botanical Gardens and Glasshouses:**

For nature enthusiasts, the Birmingham Botanical Gardens and Glasshouses offer a serene escape. Look for special events or open days when entry might be discounted or free. Annual memberships can be a cost-effective choice for regular visitors, providing unlimited access to the gardens throughout the year.

**Luxury on a Budget Tips:**

8. **Gourmet Street Food in Birmingham:**

- Experience gourmet street food in Birmingham's Digbeth Dining Club or another street food market for affordable yet delicious options.
- **Lunch at a Country Inn in the Midlands:**
    - Enjoy lunch at a country inn in the Midlands for an authentic and affordable dining experience.
- **Happy Hour in Birmingham:**
    - Explore Birmingham's vibrant bars during happy hours for discounted drinks.
- **Discounted Attraction Tickets:**
    - Look for discounted tickets or combination passes for attractions in Birmingham and the Midlands.
- **Off-Peak Travel:**
    - Plan your visit during off-peak times for lower accommodation and transportation costs.
- **Local Markets in the Midlands:**
    - Immerse yourself in local markets for fresh produce, crafts, and unique finds.
- **Nature Walks in the Midlands:**
    - Take advantage of nature walks and trails in the Midlands, such as those in Cannock Chase.
- **Student and Youth Discounts:**
    - If applicable, leverage student and youth discounts for attractions and transportation.

**Approximate Prices:**

- **Accommodation:** £60-£120 per night (varies based on type and location)
- **Train Travel:** £10-£25 for short-distance journeys
- **Attraction Entry:** £5-£20 per attraction
- **Dining:** £15-£30 per person for mid-range dining

**Birmingham:**

**Birmingham Museum and Art Gallery:**
Explore the Birmingham Museum and Art Gallery. While there may be entry fees for certain exhibitions, general admission is often free.

**Canal Walks:**
Take a leisurely walk along Birmingham's canals. Enjoy the picturesque scenery and vibrant atmosphere for free.

**Jewellery Quarter:**
Explore the Jewellery Quarter. Wander through historic streets and perhaps visit the Museum of the Jewellery Quarter.

**Cadbury World Exterior:**
Visit the exterior of Cadbury World. While there's an entry fee for the attractions, walking around the area is often free.

**Botanical Gardens:**
 Relax in the Birmingham Botanical Gardens. While there's an entry fee, it's a peaceful setting for a budget-friendly visit.


## The Midlands:

**Stratford-upon-Avon:**
 Stroll through Stratford-upon-Avon. Enjoy the birthplace of Shakespeare and explore the town for free.

**Warwick Castle Grounds:**
 Wander through the grounds of Warwick Castle. While there's an entry fee for certain areas, the exterior and gardens may be accessible for free.

**Coventry Cathedral Ruins:**
 Explore the ruins of Coventry Cathedral. While there may be entry fees for specific areas, the exterior is often free.

**Ironbridge Gorge:**
 Visit Ironbridge Gorge. While there's an entry fee for museums, walking around the gorge and enjoying the Iron Bridge is often free.

**Peak District National Park:**
 Explore the Peak District National Park. Enjoy walks amidst the stunning landscapes for free.

## Luxurious Dining:

**Purnell's in Birmingham:**
 Indulge in dining at Purnell's. Prices may range from £60-£120 per person.

**Simpsons in Edgbaston, Birmingham:**
 Enjoy a meal at Simpsons. Prices may range from £40-£80 per person.

## Local Delicacies:

**Balti Triangle in Birmingham:**
 Experience the Balti Triangle in Birmingham. Try a local Balti dish, and prices range from £10-£20 per person.

**Midlands Real Ale Tasting:**
 Sample real ales in the Midlands. Prices vary based on the venue but are generally affordable.

**Warwickshire Ice Cream:**
 Indulge in Warwickshire ice cream. Prices range from £3-£5, and it's a delightful local treat.

**Stratford-upon-Avon Tea Rooms:**
 Enjoy tea in one of Stratford-upon-Avon's traditional tea rooms. Prices vary but are generally reasonable.

## Countryside Retreats:

**Cotswold Villages:**
 Explore charming Cotswold villages. Stroll through quaint streets and enjoy the picturesque scenery.

**Shropshire Hills:**
 Hike in the Shropshire Hills. Enjoy the natural beauty and panoramic views for free.

**Malvern Hills:**

Walk in the Malvern Hills. The rolling hills offer scenic landscapes and are often free to explore.

**Chatsworth House Gardens:**

Explore the gardens of Chatsworth House. While there's an entry fee for the house, the gardens is accessible for free.

| RECAP | Cost | Cost-Saving Measure | Why It Feels Luxurious | Potential Savings |
|---|---|---|---|---|
| Accommodation | £10-£110/ night | Consider boutique hotels like Staying Cool at the Rotunda in Birmingham or budget-friendly options like YHA National Forest Hostel. | Immerse in Birmingham's modern vibe or amid the natural beauty of the Midlands. | £20-£40/ night |
| Dining | £15-£25/ meal | Opt for local gems like Lasan in Birmingham or traditional pubs in the Midlands for affordable yet delightful meals. | Savor diverse and gourmet dishes in a vibrant urban setting. | £10-£15/ meal |
| Entertainment | £10-£30/ show | Attend live music events or explore free festivals in Birmingham. Visit cultural venues like the Birmingham Museum and Art Gallery. | Enjoy cultural richness in a dynamic city or amid the historic Midlands. | £5-£20/ show |
| Transportation | £10-£15/ day | Utilize local buses or explore Birmingham and the Midlands on foot or by bike. Consider day passes for trains. | Discover urban landscapes and historic sites at a leisurely pace. | £5-£10/ day |
| Sightseeing | £0-£12/ day | Visit free attractions like the Birmingham Museum and Art Gallery or explore the Peak District in the Midlands. | Immerse in cultural history or the natural beauty of the Midlands. | £8-£12/ day |
| Total Daily Budget | | | | £50-£87/ day |

# Manchester, Liverpool and North West England

Manchester is a city pulsating with musical energy and industrial charm. Immerse yourself in the vibrant Northern Quarter, where street art, independent boutiques, and buzzing cafes create a bohemian atmosphere. Delve into the city's musical legacy at the legendary Manchester Arena or pay homage to iconic bands at the British Music Experience. Take a stroll through the revitalized Salford Quays and explore The Lowry, an arts and entertainment complex.

### Cultural Hotspots and Industrial Marvels:

Discover Manchester's cultural hotspots, including the Manchester Art Gallery and the Museum of Science and Industry, which celebrate the city's industrial past. For football enthusiasts, a pilgrimage to Old Trafford, the home of Manchester United, is a must. Engage with contemporary art at the Tate Liverpool and delve into maritime history at the Merseyside Maritime Museum in Liverpool's historic Albert Dock.

### Liverpool's Maritime Majesty:

Venture into Liverpool, a city synonymous with maritime legacy and the birthplace of The Beatles. Explore the UNESCO-listed waterfront, where the Royal Liver Building and the Cunard Building stand as symbols of the city's maritime prowess. Visit The Beatles Story museum at the Albert Dock to trace the footsteps of the Fab Four. Stroll through the bustling lanes of Bold Street for independent shops and vibrant street art.

### North West England's Natural Wonders:

As we traverse North West England, be prepared for breathtaking natural wonders. The Lake District National Park, with its serene lakes and majestic mountains, offers outdoor enthusiasts a playground for hiking, boating, and scenic drives. The charming town of Keswick provides a gateway to exploring Derwentwater and the surrounding fells. The historic city of Chester, with its Tudor-style architecture and city walls, adds a touch of medieval charm.

### Stately Homes and Gardens:

Discover the opulence of Tatton Park, a grand estate with landscaped gardens and a deer park. In Liverpool, explore Speke Hall, a Tudor manor with beautiful gardens. Manchester's Heaton Hall, set within Heaton Park, showcases neoclassical architecture surrounded by parkland.

### Gastronomic Delights and Culinary Scenes:

Indulge in Manchester's eclectic food scene, where the Curry Mile and Ancoats offer a diverse array of culinary delights. Liverpool's Baltic Triangle, known for its independent eateries, provides a gastronomic adventure. In the Lake District, traditional pubs and tearooms offer hearty fare with stunning views of the countryside.

## Nature Retreats and Scenic Drives:

Embark on scenic drives through the Lake District, where routes like the Hardknott Pass and Kirkstone Pass unveil panoramic views. Head to Formby Beach near Liverpool for coastal walks amidst sand dunes and pine forests. Explore the lush greenery of Sefton Park in Liverpool for a tranquil urban escape.

## Accommodation:

- **Chic Hotels in Manchester:**
  - Stay in chic hotels in Manchester, such as Hotel Gotham or King Street Townhouse.
- **Historic Inns in North West England:**
  - Choose historic inns or cozy bed and breakfasts in North West England, like The Old Bell Inn in Delph or The Lymm Hotel.

## Transportation:

### 3. Trains and Buses:

- Utilize trains and buses for travel within North West England. Booking in advance can secure lower fares.

## Manchester:

### 4. The John Rylands Library:

- Explore The John Rylands Library. While entry is free, donations are appreciated to support the library.
  - **Northern Quarter:**
  - Stroll through Manchester's Northern Quarter. Explore independent shops, street art, and vibrant cafes.

## North West England:

### 6. Liverpool Waterfront:

- Visit Liverpool's iconic waterfront. While some attractions have entry fees, walking along the waterfront is free.
  - **Lake District National Park:**
  - Explore the Lake District National Park. While some activities may have fees, hiking and enjoying the stunning landscapes are free.

### Paid Attractions and how to save money

**Manchester:**

**The Manchester Museum:**

The Manchester Museum is a popular attraction offering insights into archaeology, anthropology, and natural history. Save on admission by checking for discounted rates for students, seniors, or families. Some museums offer free entry on certain days or during specific hours, so plan your visit accordingly. Consider becoming a member if you anticipate multiple visits, as memberships often come with perks like free entry and exclusive events.

**Manchester Art Gallery:**

The Manchester Art Gallery showcases an impressive collection of fine art. Look for free entry days or discounted rates for special exhibitions. Many galleries offer reduced prices for evening visits, providing an affordable option. Consider exploring combo tickets if you plan to visit multiple cultural institutions in Manchester.

**LEGOLAND Discovery Centre Manchester:**

For family fun, LEGOLAND Discovery Centre Manchester is a hit. Book tickets online in advance to access discounted prices and to secure your entry for popular time slots. Combo tickets, which may include entry to other attractions, can offer additional savings. Keep an eye out for special promotions, especially during off-peak seasons.

**Chill Factore:**

Chill Factore, an indoor snow activity center, provides a unique experience. Look for online booking discounts and consider visiting during off-peak hours for potential savings. Group discounts or family packages may also be available, providing a cost-effective way to enjoy the snow activities.

**Liverpool and North West England:**

**The Beatles Story, Liverpool:**

The Beatles Story is a must-visit attraction for music enthusiasts. Book tickets online in advance to benefit from reduced prices and to ensure availability. Combo tickets, which include entry to other Liverpool attractions, can offer added value. Check for family discounts or special promotions during certain times of the year.

**Merseyside Maritime Museum:**

Explore Liverpool's maritime history at the Merseyside Maritime Museum. Look for free entry days or discounted rates for specific exhibitions. Some museums offer reduced prices for evening visits, providing a budget-friendly option. Consider checking for bundled tickets if you plan to explore multiple museums in Liverpool.

**Chester Zoo:**

Chester Zoo is a renowned wildlife attraction in the North West. Book tickets online to access discounted rates and to secure your entry. Family memberships can be cost-effective for regular visitors, offering unlimited access and additional benefits. Keep an eye on seasonal promotions or special events that may provide discounted entry.

**Tatton Park, Cheshire:**
Tatton Park offers a delightful blend of gardens, a mansion, and a deer park. Check for special events or open days when entry might be discounted or free. Annual memberships can be a cost-effective choice for frequent visitors, providing unlimited access to the park's attractions throughout the year

**Luxury on a Budget Tips:**

**8. Gourmet Street Food in Manchester:**

- Experience gourmet street food at Mackie Mayor or GRUB Manchester for affordable yet delicious options.
- **Lunch at a Country Inn in North West England:**
    - Enjoy lunch at a country inn in North West England for an authentic and affordable dining experience.
- **Happy Hour in Liverpool:**
    - Explore Liverpool's vibrant bars during happy hours for discounted drinks.
- **Discounted Attraction Tickets:**
    - Look for discounted tickets or combination passes for attractions in Manchester, Liverpool, and North West England.
- **Off-Peak Travel:**
    - Plan your visit during off-peak times for lower accommodation and transportation costs.
- **Local Markets in North West England:**
    - Immerse yourself in local markets for fresh produce, crafts, and unique finds.
- **Nature Walks in North West England:**
    - Take advantage of nature walks and trails in the Lake District or Peak District.
- **Student and Youth Discounts:**
    - If applicable, leverage student and youth discounts for attractions and transportation.

**Approximate Prices:**

- **Accommodation:** £70-£140 per night (varies based on type and location)
- **Train Travel:** £15-£30 for short-distance journeys
- **Attraction Entry:** £5-£20 per attraction
- **Dining:** £15-£30 per person for mid-range dining

## Manchester:

### Manchester Art Gallery:
Explore the Manchester Art Gallery. While there may be entry fees for special exhibitions, general admission is often free.

### Northern Quarter Street Art:
Wander through the Northern Quarter. Enjoy the vibrant street art scene for free.

### Castlefield Urban Heritage Park:
Explore Castlefield Urban Heritage Park. Wander along the canals and enjoy the historic industrial sites for free.

### Whitworth Art Gallery Gardens:
Relax in the gardens of the Whitworth Art Gallery. While there's an entry fee for certain exhibits, the gardens are often free.

### Science and Industry Museum:
Visit the Science and Industry Museum. While some exhibits may have fees, general admission is often free.

## North West England:

### Liverpool Waterfront:
Stroll along the Liverpool Waterfront. Enjoy iconic landmarks like the Liver Building and the Albert Dock for free.

### Beatles Story Exterior:
Visit the exterior of the Beatles Story. While there's an entry fee for the museum, the area around the Albert Dock is often free to explore.

### Lake District National Park:
Explore the Lake District National Park. Enjoy walks in the picturesque landscapes for free.

### Chester Rows:
Stroll along the Chester Rows. Explore the unique two-tiered medieval galleries for free.

### Blackpool Illuminations:
Experience the Blackpool Illuminations. Enjoy the dazzling light displays along the promenade for free.

## Luxurious Dining:

### The French in Manchester:
Indulge in dining at The French. Prices may range from £60-£120 per person.

### The Art School in Liverpool:
Enjoy a meal at The Art School. Prices may range from £40-£80 per person.

## Local Delicacies:

### Manchester Tart:
Try a Manchester Tart, a local delicacy. Prices range from £2-£5, and it's a delightful treat.

### Liverpool Scouse:

Experience Liverpool Scouse. Prices range from £5-£10 per person, and it's a hearty local dish.

**Cream Tea in Chester:**

Enjoy a traditional cream tea in Chester. Prices range from £5-£10 per person.

**Cumbrian Sausage:**

Try a Cumbrian sausage in the Lake District. Prices vary but are generally affordable.

## Countryside Escapes:

**Formby Beach:**

Relax at Formby Beach. Enjoy the coastal dunes and pine woods for free.

**Tatton Park Gardens:**

Explore the gardens of Tatton Park. While there may be an entry fee for certain areas, the gardens are often free.

**Lytham St Annes Promenade:**

Stroll along the Lytham St Annes Promenade. Enjoy sea views and the Victorian pier for free.

**Haworth Village:**

Visit Haworth Village in West Yorkshire. Explore the cobbled streets and the Brontë Parsonage Museum (fees may apply).

| RECAP | Cost | Cost-Saving Measure | Why It Feels Luxurious | Potential Savings |
|---|---|---|---|---|
| Accommodation | £20-£110/ night | Consider boutique hotels like King Street Townhouse in Manchester or budget-friendly options like YHA Liverpool Hostel. | Immerse in Manchester's urban vibe or amid Liverpool's cultural richness. | £20-£40/ night |
| Dining | £15-£25/ meal | Opt for local favorites like Bundobust in Manchester or traditional pubs in Liverpool for affordable yet delightful meals. | Savor diverse and gourmet dishes in a vibrant city setting. | £10-£15/ meal |
| Entertainment | £10-£30/ show | Attend live music events in Manchester or explore free festivals and events in Liverpool. Visit cultural venues like The Beatles Story. | Enjoy cultural richness in a dynamic city or amid Liverpool's iconic history. | £5-£20/ show |
| Transportation | £10-£15/ day | Utilize local buses or explore Manchester, Liverpool, and the North West on foot or by bike. Consider day passes for trains. | Discover urban landscapes and historic sites at a leisurely pace. | £5-£10/ day |
| Sightseeing | £0-£12/day | Visit free attractions like Manchester Art Gallery or explore the Lake District in the North West. | Immerse in cultural history or the natural beauty of the North West. | £8-£12/ day |
| Total Daily Budget | | | | £50-£87/ day |

# Lake District and Cumbria

Lake District is a haven of tranquility and poetic inspiration. Marvel at the beauty of Windermere, the largest natural lake in England, where gentle ripples reflect the surrounding fells. Ascend the heights of Scafell Pike, the highest peak in England, for panoramic views that stretch across lush valleys and glistening waters. Cruise along Ullswater or Coniston Water, where the dramatic landscape unfolds like a living canvas.

**Charming Villages and Market Towns:**

Explore the timeless charm of Lake District villages and Cumbrian market towns. Ambleside, with its cobbled streets and historic Bridge House, invites you to wander along the shores of Lake Windermere. Grasmere, immortalized by William Wordsworth, exudes a romantic aura, while Keswick offers a blend of cultural attractions and outdoor adventures. Discover the market town of Kendal, where medieval lanes and charming yards showcase its rich history.

**Stately Homes and Gardens:**

Uncover the elegance of stately homes and meticulously manicured gardens. Levens Hall in Cumbria boasts stunning topiary gardens that have enchanted visitors for centuries. Holker Hall, nestled on the Cartmel Peninsula, combines historic grandeur with scenic landscapes. The imposing Muncaster Castle, surrounded by woodland and gardens, adds a touch of medieval drama.

**Gastronomic Pleasures and Traditional Inns:**

Indulge in the gastronomic delights of Cumbria, where local produce takes center stage. Savour traditional Cumberland sausage, artisan cheeses, and sticky toffee pudding in welcoming country inns. Explore the foodie havens of Cartmel, home to the famous Cartmel Sticky Toffee Pudding, and sample the delights of Keswick's vibrant market scene.

**Nature Walks and Scenic Drives:**

Embark on nature walks through Cumbria's enchanting landscapes, where trails like Catbells and Helm Crag offer breathtaking views. Drive along scenic routes such as the Kirkstone Pass, winding through mountainous terrain and revealing hidden valleys. The Lake District's serene beauty invites you to explore ancient woodlands, cascading waterfalls, and idyllic meadows.

**Arts and Literary Heritage:**

Delve into the arts and literary heritage that has flourished amidst the lakes and fells. Visit the Beatrix Potter Gallery in Hawkshead, celebrating the beloved author's illustrations. Discover Dove Cottage in Grasmere, where William Wordsworth found inspiration for his poetry. Explore the Wordsworth Museum to delve into the life and works of this literary giant.

**Accommodation:**

- **Country House Hotels in the Lake District:**
  - Stay in charming country house hotels in the Lake District, such as Armathwaite Hall Hotel or Linthwaite House.
- **Cozy Inns in Cumbria:**
  - Choose cozy inns or bed and breakfasts in Cumbria, like The Pheasant Inn in Bassenthwaite or The Drunken Duck Inn in Ambleside.

**Transportation:**

3. **Buses and Boats:**

- Utilize local buses and boats for travel within the Lake District. Consider the Windermere Lake Cruises for scenic boat rides.

**Lake District:**

4. **Windermere:**

- Explore the town of Windermere and take a stroll along the lake. Enjoy the views without any cost.
  - **Catbells Hike:**
  - Hike up Catbells for panoramic views of Derwentwater and the surrounding mountains. Hiking is free, and it offers stunning landscapes.

**Cumbria:**

## 6. Grasmere:

- Visit the picturesque village of Grasmere. Explore Grasmere Lake and the charming streets.
  - **Hadrian's Wall:**
  - Explore Hadrian's Wall. While some attractions along the wall have entry fees, you can enjoy the scenic walk for free.

**Luxury on a Budget Tips:**

## 8. Gourmet Picnic by the Lakes:

- Create a gourmet picnic with local products and enjoy it by one of the beautiful lakes in the Lake District.
- **Lunch at a Village Pub in Cumbria:**
  - Enjoy lunch at a traditional village pub in Cumbria for an authentic and affordable dining experience.
- **Happy Hour in Ambleside:**
  - Explore Ambleside's pubs and bars during happy hours for discounted drinks.
- **Discounted Attraction Tickets:**
  - Look for discounted tickets or combination passes for attractions in the Lake District and Cumbria.
- **Off-Peak Travel:**
  - Plan your visit during off-peak times for lower accommodation and transportation costs.
- **Local Markets in Cumbria:**
  - Immerse yourself in local markets for fresh produce, artisanal goods, and unique finds.
- **Nature Walks in the Lake District:**
  - Take advantage of the numerous walking trails and paths throughout the Lake District.
- **Student and Youth Discounts:**
  - If applicable, leverage student and youth discounts for attractions and transportation.

**Approximate Prices:**

- **Accommodation:** £80-£150 per night (varies based on type and location)
- **Local Transport:** £5-£15 for bus or boat rides
- **Attraction Entry:** £5-£20 per attraction
- **Dining:** £15-£30 per person for mid-range dining

Lake district and Cumbria

Exploring the Lake District and Cumbria on a budget while enjoying luxurious experiences can provide a serene and picturesque getaway. Here are 20 ideas with approximate prices:

**Lake District:**

### Windermere Lake Cruise:
Enjoy a budget-friendly cruise on Lake Windermere. Prices vary but can start from £10-£15 per person.

### Orrest Head Hike:
Hike to Orrest Head for panoramic views. It's a free and rewarding experience.

### Grasmere Village:
Stroll through Grasmere Village. Enjoy the charming atmosphere and perhaps visit Dove Cottage (fees may apply).

### Tarn Hows Walk:
Take a walk around Tarn Hows. This scenic area is free to explore.

### Wray Castle Grounds:
Wander through the grounds of Wray Castle. While there may be an entry fee for the castle, the grounds are often free.

**Cumbria:**

### Carlisle Cathedral Interior:
Explore the interior of Carlisle Cathedral. While there may be entry fees for certain areas, the exterior is often free.

### Hadrian's Wall Path:
Walk along sections of Hadrian's Wall Path. Enjoy the historical significance and stunning landscapes for free.

### Keswick Market:
Immerse yourself in Keswick Market. Browse local products and enjoy the market atmosphere for free.

### Derwentwater Lakeside Walk:
Take a lakeside walk around Derwentwater. The scenery is stunning, and the walk is often free.

### Lowther Castle Gardens:
Explore the gardens of Lowther Castle. While there may be an entry fee for the castle, the gardens may be accessible for free.

**Luxurious Dining:**

### L'Enclume in Cartmel:
Indulge in dining at L'Enclume. Prices may range from £100-£200 per person.

### Sharrow Bay in Ullswater:
Enjoy a meal at Sharrow Bay. Prices may range from £80-£150 per person.

**Local Delicacies:**

### Grasmere Gingerbread:
Try Grasmere Gingerbread. Prices range from £2-£5, and it's a tasty local treat.

**Cumberland Sausage:**

Experience the Cumberland sausage. Prices vary but are generally affordable.

**Cumbrian Ale Tasting:**

Sample Cumbrian ales. Prices vary based on the venue but are generally reasonable.

**Kendal Mint Cake:**

Taste Kendal Mint Cake. Prices range from £2-£5, and it's a popular local sweet.

## Countryside Retreats:

**Ambleside Waterhead Walk:**

Take a scenic walk around Ambleside Waterhead. Enjoy views of Lake Windermere for free.

**Haweswater Reservoir:**

Explore Haweswater Reservoir. The reservoir and surrounding landscapes are often free to access.

**Coniston Water:**

Relax by Coniston Water. Enjoy the peaceful setting and perhaps embark on a budget-friendly boat trip.

**Rydal Water and Cave Walk:**

Walk around Rydal Water and explore Rydal Cave. It's a picturesque and free activity.

| RECAP | Cost | Cost-Saving Measure | Why It Feels Luxurious | Potential Savings |
|---|---|---|---|---|
| Accommodation | £10-£110/ night | Consider cozy bed and breakfasts like The Keswick B&B in the Lake District or budget-friendly options like YHA Keswick Hostel. | Immerse in the natural beauty of the Lake District with personalized stays. | £20-£40/ night |
| Dining | £15-£25/ meal | Opt for local favorites like The Drunken Duck Inn or traditional pubs for affordable yet delightful meals. | Savor locally sourced dishes in a picturesque setting. | £10-£15/ meal |
| Entertainment | £10-£30/ show | Attend local events and explore free outdoor activities in the Lake District. Visit cultural venues like The Rheged Centre in Cumbria. | Enjoy the tranquility of nature or explore cultural richness in Cumbria. | £5-£20/ show |
| Transportation | £10-£15/ day | Utilize local buses or explore the Lake District and Cumbria on foot or by bike. Consider day passes for trains. | Discover serene landscapes and charming villages at a leisurely pace. | £5-£10/ day |
| Sightseeing | £0-£12/day | Visit free attractions like Lake Windermere or explore historic sites like Hadrian's Wall in Cumbria. | Immerse in the natural wonders of the Lake District or explore historical landmarks in Cumbria. | £8-£12/ day |
| Total Daily Budget | £105-£192 | | | £50-£87/ day |

# Newcastle and northeast England

Newcastle is as defined by its iconic Tyne Bridge and the bustling quayside along the River Tyne as its people notorious accent. Immerse yourself in the lively atmosphere of Grainger Town, where historic architecture blends with modern shops and cafes. Visit the BALTIC Centre for Contemporary Art, housed in a former flour mill, and climb The Castle, offering panoramic views of the city.

**Historic Landmarks and Cultural Hotspots:**

Discover the rich history of Northeast England with visits to Durham Cathedral, a UNESCO World Heritage Site, and the medieval Durham Castle. Explore the ancient streets of Alnwick, dominated by the grand Alnwick Castle and its enchanting gardens. Uncover the maritime heritage of Sunderland at the National Glass Centre and explore its revitalized waterfront.

**Coastal Retreats and Quaint Villages:**

Venture along the rugged coastline of Northeast England, where quaint villages and hidden coves await. Explore the picturesque Seahouses and use it as a gateway to the captivating Farne Islands. Breathe in the sea air at Tynemouth, a charming coastal town with a historic priory overlooking golden sands.

**Stately Homes and Gardens:**

Embark on a journey through Northeast England's stately homes and lush gardens. Cragside, near Rothbury, was the first house in the world to be lit by hydroelectricity and offers scenic grounds. Discover the opulence of Seaton Delaval Hall, a grand country house with a turbulent history. Alnwick Garden, adjacent to Alnwick Castle, showcases stunning horticultural displays.

**Gastronomic Delights and Local Markets:**

Indulge in the local flavors of Newcastle's culinary scene, where the Ouseburn Valley is a hub of creative eateries and breweries. Explore the vibrant Grainger Market for a mix of international cuisines and fresh produce. In coastal villages, savor fish and chips with sea views or enjoy a traditional cream tea in a charming tearoom.

**Nature Walks and Scenic Drives:**

Embark on nature walks through the scenic landscapes of Northeast England. Wander along the Hadrian's Wall Path for views of the ancient Roman frontier. Drive through North Pennines Area of Outstanding Natural Beauty, where charming villages and expansive moorlands create a timeless panorama.

**Arts and Festivals:**

Engage with the vibrant arts scene in Newcastle, home to theaters like the Theatre Royal and Live Theatre. Experience the lively atmosphere of the Newcastle International Film Festival or the Sunderland International Airshow. Join the festivities at the Durham Lumiere, a dazzling light festival transforming the city's landmarks.

**Accommodation:**

- **Quayside Hotels in Newcastle:**
  - Stay in hotels along the Quayside in Newcastle, such as Malmaison Newcastle or Hotel du Vin & Bistro Newcastle.
- **Coastal Inns in Northeast England:**
  - Choose coastal inns or bed and breakfasts in Northeast England, like The Old Ship Inn in Seahouses or The Joiners Arms in Alnwick.

**Transportation:**

3. **Trains and Metro:**

- Utilize trains and the Tyne and Wear Metro for travel within Newcastle. The Metro offers convenient and affordable city transportation.

**Newcastle:**

4. **Newcastle Quayside:**

- Explore Newcastle Quayside. Stroll along the River Tyne, enjoy street performers, and take in the iconic Tyne Bridge.
  - **Grainger Town:**
  - Wander through Grainger Town, known for its historic architecture and vibrant atmosphere. Window shopping is free.

**Northeast England:**

6. **Alnwick Castle Gardens:**

- Visit the Alnwick Castle Gardens. While there's an entry fee for the castle, the gardens have a separate, more affordable fee.
  - **Northumberland Coast:**
  - Explore the Northumberland Coast. Enjoy walks along the coast, visit beaches like Bamburgh, and take in the views of historical castles.

**Luxury on a Budget Tips:**

8. **Gourmet Street Food in Newcastle:**

- Experience gourmet street food in the Grainger Market or Newcastle Quayside Market for affordable yet delicious options.

- **Lunch at Coastal Pubs:**
  - Enjoy lunch at coastal pubs in Northeast England for an authentic and affordable dining experience.
- **Happy Hour in Newcastle:**
  - Explore Newcastle's lively bars during happy hours for discounted drinks.
- **Discounted Attraction Tickets:**
  - Look for discounted tickets or combination passes for attractions in Newcastle and Northeast England.
- **Off-Peak Travel:**
  - Plan your visit during off-peak times for lower accommodation and transportation costs.
- **Local Markets in Northeast England:**
  - Immerse yourself in local markets for fresh produce, crafts, and unique finds.
- **Nature Walks on the Coast:**
  - Take advantage of nature walks along the scenic coast of Northeast England.
- **Student and Youth Discounts:**
  - If applicable, leverage student and youth discounts for attractions and transportation.

**Approximate Prices:**

- **Accommodation:** £70-£130 per night (varies based on type and location)
- **Local Transport:** £3-£5 for a day pass on the Tyne and Wear Metro
- **Attraction Entry:** £5-£20 per attraction
- **Dining:** £15-£30 per person for mid-range dining

These are approximate prices and can vary based on specific circumstances and promotions available at the time of booking. Always check for discounts, promotions, and seasonal offers to enhance your experience while staying within your budget.


Same for Newcastle and North east England


Exploring Newcastle and the North East of England on a budget while enjoying luxurious experiences can offer a mix of historical charm and vibrant culture. Here are 20 ideas with approximate prices:

**Newcastle:**

### Quayside Walk:
Take a scenic walk along the Newcastle Quayside. Enjoy the views of the River Tyne and iconic bridges for free.
### Newcastle Castle Grounds:
Explore the grounds of Newcastle Castle. While there may be entry fees for certain areas, the exterior is often free.
### BALTIC Centre for Contemporary Art:
Visit the BALTIC Centre for Contemporary Art. While there may be entry fees for specific exhibitions, general admission is often free.
### Jesmond Dene Park:

Stroll through Jesmond Dene Park. This picturesque park is free to explore.

**Grainger Market:**

Immerse yourself in Grainger Market. Browse local products and enjoy the market atmosphere for free.

## North East England:

### Durham Cathedral Interior:

Explore the interior of Durham Cathedral. While there may be entry fees for certain areas, the exterior is often free.

### Hadrian's Wall Visitor Centre:

Visit the Hadrian's Wall Visitor Centre. While there may be entry fees for certain exhibits, exploring the area around the wall is often free.

### Alnwick Castle Gardens:

Wander through the gardens of Alnwick Castle. While there's an entry fee for the castle, the gardens may be accessible for free.

### Northumberland Coast Walk:

Take a walk along the Northumberland Coast. Enjoy the stunning coastline and historic sites for free.

### Sage Gateshead Exterior:

Admire the exterior of Sage Gateshead. While there may be entry fees for performances, the exterior is often free to enjoy.

## Luxurious Dining:

### House of Tides in Newcastle:

Indulge in dining at House of Tides. Prices may range from £60-£120 per person.

### Dobson and Parnell in Newcastle:

Enjoy a meal at Dobson and Parnell. Prices may range from £40-£80 per person.

## Local Delicacies:

### Newcastle Brown Ale:

Try Newcastle Brown Ale. Prices vary based on the venue but are generally reasonable.

### Stottie Cake with Pease Pudding:

Experience a Stottie cake with Pease Pudding. Prices range from £3-£8, and it's a hearty local dish.

### Craster Kippers:

Taste Craster Kippers. Prices vary but are generally affordable.

### Greggs' Sausage Roll:

Grab a classic sausage roll from Greggs. Prices are budget-friendly.

## Countryside Escapes:

### Beamish Museum:

Explore Beamish Museum. While there's an entry fee, it provides a nostalgic journey through history.

### Holy Island of Lindisfarne:

Visit the Holy Island of Lindisfarne. While there may be parking fees, exploring the island is often free.

### Rothbury Countryside Walks:

Enjoy walks in the countryside around Rothbury. The landscapes offer tranquility and are often free to explore.

**Hexham Market:**

Experience Hexham Market. Browse local products and enjoy the market atmosphere for free.

| RECAP | Cost | Cost-Saving Measure | Why It Feels Luxurious | Potential Savings |
|---|---|---|---|---|
| Accommodation | £20-£110/ night | Consider boutique hotels like Malmaison Newcastle or budget-friendly options like YHA Newcastle Hostel. | Immerse in the vibrant atmosphere of Newcastle or amid the natural beauty of the Northeast. | £20-£40/ night |
| Dining | £15-£25/ meal | Opt for local favorites like The Broad Chare in Newcastle or traditional pubs for affordable yet delightful meals. | Savor diverse and gourmet dishes in a lively urban setting. | £10-£15/ meal |
| Entertainment | £10-£30/ show | Attend live music events in Newcastle or explore free festivals and events in the Northeast. Visit cultural venues like BALTIC Centre for Contemporary Art. | Enjoy cultural richness in a dynamic city or amid the artistic scene of the Northeast. | £5-£20/ show |
| Transportation | £10-£15/ day | Utilize local buses or explore Newcastle and the Northeast on foot or by bike. Consider day passes for trains. | Discover urban landscapes and charming coastal areas at a leisurely pace. | £5-£10/ day |
| Sightseeing | £0-£12/ day | Visit free attractions like Newcastle Castle or explore the Northumberland Coast in the Northeast. | Immerse in the city's history or explore the natural beauty of the Northeast. | £8-£12/ day |
| Total Daily Budget | | | | £50-£87/ day |

# Scotland and the Scottish highlands

*Dunrobin Castle*

Edinburgh is a tapestry of medieval and modern wonders. Wander through the cobbled streets of the Royal Mile, flanked by historic buildings, and marvel at the grandeur of Edinburgh Castle atop Castle Rock. Immerse yourself in the rich history of the city with visits to the Palace of Holyroodhouse and the National Museum of Scotland. Experience the cultural vibrancy of the Edinburgh Festival Fringe if your journey aligns with this lively event.

**Majestic Castles and Historic Sites:**

Explore the iconic Scottish castles that dot the landscape. Venture to Stirling Castle, perched atop a volcanic crag, and relive moments from Scottish history. Journey to Eilean Donan Castle, an idyllic fortress at the confluence of three lochs. Discover the mystical Urquhart Castle on the shores of Loch Ness, where legends of Nessie abound.

**Highland Glens and Enchanted Forests:**

As we journey into the Scottish Highlands, be prepared for awe-inspiring landscapes. Traverse the Great Glen, home to the mythical Loch Ness, and absorb the tranquility of Glencoe's haunting beauty. Hike through the enchanting Caledonian Forests, where ancient trees whisper tales of folklore. Ascend to the summit of Ben Nevis, the UK's highest peak, for panoramic views of the surrounding peaks and valleys.

### Lochside Legends and Scenic Drives:

Embark on scenic drives along the shores of legendary lochs. Drive the winding roads of the Trossachs, where Loch Katrine enchants with its serene beauty. Cruise the waters of Loch Lomond, the largest freshwater lake in Great Britain, surrounded by rolling hills. Explore the hidden gems along the North Coast 500, a route that unveils the rugged beauty of the northern Highlands.

### Stately Homes and Gardens:

Delve into the opulence of Scotland's stately homes and manicured gardens. Visit Drummond Castle Gardens, a formal parterre garden near Crieff. Explore the grand interiors and extensive grounds of Blair Castle in the heart of Perthshire. Wander through the walled gardens of Inveraray Castle, a neoclassical masterpiece nestled on the shores of Loch Fyne.

### Culinary Delights and Whisky Trails:

Indulge in Scotland's culinary delights, from hearty haggis to the finest Scotch whisky. Savor traditional Scottish fare in charming Highland villages and explore local markets for artisanal produce. Embark on a whisky trail through Speyside, where renowned distilleries invite you to savor the flavors of the Highlands.

### Wildlife Encounters and Nature Reserves:

Encounter Scotland's diverse wildlife in its natural habitats. Seek out red deer in the glens and spot golden eagles soaring above the mountain peaks. Visit the RSPB nature reserves, such as Forsinard Flows and Loch Garten, where rare birds and unique ecosystems thrive.

### Accommodation:

- **City-Center Boutique Hotels in Edinburgh:**
  - Stay in boutique hotels in Edinburgh's city center, such as The Rutland Hotel or The Glasshouse.
- **Cozy Inns in the Scottish Highlands:**
  - Choose cozy inns or bed and breakfasts in the Scottish Highlands, like The Dulaig in Grantown-on-Spey or The Airds Hotel in Port Appin.

### Transportation:

### 3. Trains and Buses:

- Utilize trains and buses for travel within Scotland. Scotland's scenic rail routes offer affordable and picturesque journeys.
  - **Explore the Scottish Highlands by Car:**
  - Consider renting a car to explore the vast landscapes of the Scottish Highlands independently.

**Edinburgh:**

## 5. Edinburgh Castle Esplanade:

- Enjoy the exterior views of Edinburgh Castle from the esplanade. While there's an entry fee for the castle, the exterior provides stunning photo opportunities.
  - **Royal Mile:**
  - Wander along the historic Royal Mile. Explore its nooks and crannies, and enjoy street performances.

**Scottish Highlands:**

## 7. Glencoe Valley:

- Explore Glencoe Valley. While there are guided tours with fees, hiking and enjoying the valley independently are free.
  - **Loch Ness:**
  - Visit Loch Ness. Enjoy the views, and consider taking a boat trip for a budget-friendly way to experience the lake.

**Luxury on a Budget Tips:**

## 9. Gourmet Picnic in Princes Street Gardens:

- Create a gourmet picnic with local produce and enjoy it in Edinburgh's Princes Street Gardens.
- **Lunch at Highland Tearooms:**
  - Enjoy lunch at charming tearooms in the Scottish Highlands for an authentic and affordable dining experience.
- **Happy Hour in Edinburgh's Old Town:**
  - Explore Edinburgh's Old Town during happy hours for discounted drinks.
- **Discounted Attraction Tickets:**
  - Look for discounted tickets or combination passes for attractions in Edinburgh and the Scottish Highlands.
- **Off-Peak Travel:**
  - Plan your visit during off-peak times for lower accommodation and transportation costs.
- **Local Markets in Edinburgh:**
  - Immerse yourself in local markets like the Grassmarket Market for fresh produce and handmade crafts.
- **Nature Walks in the Highlands:**
  - Take advantage of nature walks and trails in the Scottish Highlands, such as those around Fort William.
- **Student and Youth Discounts:**
  - If applicable, leverage student and youth discounts for attractions and transportation.

**Scotland:**

### Edinburgh Castle Esplanade:
Admire the Edinburgh Castle Esplanade. While there may be entry fees for certain areas, the exterior and views are often free.

### Arthur's Seat Hike:
Hike to the summit of Arthur's Seat in Edinburgh. It's a free and rewarding experience with panoramic views.

### Royal Mile Walk:
Stroll along the Royal Mile in Edinburgh. Enjoy the historic architecture and vibrant street performances for free.

### National Museum of Scotland:
Visit the National Museum of Scotland. While there may be entry fees for special exhibitions, general admission is often free.

### Glasgow Green Park:
Relax in Glasgow Green Park. This expansive park is free to explore.

## Scottish Highlands:

### Glencoe Valley:
Explore the dramatic landscapes of Glencoe Valley. Enjoy walks and hikes amidst the stunning scenery for free.

### Loch Ness Shore:
Walk along the shores of Loch Ness. While there may be fees for specific attractions, enjoying the Loch's natural beauty is often free.

### Ben Nevis Area:
Discover the area around Ben Nevis. While climbing the mountain may require preparation, exploring the foothills is free.

### Eilean Donan Castle Exterior:
Admire the exterior of Eilean Donan Castle. While there's an entry fee for the castle, the views from the outside are often free.

### Isle of Skye Coastal Walks:
Enjoy coastal walks on the Isle of Skye. The rugged beauty of the coastline is free to explore.

## Luxurious Dining:

### The Witchery in Edinburgh:
Indulge in dining at The Witchery. Prices may range from £80-£150 per person.

### Three Chimneys on the Isle of Skye:
Enjoy a meal at Three Chimneys. Prices may range from £60-£120 per person.

## Local Delicacies:

### Haggis with Neeps and Tatties:
Try traditional Haggis with Neeps and Tatties. Prices range from £5-£15 per person.

### Scottish Whisky Tasting:
Experience Scottish whisky tasting. Prices vary based on the venue but are generally affordable.

### Shortbread and Tablet:
Enjoy Scottish shortbread and tablet. Prices vary but are generally reasonable.

### Cullen Skink Soup:

Taste Cullen Skink soup. Prices range from £5-£10, and it's a hearty local dish.

**Countryside Retreats:**

### Glenfinnan Viaduct Views:

Admire views of the Glenfinnan Viaduct. The site is famous for its appearance in the Harry Potter films and is free to enjoy.

### Fairy Pools on Skye:

Explore the Fairy Pools on the Isle of Skye. While there may be parking fees, the natural pools are free to visit.

### Glenlivet Distillery Visitor Centre:

Visit the Glenlivet Distillery Visitor Centre. While there may be fees for tours, the surrounding landscapes are often free to explore.

### Loch Lomond Shoreline:

Relax along the shoreline of Loch Lomond. Enjoy the largest inland stretch of water in Great Britain for free.

| recap | Cost | Cost-Saving Measure | Why It Feels Luxurious | Potential Savings |
|---|---|---|---|---|
| Accommodation | £70-£110/ night | Consider charming guesthouses like The Bonham in Edinburgh or budget-friendly options like hostels in Inverness. | Immerse in the historic charm of Edinburgh or amid the scenic beauty of the Highlands. | £20-£40/ night |
| Dining | £15-£25/ meal | Opt for local gems like The Witchery in Edinburgh or traditional pubs for affordable yet delightful meals. | Savor authentic Scottish cuisine in a unique and atmospheric setting. | £10-£15/ meal |
| Entertainment | £10-£30/ show | Attend traditional music performances or explore free festivals in Scotland. Visit cultural venues like the National Museum of Scotland. | Enjoy the rich cultural heritage of Scotland or explore artistic venues. | £5-£20/ show |
| Transportation | £10-£15/ day | Utilize local buses or explore Scotland and the Highlands on foot or by bike. Consider day passes for trains. | Discover historic sites and natural wonders at a leisurely pace. | £5-£10/ day |
| Sightseeing | £0-£12/ day | Visit free attractions like Edinburgh Castle or explore the Isle of Skye in the Highlands. | Immerse in the history of Edinburgh or explore the breathtaking landscapes of the Highlands. | £8-£12/ day |
| Total Daily Budget | | | | £50-£87/ day |

# Northern Ireland

*Giants Causeway*

### Belfast's Urban Resurgence:

Our exploration begins in Belfast, a city that seamlessly intertwines history and modernity. Delve into the Titanic Quarter, where the world's most famous ship was built, and explore the Titanic Belfast museum for a captivating journey through maritime history. Stroll through the vibrant Cathedral Quarter, where street art and lively pubs add to the city's creative atmosphere. Admire the grandeur of Belfast City Hall and relax in the tranquil surroundings of Botanic Gardens.

### Giant's Causeway and Coastal Marvels:

Venturing to the north coast, behold the wonder of Giant's Causeway, an otherworldly landscape of hexagonal basalt columns formed by ancient volcanic activity. Marvel at the rugged cliffs of Carrick-a-Rede, connected to the mainland by a thrilling rope bridge with panoramic sea views. Explore the mystical Dark Hedges, an enchanting avenue of intertwined beech trees featured in popular TV series.

### Historic Castles and Stately Homes:

Discover the historic treasures that dot the Northern Irish landscape. Wander through the medieval ruins of Dunluce Castle, perched dramatically on cliffs overlooking the North Atlantic. Visit Carrickfergus Castle, a well-preserved Norman fortress with a rich history. Explore the opulent gardens and grounds of Mount Stewart, a neoclassical estate on the shores of Strangford Lough.

### Mourne Mountains and Loughs:

Embark on an adventure through the Mourne Mountains, an area of outstanding natural beauty with panoramic vistas and challenging hiking trails. Cruise the tranquil waters of Strangford Lough, a designated Area of Outstanding Natural Beauty, and discover its diverse birdlife and picturesque villages. Immerse yourself in the serene landscapes surrounding Fermanagh's enchanting lakes.

### Cultural Heritage and Murals:

Dive into Northern Ireland's complex history by exploring its vibrant murals and cultural sites. In Derry/Londonderry, stroll along the city walls and learn about the Troubles at the Museum of Free Derry. Discover the Peace Walls adorned with powerful murals, reflecting the city's journey towards reconciliation. Visit the Ulster Museum in Belfast to explore the region's rich cultural heritage.

### Whiskey Distilleries and Culinary Delights:

Indulge in Northern Ireland's culinary offerings and savor the flavors of local produce. Discover the thriving food scene in Belfast's St. George's Market, where artisanal treats and fresh produce abound. Embark on a whiskey trail, visiting distilleries like Bushmills, where centuries of tradition meet modern craftsmanship.

### Nature Reserves and Wildlife Sanctuaries:

Explore the diverse ecosystems of Northern Ireland in its nature reserves. Stride along the trails of the Murlough National Nature Reserve, a coastal dune system teeming with wildlife. Visit Rathlin Island, a haven for seabirds, and witness puffins and seals in their natural habitat.

### Accommodation:

- **Boutique Hotels in Belfast:**
    - Stay in boutique hotels in Belfast, such as The Fitzwilliam Hotel or The Bullitt Hotel.
- **Coastal Inns in Northern Ireland:**
    - Choose coastal inns or bed and breakfasts, like The Whitepark House in Ballintoy or The Bushmills Inn.

### Transportation:

### 3. Buses and Trains:

- Utilize buses and trains for travel within Northern Ireland. Public transportation is affordable and connects key cities.
    - **Causeway Coast Route by Car:**
    - Consider renting a car to explore the scenic Causeway Coast Route independently.

**Belfast:**

### 5. Titanic Quarter:

- Explore the Titanic Quarter in Belfast. While there's an entry fee for the Titanic Belfast museum, walking around the area is free.
    - **Botanic Gardens:**
    - Visit Botanic Gardens. Enjoy the greenery and architecture, and entry is free.

**Causeway Coast:**

### 7. Giant's Causeway:

- Explore the Giant's Causeway. While there's an entry fee for the visitor center, walking along the causeway is free.
    - **Carrick-a-Rede Rope Bridge:**
    - Cross the Carrick-a-Rede Rope Bridge. While there's an entry fee, the coastal views are spectacular.

**Paid Attractions and how to save**

**Giant's Causeway:**

Giant's Causeway, a unique geological wonder, has an entrance fee for the visitor center. Save on admission by booking tickets online in advance, and consider exploring combo tickets that include other nearby attractions. Some National Trust memberships may offer free or discounted entry.

**Titanic Belfast:**

Titanic Belfast, a tribute to the ill-fated ship, requires an entrance fee. Book tickets online to secure lower prices and skip the queue. Family packages or combo tickets with other Titanic Quarter attractions may provide additional savings. Check for special events or themed tours.

**Carrick-a-Rede Rope Bridge:**

The Carrick-a-Rede Rope Bridge offers a thrilling experience with an associated fee. Book tickets in advance to avoid disappointment, and check for any online discounts. Consider visiting during off-peak hours to enjoy the bridge with fewer crowds. Some National Trust memberships may offer benefits.

**Ulster Museum:**

The Ulster Museum in Belfast provides free entry to its diverse collections. Check for free events, workshops, or educational programs. Some temporary exhibitions may have admission fees, so plan your visit accordingly. Explore membership options for exclusive benefits.

**Dark Hedges:**

The Dark Hedges, a famous avenue of beech trees, is a free-to-visit attraction. Stroll along the picturesque avenue and explore the surrounding area. Keep in mind that this site has gained popularity due to its appearance in popular TV shows, so consider visiting during quieter times.

**Carrickfergus Castle:**

Carrickfergus Castle, a well-preserved medieval fortress, has an entrance fee. Book tickets online for potential discounts and to secure your entry. Consider exploring combo tickets that include other local attractions for added value. Some memberships may offer benefits for regular visitors.

**Mussenden Temple and Downhill Demesne:**

The Mussenden Temple and Downhill Demesne offer stunning coastal views. While access to the grounds is often free, check for any associated fees for guided tours or special events. Consider visiting during open days or public events for a unique experience.

**Bushmills Distillery:**

The Old Bushmills Distillery, known for its whiskey, may have a fee for guided tours. Book tours in advance to secure your spot and potentially benefit from online discounts. Check for tasting packages or group discounts for added value.

**Luxury on a Budget Tips:**

9. **Gourmet Street Food in St. George's Market:**

- Experience gourmet street food in St. George's Market in Belfast for affordable yet delicious options.
- **Lunch at Coastal Pubs:**
  - Enjoy lunch at coastal pubs for an authentic and affordable dining experience.
- **Happy Hour in Belfast City Center:**
  - Explore Belfast's city center during happy hours for discounted drinks.
- **Discounted Attraction Tickets:**
  - Look for discounted tickets or combination passes for attractions in Belfast and Northern Ireland.
- **Off-Peak Travel:**
  - Plan your visit during off-peak times for lower accommodation and transportation costs.
- **Local Markets in Belfast:**
  - Immerse yourself in local markets, such as St. George's Market, for fresh produce and unique finds.
- **Nature Walks along the Causeway Coast:**
  - Take advantage of nature walks and trails along the Causeway Coast.
- **Student and Youth Discounts:**
  - If applicable, leverage student and youth discounts for attractions and transportation.

**Approximate Prices:**

- **Accommodation:** £70-£120 per night (varies based on type and location)
- **Local Transport:** £5-£15 for short-distance journeys
- **Attraction Entry:** £8-£20 per attraction
- **Dining:** £15-£30 per person for mid-range dining

- **Explore Giant's Causeway:** Immerse yourself in the otherworldly landscape of hexagonal basalt columns formed by volcanic activity. Entrance to the visitor center, providing audio guides and exhibitions, is around £12 per adult.
- **Visit Dark Hedges:** Step into the magical world of the Dark Hedges, an iconic avenue of beech trees featured in "Game of Thrones." This enchanting location is free to visit, allowing you to capture the essence of the Seven Kingdoms.
- **Carrick-a-Rede Rope Bridge:** Experience an adrenaline rush as you cross this suspended bridge connecting the mainland to a small island. Admission to cross the bridge is approximately £9 per adult, offering stunning views of the coastal scenery.
- **Stroll through Belfast Botanic Gardens:** Escape to this botanical oasis in the heart of Belfast, featuring exotic plant collections, a palm house, and a tropical ravine—all for free.
- **Titanic Belfast:** Delve into the tragic yet fascinating history of the Titanic at this world-class museum. While adult admission is around £19.50, consider visiting during off-peak times for potential discounts and a more intimate experience.
- **Hike in Mourne Mountains:** Embark on a scenic hike through the majestic Mourne Mountains, taking in panoramic views of rolling hills and serene landscapes. The experience is free, with potential parking fees depending on the chosen trailhead.
- **Visit Belfast Cathedral:** Marvel at the grandeur of St. Anne's Cathedral, with its stunning architecture and intricate stained glass windows. Entry is by donation, making it an accessible cultural experience.

- **Enjoy Street Art in Belfast:** Wander through the vibrant streets of the Cathedral Quarter, adorned with captivating street art. This open-air art gallery is free to explore, providing an urban luxury for art enthusiasts.
- **Discover Dunluce Castle:** Explore the dramatic ruins of Dunluce Castle perched on the coastal cliffs. Entrance is around £6 per adult, allowing you to step back in time and imagine the castle's storied history.
- **Cave Hill Country Park:** Hike to the top of Cave Hill for breathtaking views of Belfast and its surroundings. The park offers free entry, making it an ideal spot for nature lovers on a budget.
- **Attend a Traditional Music Session:** Immerse yourself in Northern Ireland's rich musical heritage by joining a traditional music session in a local pub. While enjoying the tunes, sip on affordable drinks, especially during traditional music nights.
- **Botanic Inn Happy Hour:** Unwind at the Botanic Inn during happy hour, where you can enjoy discounted drinks in a lively and welcoming atmosphere.
- **Lagan Towpath Cycling:** Rent a bike and cycle along the scenic Lagan Towpath, a picturesque trail following the river. Bike rental prices can start from £10-£15 per day, providing an affordable and active way to explore.
- **Ulster Museum:** Discover art, history, and natural sciences at the Ulster Museum, with free entry that welcomes donations to support ongoing exhibitions and educational programs.
- **Visit Armagh Observatory:** Explore the wonders of the universe at Armagh Observatory, which occasionally offers free or discounted events, providing a celestial experience on a budget.
- **Game of Thrones Locations:** Embark on a self-guided tour or join a guided tour to visit iconic "Game of Thrones" filming locations across Northern Ireland. Tours may cost around £25-£40, offering a touch of fantasy and cinematic history.
- **Belfast City Hall:** Admire the architectural beauty of Belfast City Hall, and take advantage of free guided tours to delve into the city's history and culture.
- **Blackhead Path:** Take a leisurely walk along Blackhead Path in Whitehead, enjoying the fresh sea breeze and panoramic coastal views. The path is free to explore, providing a serene escape.
- **Explore Enniskillen Castle:** Immerse yourself in history at Enniskillen Castle, featuring museums and exhibitions. Admission is around £6 per adult, offering an affordable cultural experience.
- **Fermanagh Lakelands:** Unwind by the tranquil Fermanagh Lakelands, where lush landscapes and serene waters create a luxurious natural escape, all for free.

| RECAP | Cost | Cost-Saving Measure | Why It Feels Luxurious | Potential Savings |
|---|---|---|---|---|
| Accommodation | £70-£110/ night | Consider boutique hotels like The Fitzwilliam Hotel in Belfast or budget-friendly options like hostels in Derry. | Immerse in the urban charm of Belfast or amid the historic atmosphere of Derry. | £20-£40/ night |
| Dining | £15-£25/ meal | Opt for local gems like Deanes in Belfast or traditional pubs for affordable yet delightful meals. | Savor authentic Northern Irish cuisine in a welcoming and unique setting. | £10-£15/ meal |
| Entertainment | £10-£30/ show | Attend traditional music sessions or explore free events and festivals in Northern Ireland. Visit cultural venues like the Titanic Belfast. | Enjoy the rich cultural scene of Northern Ireland or explore historic sites. | £5-£20/ show |
| Transportation | £10-£15/ day | Utilize local buses or explore Northern Ireland on foot or by bike. Consider day passes for trains. | Discover charming towns and coastal landscapes at a leisurely pace. | £5-£10/ day |
| Sightseeing | £0-£12/day | Visit free attractions like the Giant's Causeway or explore the historic walls of Derry. | Immerse in the natural wonders of Northern Ireland or explore the rich history of Derry. | £8-£12/ day |
| Total Daily Budget | | | | £50-£87/ day |

# Wales

*Carew Castle*

Snowdonia, a haven for outdoor enthusiasts. Ascend to the summit of Mount Snowdon, the highest peak in Wales, for panoramic views of glacial valleys and shimmering lakes. Explore the enchanting village of Beddgelert, nestled amidst ancient forests and cradled by mountains. Wander through the scenic Ogwen Valley, where Tryfan's distinctive peak entices climbers.

**Coastal Trails and Hidden Coves:**

Discover the rugged beauty of the Welsh coastline, where cliffs plunge into the sea and hidden coves await exploration. Hike along the Pembrokeshire Coast Path, encountering dramatic seascapes and wildlife havens. Visit the quaint village of Tenby, with its pastel-hued houses overlooking sandy shores. Explore the serene beauty of the Gower Peninsula, where Three Cliffs Bay and Rhossili Bay showcase nature's artistry.

**Medieval Castles and Stately Homes:**

Uncover Wales' medieval heritage through its formidable castles and stately homes. Marvel at Conwy Castle, a UNESCO World Heritage Site with imposing walls and medieval architecture. Explore Caerphilly Castle, a striking fortress surrounded by water. Wander through the lavish interiors of Chirk Castle, set against the backdrop of rolling hills.

## Brecon Beacons National Park:

Embark on an adventure through the green landscapes of Brecon Beacons National Park, where rolling hills and hidden waterfalls await. Hike along the scenic trails of Pen y Fan, the highest peak in southern Britain, and soak in the tranquility of Llyn y Fan Fach, a mystical lake surrounded by legends. Visit the picturesque town of Brecon, nestled along the River Usk.

## Celtic Folklore and Literary Heritage:

Immerse yourself in the rich tapestry of Celtic folklore and literary heritage. Explore Hay-on-Wye, a town known for its bookshops and the annual Hay Festival. Visit Laugharne, where the boathouse of Dylan Thomas overlooks the estuary, offering insights into the poet's life and work. Discover the mystical landscapes that inspired the tales of the Mabinogion.

## Welsh Culinary Delights:

Indulge in the flavors of Welsh cuisine, where local produce takes center stage. Enjoy traditional dishes like Welsh rarebit, cawl (a hearty soup), and bara brith (fruit loaf). Visit local markets, such as Abergavenny Food Festival, to savor artisanal treats and regional specialties

## Accommodation:

- **Boutique Guesthouses in Cardiff:**
    - Stay in boutique guesthouses in Cardiff, such as Jolyon's Boutique Hotel or Cathedral 73.
- **Country Inns in Welsh Countryside:**
    - Choose country inns or bed and breakfasts in the Welsh countryside, like The Old Rectory Country Hotel in Pembrokeshire or Ty Mawr Country Hotel in Brecon.

## Transportation:

## 3. Trains and Buses:

- Utilize trains and buses for travel within Wales. The train network connects major cities, and buses offer access to rural areas.
    - **Snowdonia National Park by Car:**
    - Consider renting a car to explore scenic areas like Snowdonia National Park independently. carrentals.com has some budget options.

## Cardiff:

## 5. Cardiff Castle Grounds:

- Explore the grounds of Cardiff Castle. While there's an entry fee for the castle, walking around the exterior is free.
  - **Bute Park:**
    - Visit Bute Park. Enjoy a stroll along the River Taff, and entry to the park is free.

## Snowdonia National Park:

### 7. Snowdon Summit:

- Hike or take the train to the summit of Snowdon. While there are fees for the train and guided hikes, independent hiking is free.
  - **Swallow Falls in Betws-y-Coed:**
    - Explore Swallow Falls in Betws-y-Coed. While there's a small entry fee, witnessing the cascading waterfalls is worth it.

## Luxury on a Budget Tips:

### 9. Gourmet Street Food in Cardiff Market:

- Experience gourmet street food in Cardiff Central Market for affordable yet delicious options.
- **Lunch at Traditional Welsh Pubs:**
  - Enjoy lunch at traditional Welsh pubs for an authentic and affordable dining experience.
- **Happy Hour in Cardiff Bay:**
  - Explore Cardiff Bay during happy hours for discounted drinks.
- **Discounted Attraction Tickets:**
  - Look for discounted tickets or combination passes for attractions in Cardiff and Wales.
- **Off-Peak Travel:**
  - Plan your visit during off-peak times for lower accommodation and transportation costs.
- **Local Markets in Wales:**
  - Immerse yourself in local markets for fresh produce, crafts, and unique finds.
- **Nature Walks in National Parks:**
  - Take advantage of nature walks and trails in national parks like Snowdonia and Brecon Beacons.
- **Student and Youth Discounts:**
  - If applicable, leverage student and youth discounts for attractions and transportation.

## Approximate Prices:

- **Accommodation:** £70-£120 per night (varies based on type and location)
- **Local Transport:** £5-£15 for short-distance journeys
- **Attraction Entry:** £8-£20 per attraction
- **Dining:** £15-£30 per person for mid-range dining

These are approximate prices and can vary based on specific circumstances and promotions available at the time of booking. Always check for discounts, promotions, and seasonal offers to enhance your experience while staying within your budget.

**Wales:**

### Snowdonia National Park:
Explore Snowdonia National Park. Enjoy walks amidst the stunning landscapes, and some trails are free.

### Cardiff Bay Walk:
Take a stroll around Cardiff Bay. Enjoy the waterfront views and the atmosphere for free.

### Conwy Castle Exterior:
Admire the exterior of Conwy Castle. While there's an entry fee for the castle, the views from outside are often free.

### Brecon Beacons Waterfalls:
Discover the waterfalls in the Brecon Beacons. Some trails are free, offering views of picturesque falls.

### St. Fagans National Museum of History:
Visit St. Fagans National Museum of History. While there may be fees for parking, general admission is often free.

## Luxurious Dining:

### The Walnut Tree in Abergavenny:
Indulge in dining at The Walnut Tree. Prices may range from £60-£120 per person.

### The Hardwick in Abergavenny:
Enjoy a meal at The Hardwick. Prices may range from £40-£80 per person.

## Local Delicacies:

### Welsh Cakes:
Try Welsh cakes. Prices range from £2-£5, and they're a delightful local treat.

### Welsh Rarebit:
Experience Welsh Rarebit. Prices range from £5-£10 per person, and it's a savory Welsh dish.

### Bara Brith:
Taste Bara Brith, a traditional Welsh fruitcake. Prices vary but are generally affordable.

## Countryside Retreats:

### Pembrokeshire Coast Path:
Explore the Pembrokeshire Coast Path. Enjoy coastal walks with stunning views, and some sections are free.

### Llyn Peninsula Beaches:
Relax on the beaches of the Llyn Peninsula. Some beaches are free to access and offer beautiful scenery.

### Blaenavon Industrial Landscape:
Visit the Blaenavon Industrial Landscape. While there may be fees for specific attractions, the landscape is often free to explore.

### Tintern Abbey Ruins:
Explore the ruins of Tintern Abbey. While there's an entry fee for specific areas, the exterior is often free.

### Aberglasney Gardens:
Wander through Aberglasney Gardens. While there may be an entry fee, the gardens are a beautiful setting.

**City Exploration:**

### Cardiff Castle Grounds:
Stroll through the grounds of Cardiff Castle. While there's an entry fee for certain areas, the exterior is often free.

### National Waterfront Museum in Swansea:
Visit the National Waterfront Museum. While there may be fees for specific exhibits, general admission is often free.

### Caernarfon Town Walk:
Take a walk around Caernarfon. Enjoy the medieval town and perhaps visit Caernarfon Castle (fees may apply).

### Swansea Marina:
Explore Swansea Marina. Enjoy the maritime atmosphere and the views of sailboats for free.

### Aberystwyth Cliff Railway Views:
Admire views from the Aberystwyth Cliff Railway. While there's an entry fee for the railway, the views from the top are often spectacular.

| RECAP | Cost | Cost-Saving Measure | Why It Feels Luxurious | Potential Savings |
|---|---|---|---|---|
| Accommodation | £10-£110/ night | Consider boutique hotels like The St. David's Hotel in Cardiff or budget-friendly options like hostels in Snowdonia. | Immerse in the urban charm of Cardiff or amid the natural beauty of Snowdonia. | £20-£40/ night |
| Dining | £15-£25/ meal | Opt for local gems like The Potted Pig in Cardiff or traditional pubs for affordable yet delightful meals. | Savor authentic Welsh cuisine in a welcoming and unique setting. | £10-£15/ meal |
| Entertainment | £10-£30/ show | Attend traditional music sessions or explore free events and festivals in Wales. Visit cultural venues like the National Museum Cardiff. | Enjoy the rich cultural scene of Wales or explore historic sites. | £5-£20/ show |
| Transportation | £10-£15/ day | Utilize local buses or explore Wales on foot or by bike. Consider day passes for trains. | Discover charming towns, coastal landscapes, and mountainous regions at a leisurely pace. | £5-£10/ day |
| Sightseeing | £0-£12/day | Visit free attractions like Cardiff Castle or explore the Brecon Beacons. | Immerse in the historic charm of Cardiff or explore the breathtaking landscapes of the Brecon Beacons. | £8-£12/ day |
| Total Daily Budget | £105-£192 | | | £50-£87/ day |

# Truly weird and wonderful things to do in the UK

The UK is full of quirky and unusual experiences. Here are some truly weird and wonderful things to do:

### Bog Snorkeling in Wales:

Dive into the quirky World Bog Snorkeling Championships in Llanwrtyd Wells, Wales, where competitors don snorkels and navigate the challenging waters of a peat bog. The surreal experience is not only an adventurous endeavor but also an opportunity to witness the hilarity and determination of participants. Prices for registration typically range from £10 to £20, ensuring a memorable and affordable day of unconventional aquatic fun.

### Cheese Rolling in Gloucestershire:

Participate in the exhilarating annual Cheese Rolling event on Cooper's Hill, Gloucestershire, where enthusiasts chase a wheel of cheese down a steep hill. The adrenaline-packed race is a testament to both skill and daring, and spectators can join the excitement for free. While the physical toll on participants is considerable, the priceless experience makes it a must-see event for thrill-seekers and cheese lovers alike.

### The Big Sheep in Devon:

Head to The Big Sheep in Devon for a day of family-friendly amusement, featuring attractions like sheep racing and sheepdog trials. This whimsical theme park offers a unique blend of entertainment and agricultural experiences. Admission prices vary, but a family ticket can range from £40 to £50, making it an affordable outing filled with laughter and woolly adventures.

### Edinburgh Festival Fringe:

Immerse yourself in the creative extravaganza of the Edinburgh Festival Fringe, the world's largest arts festival. With a plethora of bizarre and avant-garde performances, the festival caters to all tastes. Ticket prices vary depending on the shows, but numerous free and low-cost events ensure accessibility for all. Get ready to be captivated by the artistic vibrancy and cultural diversity that define this renowned festival.

### The Museum of Witchcraft and Magic in Cornwall:

Embark on a mystical journey at the Museum of Witchcraft and Magic in Boscastle, Cornwall, where artifacts related to witchcraft and the occult are on display. Admission prices typically range from £5 to £10, offering a fascinating exploration of esoteric history and folklore in a bewitching setting. Delve into the mysterious realms of magic and superstition, surrounded by the enchanting landscapes of Cornwall.

### The Bakewell Pudding Shop in Derbyshire:

Indulge your taste buds at the Bakewell Pudding Shop in Derbyshire, where you can sample the famous Bakewell Pudding, a local delicacy. Engage in the age-old debate of Pudding versus Tart while enjoying the sweet treat. Prices for a delectable Bakewell Pudding vary but generally range from £5 to £10, providing a delightful culinary experience in the charming town of Bakewell.

### The Forbidden Corner in North Yorkshire:

Embark on an enchanting adventure through The Forbidden Corner in North Yorkshire, a labyrinthine garden filled with peculiar statues, tunnels, and hidden surprises. Admission prices range from £12 to £15, offering a surreal journey through this whimsical landscape. Prepare to be mystified as you navigate the twists and turns of one of England's most peculiar gardens.

### Avenue of the Baobabs in Cornwall:

Discover the surreal beauty of the Avenue of the Baobabs in Adeney, Cornwall, where giant tree sculptures stand sentinel in the landscape. This unique attraction is often free to explore, allowing visitors to marvel at the whimsical creations that blend seamlessly with the natural surroundings. Take a leisurely stroll among these captivating baobabs and embrace the artistic charm of Cornwall.

### The Last Invasion Tapestry in Pembrokeshire:

Admire The Last Invasion Tapestry in Fishguard, Pembrokeshire, depicting a little-known French invasion in 1797. Entrance to the tapestry exhibition typically costs around £3 to £5, providing a historical journey through vivid textile storytelling. Explore the details of this remarkable creation, celebrating a pivotal moment in Welsh history.

### Dunmore Pineapple in Scotland:

Marvel at the architectural curiosity of Dunmore Pineapple in Airth, Scotland, shaped like a giant pineapple. While the exterior can be admired from the grounds for free, entrance to the interior costs approximately £3 to £5. Explore the eccentricity of this unique summerhouse and its lush surroundings, offering a delightful blend of history and horticulture.

### The Horniman Museum's Walrus in London:

Visit the Horniman Museum in London to witness the peculiar taxidermy exhibit of the famous overstuffed walrus. Entrance to the museum is generally free, allowing you to marvel at the walrus's comically large proportions and the extensive collection of anthropological and natural history artifacts. Immerse yourself in the diverse exhibitions housed within this captivating museum.

**The Shell Grotto in Margate:**

Explore the mysterious Shell Grotto in Margate, an underground chamber adorned with intricate mosaics made entirely of seashells. Admission to the grotto typically costs around £4 to £6, offering a mesmerizing experience surrounded by the beauty of shell artistry. Uncover the secrets of this subterranean wonder and appreciate the craftsmanship displayed in every corner.

**Portmeirion in Wales:**

Wander through the enchanting Italian-inspired village of Portmeirion in Wales, famously featured in the TV series "The Prisoner." Admission prices vary, with a standard adult ticket costing approximately £12 to £15. Immerse yourself in the architectural splendor and picturesque landscapes of this unique village, blending fantasy and reality seamlessly.

**The Angel of the North in Gateshead:**
Gaze upon The Angel of the North, a massive sculpture by Antony Gormley, standing tall near Gateshead. The iconic landmark can be viewed from the surrounding area for free, offering a striking silhouette against the sky. Marvel at the grandeur of this contemporary masterpiece that symbolizes the spirit of the North

**Be part of a TV audience in the UK**
There are agencies that specialize in providing TV audience tickets. Websites like Applause Store and SRO Audiences often offer free tickets to various shows.

# What to do for free at night in the UK

Discover a plethora of free nighttime activities across the UK, offering a diverse range of experiences to illuminate your evenings.

**Night Markets:**

Embark on a sensory journey at night markets scattered across vibrant cities like London and Manchester. Engage with local vendors, relish culinary delights from food stalls, and immerse yourself in the lively atmosphere of live entertainment.

**City Skylines:**

Indulge in the mesmerizing beauty of city skylines as landmarks come to life with enchanting illumination. Take a leisurely stroll or find a strategic vantage point to marvel at the architectural wonders that create a stunning and picturesque view.

**Free Events and Performances:**

Peruse local event listings for an array of free cultural experiences. From open-air concerts to captivating outdoor performances, there's a wealth of artistic expression awaiting discovery in your area.

**Museums and Galleries:**

Unlock the secrets of museums and galleries during special late-night openings. Experience cultural attractions in a unique light as you explore exhibitions and installations after the hustle and bustle of regular hours.

**Night Photography:**

For photography enthusiasts, the night unveils a canvas of illuminated streets, buildings, and landmarks. Capture the magic of your city at night, transforming ordinary scenes into extraordinary photographic masterpieces.

**Stargazing:**

Escape the city lights for a tranquil stargazing experience. Keep an eye out for astronomy events or meteor showers, adding a celestial touch to your nocturnal adventures.

**Outdoor Film Screenings:**

During balmy summer nights, parks transform into open-air cinemas hosting free film screenings. Bring a blanket, pack some snacks, and relish the magic of cinema under the twinkling stars.

**River Walks:**

Wander along riverside paths in iconic cities like London or Edinburgh. The serene ambiance, complemented by beautifully lit bridges and waterfronts, creates an enchanting setting for an evening stroll.

**Public Art Installations:**

Embark on a quest to discover public art installations and light displays. Cities showcase temporary art projects that enhance the urban landscape, creating an immersive experience for nocturnal explorers.

**Local Parks:**

Find solace in the tranquility of local parks that may host evening events or provide a serene backdrop for a leisurely walk. Breathe in the fresh night air as you unwind amidst nature.

**Street Performers:**

City centers come alive with the captivating performances of street artists and buskers. Enjoy entertaining shows that add a touch of magic to your nighttime urban escapade, all free of charge.

**City Squares and Gardens:**

Unwind in city squares or gardens that reveal their charm at night. Well-lit pathways and inviting benches beckon, providing ideal spots for relaxation and reflection.

**Cultural Festivals:**

Immerse yourself in the cultural tapestry of your surroundings by exploring free events, music, and performances at local festivals. Unearth the hidden gems that bring communities together in celebration.

**Community Events:**

Participate in community events and gatherings where local neighborhoods organize free activities, ranging from outdoor concerts to community meetings. Experience the warmth and camaraderie of shared moments.

**Historical Tours:**

Embark on a journey through time with free historical walking tours offered by some cities. Explore architectural wonders and delve into the rich history that defines the character of the city.

**Libraries and Bookshops:**

Enter the literary realm during free evening events hosted by libraries or bookshops. From engaging book readings to literary discussions, these cultural hubs offer intellectual stimulation against the backdrop of the night.

**Public Lectures:**
Fuel your curiosity by attending free public lectures or talks hosted by universities and cultural institutions. Explore a spectrum of intriguing topics that align with your interests, expanding your knowledge under the evening sky.

# Getting Out Cheaply

**Tips:**

### Book in Advance:
Generally, booking flights well in advance can help you secure lower prices. Prices tend to rise as the departure date approaches.

### Flexible Dates:
If your travel dates are flexible, use search engines that allow you to compare prices across a range of dates. Sometimes flying on weekdays or at off-peak times can be more economical.

### Use Flight Comparison Websites:
Utilize flight comparison websites like Skyscanner, Kayak, or Google Flights to compare prices from various airlines. These platforms often highlight the most budget-friendly options.

### Consider Nearby Airports:
Check prices for nearby airports, as flying from or to a different airport might offer more cost-effective options.

### Budget Airlines:
Explore flights with budget airlines, which are known for offering competitive prices. However, be mindful of additional fees for baggage, seat selection, and other services.

### Sign Up for Alerts:
Subscribe to fare alerts or newsletters from airlines and travel websites. This way, you'll be notified of any special promotions or discounts.

### One-Way Tickets:
Sometimes booking one-way tickets with different airlines can be cheaper than round-trip options.

## Budget Airline Providers flying out of the UK:

### Ryanair:
A well-known Irish budget airline, Ryanair often offers low-cost flights across Europe.

### easyJet:
Another prominent budget airline, easyJet operates a large number of routes within Europe.

### Wizz Air:
Specializing in flights to Eastern and Central Europe, Wizz Air is a budget-friendly option for certain destinations.

### Jet2.com:
Jet2.com is a low-cost airline with a focus on flights to popular European destinations, particularly holiday hotspots.

### Norwegian Air Shuttle:
Norwegian Air Shuttle provides budget flights, including long-haul routes, making it an option for both European and intercontinental travel.

### TUI Airways:

Formerly known as Thomson Airways, TUI Airways is a charter airline that offers budget-friendly flights, especially for holiday destinations.

**Vueling:**

Vueling is a Spanish low-cost carrier that operates flights within Europe.

**Flybe:**

While Flybe faced financial challenges and ceased operations in 2020, its assets have been acquired by Thyme Opco Limited. Keep an eye on developments, as it may resume operations.

**Always double-check baggage fees, travel restrictions, and other terms and conditions when booking with budget airlines. Additionally, be aware that these airlines may operate from different airports, so consider the overall cost and convenience of your journey.**

**Eurostar:**

Check for advance booking deals on Eurostar trains, especially if you're traveling to continental Europe. Booking well in advance can often yield significant savings.

**Buses:**

Consider using long-distance bus services, such as FlixBus or Eurolines. These bus companies often provide budget-friendly options for traveling to neighboring countries.

**Ferries:**

Ferries can be a cost-effective way to travel, particularly to destinations like France, Belgium, or Ireland. Companies like DFDS, P&O Ferries, and Stena Line offer various routes.

**Trains:**

For destinations within the UK and nearby European countries, explore train options. Booking in advance and being flexible with travel times can result in lower fares.

**Budget Airlines:**

Consider low-cost airlines for flights to European destinations. Airlines like Ryanair and easyJet often provide affordable options, especially when booked in advance.

**Car Sharing:**

Explore car-sharing options. Websites like BlaBlaCar connect drivers with empty seats to passengers traveling in the same direction, offering a cost-effective alternative.

**Comparison Websites:**

Use travel comparison websites to find the best deals. Platforms like Skyscanner or Rome2Rio allow you to compare prices across various modes of transportation.

**Flexible Dates:**

Be flexible with your travel dates. Prices can vary significantly depending on the day and time of travel, so adjusting your schedule may result in lower costs.

**Rail and Sail Packages:**

Some companies offer combined rail and ferry packages. This can be a convenient and economical way to travel, especially for routes involving both land and sea.

**Student or Youth Discounts:**

If you're a student or a young traveler, check for special discounts. Many transportation providers offer reduced rates for students or youth.

**Off-Peak Travel:**

Opt for off-peak travel times to take advantage of lower fares. This is applicable to trains, buses, and even some ferries.

**Travel Passes:**

Investigate whether any regional or European travel passes suit your itinerary. For example, Interrail and Eurail passes can offer cost-effective options for train travel.

**Consider Nearby Airports:**

Check prices from nearby airports. Sometimes flying from a different airport can result in lower fares.

**Package Deals:**

Explore package deals that combine transportation and accommodation. Some travel agencies offer bundled deals that may be more economical than booking each component separately.

# Airport Lounges

What better way to say goodbye to blighty than relaxing in an airport lounge before your flight home? While lounge prices can vary, some options offer more budget-friendly access.

### No.1 Lounges:

No.1 Lounges operate at various UK airports, including Gatwick, Heathrow, and Birmingham. They often provide a range of amenities such as complimentary snacks, drinks, and comfortable seating. Prices can be more reasonable compared to exclusive lounges, and occasional promotions or advance bookings might offer additional savings.

### Aspire Lounges:

Aspire Lounges are part of the Swissport network and can be found in multiple UK airports like Manchester and Birmingham. These lounges typically provide a tranquil atmosphere with complimentary snacks and beverages. Prices are often more affordable, especially when booked in advance.

### Escape Lounges:

Escape Lounges, available at airports like Manchester, East Midlands, and Stansted, offer a comfortable space with complimentary refreshments. Prices are generally competitive, and some lounges provide discounts for advance bookings or loyalty program members.

### Executive Lounges by Holiday Inn:

Some airports feature Executive Lounges operated by Holiday Inn. These lounges offer a cost-effective option for travelers seeking a quiet space, light snacks, and beverages. Prices can be relatively reasonable compared to premium lounges.

### Priority Pass Access:

If you travel frequently, consider a Priority Pass membership, which provides access to a network of lounges worldwide, including those in the UK. While the membership itself has a cost, it can be a cost-effective way to access lounges regularly without paying per visit.

# Breakdown of a luxury £10,000 trip to the United Kingdom on a £1000 budget

Creating a luxury trip to the United Kingdom with a budget of £1,000 requires careful planning and prioritization. Here's a rough breakdown, keeping in mind that prices can vary based on factors such as location, time of year, and personal preferences. This budget assumes you are focusing on key experiences and staying within a reasonable range:

| Expense Category | Estimated Cost (£) | Hacks & Savings |
|---|---|---|
| Accommodation | £400 | Opt for boutique hotels or consider upscale lastminute hotels for huge savings. |
| Transportation | £100 | Use megabus £1 tickets, advance train booking, rail passes, and off-peak deals for massive savings. |
| Dining & Entertainment | £400 | Leverage lunch specials, explore local markets, and use too good to go. |
| Attractions & Experiences | £100 | Purchase bundled attraction passes and explore free activities. |
| Total Budget | £1,000 | Hacks & Savings Total: £9,000 |

**Total: £1,000**

Tips for Saving:

- **Blindbook**: Especially in cities.
- **Buy a discount pass:** Explore hundreds of attractions for just £65 with passes like the National Trust membership.
- **Local Cuisine:** Opt for local markets or too good to go bags to experience the cuisine without breaking the bank.
- **Public Transportation:** Use cost-effective public transportation options, and consider walking to explore cities.

# Money Mistakes

| Mistake | Solution | Notes |
| --- | --- | --- |
| Not Using Pounds | Embrace cards where you can pre convert money into pounds to avoid conversion fees. Look at Wise or Revolut cards or | Many places in the UK widely accept contactless payments, making transactions quick and efficient. Conversion fees can take $5 everytime! |
| Overlooking Travel Insurance | Purchase comprehensive travel insurance | Healthcare costs in the UK can be high for non-residents; travel insurance covers medical emergencies and unexpected trip disruptions. |
| Ignoring the Oyster Card in London | Use an Oyster card for affordable and convenient travel | Oyster cards offer discounted fares on public transport in London; loading credit in advance can save money compared to individual tickets. |
| Exchanging Currency at Airports | Avoid currency exchange at airports | Rates at airport currency exchanges tend to be less favorable; exchange currency at banks, local shops, or use ATMs for better rates. |
| Not Taking Advantage of Discount passes | Explore the numerous palaces, stately homes, museums and attractions for £65 instead of thousands in entry fees! | Many museums in the UK offer free entry or specific free days; plan visits to these attractions to save on admission fees if you choose not to buy passes. |
| Booking trains instead of buses | Buses are always cheaper. And you always get a seat. | If you want to travel by train, pre-book your tickets. |
| Overlooking Railcard Discounts | Purchase a railcard for discounted train travel | Railcards offer significant discounts for various groups (e.g., young travelers, seniors); investing in one can result in substantial savings on train tickets. |
| Neglecting Tap Water in Restaurants | Ask for free tap water instead of buying bottled water | Restaurants in the UK typically provide free tap water; opting for this instead of bottled water helps save money and reduces plastic waste. |
| Ignoring Meal Deals and Vouchers | Look for too good to go bags, meal deals and discount vouchers | Many restaurants and cafes offer meal deals, and discount vouchers can be found online; taking advantage of these can cut down on food expenses. |

# Quick Luxury on a Budget Reference Guide

## London:

- **Attractions:**
  - Buckingham Palace, The British Museum, Tower of London, Hyde Park, West End Theatres.
- **Luxury on a Budget:**
  - **Accommodation:** Consider boutique hotels in neighborhoods like Kensington or Covent Garden for a touch of luxury at more affordable prices.
  - **Dining:** Enjoy Michelin-starred lunch deals or explore upscale food markets like Borough Market.
  - **Transportation:** Use Oyster cards for affordable travel on public transportation.

## Edinburgh:

- **Attractions:**
  - Edinburgh Castle, The Royal Mile, Arthur's Seat, Holyrood Palace.
- **Luxury on a Budget:**
  - **Accommodation:** Look for boutique guesthouses in charming areas like Stockbridge or Dean Village.
  - **Dining:** Opt for lunch deals in renowned restaurants or explore local pubs for affordable gourmet experiences.
  - **Activities:** Many attractions offer discounted rates during off-peak hours.

## Bath:

- **Attractions:**
  - The Roman Baths, Bath Abbey, The Royal Crescent, Pulteney Bridge.
- **Luxury on a Budget:**
  - **Accommodation:** Choose stylish B&Bs or boutique hotels for a more intimate stay.
  - **Dining:** Explore local bistros or take advantage of set-menu deals in upscale restaurants.
  - **Thermal Bath Spa:** Visit during weekdays for more budget-friendly rates.

## Oxford:

- **Attractions:**
  - The Bodleian Library, Radcliffe Camera, Christ Church College, Ashmolean Museum.
- **Luxury on a Budget:**
  - **Accommodation:** Stay in boutique hotels or charming guesthouses near the city center.
  - **Dining:** Explore historic pubs and local eateries for gourmet experiences without breaking the bank.
  - **Walking Tours:** Many colleges offer guided tours at reasonable prices.

## Cambridge:

- **Attractions:**
  - University of Cambridge, King's College Chapel, The Backs, Fitzwilliam Museum.
- **Luxury on a Budget:**
  - **Accommodation:** Choose cozy guesthouses or boutique B&Bs for a more personalized experience.
  - **Dining:** Visit local restaurants or enjoy riverside picnics along the Cam.
  - **Punting:** Rent a punt and explore the River Cam for a relaxing experience.

## Stratford-upon-Avon:

- **Attractions:**
  - Shakespeare's Birthplace, Royal Shakespeare Theatre, Anne Hathaway's Cottage.
- **Luxury on a Budget:**
  - **Accommodation:** Stay in charming inns or boutique hotels for a touch of luxury.
  - **Dining:** Explore local pubs and bistros offering Shakespearean-themed menus.
  - **Theatrical Performances:** Take advantage of discounted theater tickets during off-peak times.

## Liverpool:

- **Attractions:**
  - The Beatles Story, Albert Dock, Liverpool Cathedral, Tate Liverpool.
- **Luxury on a Budget:**
  - **Accommodation:** Look for stylish budget hotels or boutique hostels in the city center.
  - **Dining:** Explore the diverse food scene in areas like Bold Street for affordable gourmet options.
  - **Free Attractions:** Enjoy the city's many free attractions and waterfront activities.

## Manchester:

- **Attractions:**
  - Manchester Museum, Old Trafford, Science and Industry Museum, Manchester Art Gallery.
- **Luxury on a Budget:**
  - **Accommodation:** Choose trendy budget hotels or boutique guesthouses in neighborhoods like Northern Quarter.
  - **Dining:** Explore affordable Michelin Bib Gourmand restaurants and eclectic food markets.
  - **Cultural Events:** Attend free cultural events and exhibitions at museums and galleries.

# Scams to avoid

**Fake Police Scams:**

Be cautious of individuals posing as police officers. Genuine police will always carry identification, and you have the right to request it.

**Pickpocketing in Crowded Areas:**

Exercise vigilance in crowded tourist spots and public transportation. Keep valuables secure, and be aware of your surroundings.

**ATM Skimming:**

Check ATMs for any unusual devices. Use machines in well-lit, secure areas, and cover the keypad when entering your PIN.

**Unofficial Tour Guides:**

Avoid unsolicited tour guides offering services, especially near popular attractions. Stick to reputable tour companies to ensure a safe and legitimate experience.

**Taxi Scams:**

Use licensed taxis with proper identification. Be wary of unmarked vehicles and agree on fares before starting your journey.

**Card Skimming in Restaurants:**

Be cautious when paying with cards in restaurants. Ensure your card remains visible throughout the transaction to prevent skimming.

**Overcharging in Restaurants:**

Check the menu prices and review the bill for discrepancies. Some establishments may attempt to overcharge unsuspecting tourists.

**Public Wi-Fi Risks:**

Avoid accessing sensitive information on public Wi-Fi networks. Use secure connections or virtual private networks (VPNs) to protect your data.

**Petty Street Crime:**

Stay vigilant against petty crimes like bag snatching or phone theft, especially in crowded areas. Keep belongings secure and maintain awareness.

**Rental Scams:**

Use reputable rental services for accommodations and vehicles. Verify the legitimacy of rental agreements and check online reviews.

# Historical events to help you make sense of the United Kingdom

Understanding the United Kingdom and its cultural traditions involves exploring a rich tapestry of historical events, shaping both its society and traditions. Here are key historical events that provide insights into the UK's cultural and social landscape:

Roman Britain (43–410 AD):

The influence of the Romans during this period left an enduring mark on British culture. Their impact is evident in the infrastructure, language, and governance structures that form the foundation of British society.

Anglo-Saxon Period (410–1066):

With the arrival of the Anglo-Saxons came the establishment of seven Anglo-Saxon kingdoms, laying the groundwork for the English language and contributing significantly to cultural development during this period.

Viking Invasions (8th–11th centuries):

Viking invasions left a lasting imprint on local governance, trade, and language. Today, place names and cultural elements bear witness to the influence of the Vikings.

Norman Conquest (1066):

The Battle of Hastings in 1066 led to Norman rule, shaping medieval England and introducing elements such as feudalism, which had a profound impact on architecture and language.

Magna Carta (1215):

The signing of the Magna Carta in 1215 marked a pivotal moment in the development of constitutional governance. Its principles went on to influence later legal and political developments.

The Hundred Years' War (1337–1453):

The protracted conflict with France during this period had a profound impact on nationalism and triggered social changes that left a lasting mark on English identity.

The Wars of the Roses (1455–1487):

The Wars of the Roses, a series of civil wars between the Houses of York and Lancaster, concluded with the establishment of the Tudor dynasty, marking a transformative period in English history.

Tudor Era (1485–1603):

The Tudor era witnessed the Renaissance, the Reformation, and exploration, contributing to significant cultural and political shifts that laid the groundwork for the modern United Kingdom.

English Civil War (1642–1651):

The conflict between Parliamentarians and Royalists during this period resulted in the temporary establishment of the Commonwealth under Oliver Cromwell.

Glorious Revolution (1688):

The Glorious Revolution solidified constitutional monarchy, limiting the power of the monarchy and establishing parliamentary sovereignty, shaping the political landscape for centuries.

Industrial Revolution (18th–19th centuries):

The Industrial Revolution brought about profound social and economic transformations, including urbanization, technological advancements, and significant societal changes.

Victorian Era (1837–1901):

Queen Victoria's reign saw the expansion of the British Empire, significant societal reforms, and the rise of the middle class, leaving a lasting impact on British society.

World Wars (1914–1918, 1939–1945):

Both World Wars profoundly shaped the national identity of the UK, triggering social reforms and contributing to the decline of the British Empire.

Post-War Period and Welfare State (1945–):

The establishment of the welfare state after World War II aimed to address social inequalities and improve citizens' well-being.

Decolonization (20th century):

The decolonization process marked the end of the British Empire, influencing international relations and migration patterns.

Cultural Revolutions of the 1960s:

Social and cultural changes in the 1960s, including the rise of youth culture and musical movements, had a lasting impact on British society.

European Union Membership (1973–2020):

The UK's membership in the EU and the subsequent Brexit referendum reflect ongoing debates about national identity, sovereignty, and global relationships. The UK continues to navigate the consequences of its withdrawal from the European Union (Brexit), including trade relations, regulatory changes, and the Northern Ireland Protocol.

# Weird and wonderful facts about the UK that most people don't know about

### The Longest Place Name:

Nestled in Wales, the village of Llanfairpwllgwyngyllgogerychwyrndrobwllllantysiliogogogoch proudly boasts one of the world's longest place names. Locals, with a wink to brevity, affectionately abbreviate it to Llanfairpwllgwyngyll.

### A Library for Sheep:

Venture to the Lake District, where a library tailored for ovine literary tastes awaits. Shelves stocked with sheep-friendly books create a unique blend of rural charm and literary appreciation in this woolly haven.

### The Oldest Working Clock:

Within the hallowed halls of Salisbury Cathedral, time takes on a new meaning with the world's oldest working clock, dating back to 1386. Ticking faithfully for over 600 years, it's a testament to the enduring passage of time, especially in the UK.

### Royal Ravens:

Legends guard the Tower of London, where a group of ravens watches over the kingdom. Clipped wings prevent their departure, as folklore warns that if they leave, the kingdom shall fall, and so they enjoy a royal diet in their feathered vigil.

### The Subterranean Mail Train:

Beneath the bustling streets of London lies a hidden world – the Mail Rail. This Victorian underground train network transported mail between sorting offices, showcasing the ingenuity of a bygone era.

### The Town of Sandwich:

Journey to Kent, where the town of Sandwich is more than a delicious coincidence. According to lore, the Earl of Sandwich invented the iconic snack, requesting meat between slices of bread to avoid interrupting his gambling sessions.

**Unicorn on the Royal Coat of Arms:**

Explore the Royal Coat of Arms of the United Kingdom, where a unicorn graces the emblem. In Scottish heraldry, the unicorn symbolizes purity and power, adding a touch of mythical charm to this regal symbol.

**A Museum of Broken Relationships:**

London hosts a Museum of Broken Relationships, where artifacts from failed romances become art. It's a poignant reminder that love's journey, as showcased in these exhibits, isn't always smooth but possesses a unique beauty.

# Checklist

**1-10: Iconic Landmarks and Attractions:**

- O Visit Buckingham Palace.
- O Explore the Tower of London.
- O Marvel at Stonehenge.
- O Walk along the historic streets of Edinburgh.
- O Tour Windsor Castle.
- O Take a photo at Big Ben and the Houses of Parliament.
- O Discover the British Museum.
- O Stroll through Hyde Park.
- O Explore the city walls of York.
- O Visit the Roman Baths in Bath.

**11-20: Cultural and Artistic Highlights:**

- O Attend a West End show in London.
- O Explore the Tate Modern and Tate Britain.
- O Experience the Edinburgh Festival Fringe.
- O Visit the Royal Opera House.
- O Wander through the National Gallery.
- O Attend the Royal Edinburgh Military Tattoo.
- O Discover the Victoria and Albert Museum.
- O Explore the Royal Albert Hall.
- O Visit the Scottish National Gallery.
- O Experience Shakespeare's Globe Theatre.

**21-30: Natural Beauty and Landscapes:**

- O Take a scenic drive through the Lake District.
- O Explore the Giant's Causeway in Northern Ireland.
- O Hike in the Scottish Highlands.
- O Visit the Cliffs of Moher in Ireland.
- O Enjoy the beaches of Cornwall.
- O Discover the Peak District National Park.
- O Cruise on Loch Ness.
- O Walk along the White Cliffs of Dover.
- O Explore the Isle of Skye.
- O Visit the Royal Botanic Garden Edinburgh.

**31-40: Historic and Architectural Wonders:**

- O Tour St. Paul's Cathedral.
- O Explore Canterbury Cathedral.
- O Wander through the historic streets of Cambridge.

o  Visit the Tower Bridge Exhibition.
o  Discover the historic city of Bath.
o  Explore Durham Cathedral and Castle.
o  Visit St. Giles' Cathedral in Edinburgh.
o  Explore Stirling Castle.
o  Wander through Oxford's historic colleges.
o  Visit the Royal Observatory Greenwich.

**41-50: Local Experiences and Culinary Delights:**

o  Experience a traditional afternoon tea.
o  Wander through the streets of Notting Hill.
o  Attend the Changing of the Guard at Buckingham Palace.
o  Explore the vibrant markets of London (e.g., Borough Market).
o  Take a Harry Potter-themed tour in Edinburgh.
o  Experience a traditional pub night.
o  Attend a football match (soccer game).
o  Explore the historic town of Stratford-upon-Avon.
o  Take a scenic train journey (e.g., Jacobite Steam Train).
o  Enjoy traditional fish and chips by the seaside.

# The secret to saving HUGE amounts of money when travelling to UK is...

Your mindset. Money is an emotional topic, if you associate words like cheapskate, Miser (and its £9.50 to go into Charles Dickens London house, oh the Irony) with being thrifty when traveling you are likely to say 'F-it' and spend your money needlessly because you associate pain with saving money. You pay now for an immediate reward. Our brains are prehistoric; they focus on surviving day to day. Travel companies and hotels know this and put trillions into making you believe you will be happier when you spend on their products or services. Our poor brains are up against outdated programming and an onslaught of advertisements bombarding us with the message: spending money on travel equals PLEASURE. To correct this carefully lodged propaganda in your frontal cortex, you need to imagine your future self.

Saving money does not make you a cheapskate. It makes you smart. How do people get rich? They invest their money. They don't go out and earn it; they let their money earn more money. So every time you want to spend money, imagine this: while you travel, your money is working for you, not you for money. While you sleep, the money, you've invested is going up and up. That's a pleasure a pricey entrance fee can't give you. Thinking about putting your money to work for you tricks your brain into believing you are not withholding pleasure from yourself, you are saving your money to invest so you can go to even more amazing places. You are thus turning thrifty travel into a pleasure fueled sport.

When you've got money invested - If you want to splash your cash on a first-class airplane seat - you can. I can't tell you how to invest your money, only that you should. Saving $20 on taxis doesn't seem like much, but over time you could save upwards of $15,000 a year, which is a deposit for a house which you can rent on Airbnb to finance more travel. Your brain making money looks like your brain on cocaine, so tell yourself saving money is making money.

Scientists have proved that imagining your future self is the easiest way to associate pleasure with saving money. You can download FaceApp — which will give you a picture of what you will look like older and grayer, or you can take a deep breath just before spending money and ask yourself if you will regret the purchase later.

The easiest ways to waste money traveling are:

Getting a taxi. The solution to this is to always download the google map before you go. Many taxi drivers will drive you around for 15 minutes when the place you were trying to get to is a 5-minute walk... remember while not getting an overpriced taxi to tell yourself, 'I am saving money to free myself for more travel.'
Spending money on overpriced food when hungry. The solution: carry snacks. A banana and an apple will cost you, in most places, less than a dollar.

Spending on entrance fees to top-rated attractions. If you really want to do it, spend the money happily. If you're conflicted, sleep on it. I don't regret spending $200 on a sky dive over the Great Barrier Reef; I regret going to the top of the shard on a cloudy day in UK for $60. Only you can know, but make sure it's your decision and not the marketing directors at said top-rated attraction.

Telling yourself 'you only have the chance to see/eat/experience it now'. While this might be true, make sure YOU WANT to spend the money. Money spent is money you can't invest, and often you can have the same experience for much less.

You can experience luxurious travel on a small budget, which will trick your brain into thinking you're already a high-roller, which will mean you'll be more likely to act like one and invest your money. Stay in five-star hotels for $5 by booking on the day of your stay on booking.com to enjoy last-minute deals. You can go to fancy restaurants using daily deal sites. Ask your airline about last-minute upgrades to first-class or business. I paid $100 extra on a $179 ticket to Cuba from Germany to be bumped to Business Class. When you ask, it will surprise you what you can get both at hotels and airlines.

Travel, as the saying goes, is the only thing you spend money on that makes you richer. You can easily waste money, making it difficult to enjoy that metaphysical wealth. The biggest money saving secret is to turn bargain hunting into a pleasurable activity, not an annoyance. Budgeting consciously can be fun, don't feel disappointed because you don't spend the $60 to go into an attraction. Feel good because soon that $60 will soon earn money for you. Meaning, you'll have the time and money to enjoy more metaphysical wealth while your bank balance increases.

## Mindset Tips:

- Instead of focusing solely on material luxuries, prioritize experiences. Enjoying a breathtaking view, attending a cultural event, or exploring historical sites can provide a sense of luxury without a hefty price tag.
- Immerse yourself in the local culture by participating in free or low-cost events, festivals, or community activities. This can add a layer of richness to your experience without extravagant spending.
- Be flexible with your travel dates and plans. Spontaneous opportunities, such as last-minute deals or unexpected local events, can provide a taste of luxury without the luxury price tag.
- Research thoroughly before your trip to identify free or low-cost activities and dining options. Planning ahead allows you to make informed decisions and optimize your budget.
- Remember, buses are way cheaper than trains, unless the train is booked in advance. Use public transportation, walk, or consider budget-friendly transportation options. Luxury doesn't always mean extravagant cars; sometimes, the joy is in the journey itself.

So there it is. You can save a small fortune by being strategic with your trip planning. We've arranged everything in the guide to offer the best bang for your buck. Which means we took the view that if it's not an excellent investment for your money, we wouldn't include it. Why would a guide called 'Super Cheap' include lots of overpriced attractions? That said, if you think we've missed something or have unanswered questions, ping me an email: philgtang@gmail.com I'm on central Europe time and usually reply within 8 hours of getting your mail. We like to think of our guide books as evolving organisms helping our readers travel better cheaper. We use reader questions via email to update this book year round so you'll be helping other readers and yourself.

**Don't put your dreams off!**

Time is a currency you never get back and travel is its greatest return on investment. Plus, now you know you can visit UK for a fraction of the price most would have you believe.

# Thank you for reading

Dear **Lovely Reader**,

**If you have found this book useful, please consider writing a quick review on Online Retailers.**

One person from every 1000 readers leaves a review on Online Retailers. It would mean more than you could ever know if you were one of our 1 in 1000 people to take the time to write a brief review.

Thank you so much for reading again and for spending your time and investing your trips future in Super Cheap Insider Guides.

One last note, please don't listen to anyone who says 'Oh no, you can't visit UK on a budget'. Unlike you, they didn't have this book. You can do ANYWHERE on a budget with the right insider advice and planning. Sure, learning to travel to UK on a budget that doesn't compromise on anything or drastically compromise on safety or comfort levels is a skill, but this guide has done the detective work for you. Now it is time for you to put the advice into action.

Phil and the Super Cheap Insider Guides Team

P.S If you need any more super cheap tips we'd love to hear from you e-mail me at philgtang@gmail.com, we have a lot of contacts in every region, so if there's a specific bargain you're hunting we can help you find it.

# Your Next Travel Guide is on me

Simply leave an honest, verified purchase review on Amazon and choose your next guide for free!
Email me a screenshot and the name of the book you want: philgtang@gmail.com

## COUNTRY GUIDES

Super Cheap AUSTRALIA
Super Cheap Austria
Super Cheap BAHAMAS
Super Cheap BARBADOS
Super Cheap BERMUDA
Super Cheap BRAZIL
Super Cheap CANADA
Super Cheap DENMARK
Super Cheap Dominican Republic
Super Cheap FIJI
Super Cheap FINLAND
Super Cheap FRANCE
Super Cheap GRENADA
Super Cheap GERMANY
Super Cheap GREECE
Super Cheap ICELAND
Super Cheap ITALY
Super Cheap IRELAND
Super Cheap JAMAICA
Super Cheap JAPAN
Super Cheap LUXEMBOURG
Super Cheap MALAYSIA
Super Cheap MALDIVES
Super Cheap MEXICO
Super Cheap NETHERLANDS
Super Cheap NEW ZEALAND
Super Cheap NORWAY
Super Cheap Saint Martin/ Sint Maarten
Super Cheap SOUTH KOREA
Super Cheap SPAIN
Super Cheap SWITZERLAND
Super Cheap UAE
Super Cheap UNITED KINGDOM
Super Cheap UNITED STATES

## CITIES / TOWNS

Super Cheap ADELAIDE
Super Cheap ALASKA
Super Cheap AUSTIN
Super Cheap BANFF
Super Cheap BANGKOK

Super Cheap BARCELONA
Super Cheap BELFAST
Super Cheap BERMUDA
Super Cheap BORA BORA
Super Cheap BRITISH VIRGIN ISLANDS
Super Cheap BUDAPEST
Super Cheap Great Barrier Reef
Super Cheap CAMBRIDGE
Super Cheap CANCUN
Super Cheap CHIANG MAI
Super Cheap CHICAGO
Super Cheap Copenhagen
Super Cheap DOHA
Super Cheap DUBAI
Super Cheap DUBLIN
Super Cheap EDINBURGH
Super Cheap GALWAY
Super Cheap Guadeloupe
Super Cheap HELSINKI
Super Cheap LIMA
Super Cheap LISBON
Super Cheap MALAGA
Super Cheap Martinique
Super Cheap Machu Pichu
Super Cheap MIAMI
Super Cheap Milan
Super Cheap Montpellier
Super Cheap NASHVILLE
Super Cheap NAPA
Super Cheap NEW ORLEANS
Super Cheap NEW YORK
Super Cheap PARIS
Super Cheap PRAGUE
Super Cheap SANTORINI
Super Cheap SEATTLE
Super Cheap St. Vincent and the Grenadines
Super Cheap SEYCHELLES
Super Cheap SINGAPORE
Super Cheap ST LUCIA
Super Cheap TORONTO
Super Cheap Turks and Caicos
Super Cheap VANCOUVER
Super Cheap VENICE
Super Cheap VIENNA
Super Cheap YOSEMITE
Super Cheap ZURICH
Super Cheap ZANZIBAR

# Bonus Travel Hacks

I've included these bonus travel hacks to help you plan and enjoy your trip to Great Britain cheaply, joyfully, and smoothly. Perhaps they will even inspire you to start or renew a passion for long-term travel.

# Common pitfalls when it comes to allocating money to <u>your desires</u> while traveling

### Beware of Malleable mental accounting

Let's say you budgeted spending only $30 per day in Great Britain but then you say well if I was at home I'd be spending $30 on food as an everyday purchase so you add another $30 to your budget. Don't fall into that trap as the likelihood is you still have expenses at home even if its just the cost of keeping your freezer going.

### Beware of impulse purchases in Great Britain

Restaurants that you haven't researched and just idle into can sometimes turn out to be great, but more often, they turn out to suck, especially if they are near tourist attractions. Make yourself a travel itinerary including where you'll eat breakfast and lunch. Dinner is always more expensive, so the meal best to enjoy at home or as a takeaway. This book is full of incredible cheap eats. All you have to do is plan to go to them.

### Social media and FOMO (Fear of Missing Out)

'The pull of seeing acquaintances spend money on travel can often be a more powerful motivator to spend more while traveling than seeing an advertisement.' Beware of what you allow to influence you and go back to the question, what's the best money I can spend today?

### Now-or-never sales strategies

One reason tourists are targeted by salespeople is the success of the now-or-never strategy. If you don't spend the money now… your never get the opportunity again. Rarely is this true.

Instead of spending your money on something you might not actually desire, take five minutes. Ask yourself, do I really want this? And return to the answer in five minutes. Your body will either say an absolute yes with a warm, excited feeling or a no with a weak, obscure feeling.

### Unexpected costs

**"Holding on to anger is like grasping a hot coal with the intent of throwing it at someone else; you only hurt yourself." The Buddha.**

One downside to traveling is unexpected costs. When these spring up from airlines, accommodation providers, tours and on and on, they feel like a punch in the gut. During the pandemic my earnings fell to 20% of what they are normally. No one was traveling, no one was buying travel guides. My accountant out of nowhere significantly raised his fee for the year despite the fact there was a lot less money to count. I was so angry I consulted a lawyer who told me you will spend more taking him to court than you will paying his bill. I had to get myself into a good feeling place before I paid his bill, so I googled how to feel good paying someone who has scammed you.

The answer: Write down that you will receive 10 times the amount you are paying from an unexpected source. I did that. Four months later, the accountant wrote to me. He had applied for a COVID subsidy for me and I would receive… you guessed it almost exactly 10 times his fee.

Make of that what you want. I don't wish to get embroiled in a conversation about what many term 'woo-woo', but the result of my writing that I would receive 10 times the amount made me feel much, much better when paying him. And ultimately, that was a gift in itself. So next time some airline or train operator or hotel/ Airbnb sticks you with an unexpected fee, immediately write that you will receive 10 times the amount you are paying from an unexpected source. Rise your vibe and skip the added price of feeling angry.

# Hack your allocations for your Great Britain Trip

**"The best trick for saving is to eliminate the decision to save." Perry Wright of Duke University.**

Put the money you plan to spend in Great Britain on a pre-paid card in the local currency. This cuts out two problems - not knowing how much you've spent and totally avoiding expensive currency conversion fees.

You could even create separate spaces. This much for transportation, this for tours/ entertainment, accommodation and food. We are reluctant to spend money that is pre-assigned to categories or uses.

Write that you want to enjoy a $3,000 trip for $500 to your Great Britain trip. Countless research shows when you put goals in writing, you have a higher chance of following through.

**Spend all the money you want to on buying experiences in Great Britain**

**"Experiences are like good relatives that stay for a while and then leave. Objects are like relatives who move in and stay past their welcome." Daniel Gilbert, psychologist from Harvard University.**

Economic and psychological research shows we are happier buying brief experiences on vacation rather than buying stuff to wear so give yourself freedom to spend on experiences knowing that the value you get back is many many times over.

**Make saving money a game**

There's one day a year where all the thrift shops where me and my family live sell everything there for a $1. My wife and I hold a contest where we take $5 and buy an entire outfit for each other. Whoever's outfit is liked more wins. We also look online to see whose outfit would have cost more to buy new. This year, my wife even snagged me an Armani coat for $1. I liked the coat when she showed it to me, but when I found out it was $500 new; I liked it and wore it a lot more.

**Quadruple your money**

Every-time you want to spend money, imagine it quadrupled. So the $10 you want to spend is actually $40. Now imagine that what you want to buy is four times the price. Do you still want it? If yes, go enjoy. If not, you've just saved yourself money, know you can choose to invest it in a way that quadruples or allocate it to something you really want to give you a greater return.

**Understand what having unlimited amounts of money to spend in Great Britain actually looks like**

Let's look at what it would be like to have unlimited amounts of money to spend on your trip to Great Britain.

## Isolation

You take a private jet to your private Great Britain hotel. There you are lavished with the best food, drink, and entertainment. Spending vast amounts of money on vacation equals being isolated.

If you're on your honeymoon and you want to be alone with your Amore, this is wonderful, but it can be equally wonderful to make new friends. Know this a study 'carried out by Brigham Young University, Utah found that while obesity increased risk of death by 30%, loneliness increased it by half.'

## Comfort

Money can buy you late check outs of five-star hotels and priority boarding on airlines, all of which add up to comfort. But as this book has shown you, saving money in Great Britain doesn't minimize comfort, that's just a lie travel agencies littered with glossy brochures want you to believe.

You can do late-check outs for free with the right credit cards and priority boarding can be purchased with a lot of airlines from $4. If you want to go big with first-class or business, flights offset your own travel costs by renting your own home or you can upgrade at the airport often for a fraction of what you would have paid booking a business flight online.

# MORE TIPS TO FIND CHEAP FLIGHTS

"The use of travelling is to regulate imagination by reality, and instead of thinking how things may be, to see them as they are." Samuel Jackson

If you're working full-time, you can save yourself a lot of money by requesting your time off from work starting in the middle of the week. Tuesdays and Wednesdays are the cheapest days to fly. You can save thousands just by adjusting your time off.

The simplest secret to booking cheap flights is open parameters. Let's say you want to fly from Chicago to Paris. You enter the USA in from and select Great Britain under to. You may find flights from New York City to Paris for $70. Then you just need to find a cheap flight to NYC. Make sure you calculate full costs, including if you need airport accommodation and of course getting to and from airports, **but in nearly every instance open parameters will save you at least half the cost of the flight.**

If you're not sure about where you want to go, use open parameters to show you the cheapest destinations from your city. Start with skyscanner.net they include the low-cost airlines that others like Kayak leave out. Google Flights can also show you cheap destinations. To see these leave the WHERE TO section blank. Open parameters can also show you the cheapest dates to fly. If you're flexible, you can save up to 80% of the flight cost. Always check the weather at your destination before you book. Sometimes a $400 flight will be $20, because it's monsoon season. But hey, if you like the rain, why not?

## ALWAYS USE A PRIVATE BROWSER TO BOOK FLIGHTS

Skyscanner and other sites track your IP address and put prices up and down based on what they determine your strength of conviction to buy. e.g. if you've booked one-way and are looking for the return, these sites will jack the prices up by in most cases 50%. Incognito browsing pays.

**Use a VPN such as Hola to book your flight from your destination**

Install Hola, change your destination to the country you are flying to. The location from which a ticket is booked can affect the price significantly as algorithms consider local buying power.

### Choose the right time to buy your ticket.

Choose the right time to buy your ticket, as purchasing tickets on a Sunday has been proven to be cheaper. If you can only book during the week, try to do it on a Tuesday.

### Mistake fares

Email alerts from individual carriers are where you can find the best 'mistake fares". This is where a computer error has resulted in an airline offering the wrong fare. In my experience, it's best to sign up to individual carriers email lists, but if you ARE lazy Secret Flying puts together a daily roster of mistake fares. Visit https://www.secretflying.com/errorfare/ to see if there're any errors that can benefit you.

### Fly late for cheaper prices

Red-eye flights, the ones that leave later in the day, are typically cheaper and less crowded, so aim to book that flight if possible. You will also get through the airport much quicker at the end of the day. Just make sure there's ground transport available for when you land. You don't want to save $50 on the airfare and spend it on a taxi to your accommodation.

### Use this APP for same day flights

If your plans are flexible, use 'Get The Flight Out' (http://www.gtfoflights.com/) a fare tracker Hopper that shows you same-day deeply discounted flights. This is best for long-haul flights with major carriers. You can often find a British Airways round-trip from JFK Airport to Heathrow for $300. If you booked this in advance, you'd pay at least double.

### Take an empty water bottle with you

Airport prices on food and drinks are sky high. It disgusts me to see some airports charging $10 for a bottle of water. ALWAYS take an empty water bottle with you. It's relatively unknown, but most airports have drinking water fountains past the security check. Just type in your airport name to wateratairports.com to locate the fountain. Then once you've passed security (because they don't allow you to take 100ml or more of liquids) you can freely refill your bottle with water.

### Round-the-World (RTW) Tickets

It is always cheaper to book your flights using a DIY approach. First, you may decide you want to stay longer in one country, and a RTW will charge you a hefty fee for changing your flight. Secondly, it all depends on where and when you travel and as we have discussed, there are many ways to ensure you pay way less than $1,500 for a year of flights. If you're travelling long-haul, the best strategy is to buy a return ticket, say New York, to Bangkok and then take cheap flights or transport around Asia and even to Australia and beyond.

### Cut your costs to and from airports

Don't you hate it when getting to and from the airport is more expensive than your flight! And this is true in so many cities, especially European ones. For some reason, Google often shows the most expensive options. Use Omio to compare the cheapest transport options and save on airport transfer costs.

**Car sharing instead of taxis**

Check if Great Britain has car sharing at the airport. Often they'll be tons of cars parked at the airport that are half the price of taking a taxi into the city. In most instances, you register your driving licence on an app and scan the code on the car to get going.

**Checking Bags**

Sometimes you need to check bags. If you do, put an AirTag inside. That way, you'll be about to see when you land where your bag is. This saves you the nail biting wait at baggage claim. And if worse comes to worst, and you see your bag is actually in another city, you can calmly stroll over to customer services and show them where your bag is.

**Is it cheaper and more convenient to send your bags ahead?**

Before you check your bags, check if it's cheaper to send them ahead of you with sendmybag.com obviously if you're staying in an Airbnb, you'll need to ask the hosts permission or you can time them to arrive the day after you. Hotels are normally very amenable.

# What Credit Card Gives The Best Air Miles?

You can slash the cost of flights just for spending on a piece of plastic.

**LET'S TALK ABOUT DEBT**

Before we go into the best cards for each country, let's first talk about debt. The US system offers the best and biggest rewards. Why? Because they rely on the fact that many people living in the US will not pay their cards in full and the card will earn the bank significant interest payments. Other countries have a very different attitude towards money, debt, and saving than Americans. Thus in Germany and Austria the offerings aren't as favourable as the UK, Great Britain and Australia, where debt culture is more widely embraced. The takeaway here is this: **Only spend on one of these cards when you have set-up an automatic total monthly balance repayment. Don't let banks profit from your lizard brain!**

**The best air-mile credit cards for those living in the UK**

Amex Preferred Rewards Gold comes out top for those living in the UK for 2024.

Here are the benefits:

- 20,000-point bonus on £3,000 spend in first three months. These can be used towards flights with British Airways, Virgin Atlantic, Emirates and Etihad, and often other rewards, such as hotel stays and car hire.
- 1 point per £1 spent
- 1 point = 1 airline point
- Two free visits a year to airport lounges
- No fee in year one, then £140/yr

The downside:

- Fail to repay fully and it's 59.9% rep APR interest, incl fee

You'll need to cancel before the £140/yr fee kicks in year two if you want to avoid it.

**The best air-mile credit cards for those living in Canada**

Aeroplan is the superior rewards program in Canada. The card has a high earn rate for Aeroplan Points, generating 1.5 points per $1 spent on eligible purchases. Look at the specifics of the eligible purchases https://www.aircanada.com/ca/en/aco/home/aeroplan/earn.html. If you're not spending on these things AMEX's Membership Rewards program offers you the best returns in Canada.

**The best air-mile credit cards for those living in Germany**

If you have a German bank account, you can apply for a Lufthansa credit card.

Earn 50,000 award miles if you spend $3,000 in purchases and paying the annual fee, both within the first 90 days.

Earn 2 award miles per $1 spent on ticket purchases directly from Miles & More integrated airline partners.

Earn 1 award mile per $1 spent on all other purchases.

The downsides

the €89 annual fee

Limited to fly with Lufthansa and its partners but you can capitalise on perks like the companion pass and airport lounge vouchers.

You need excellent credit to get this card.

### The best air-mile credit cards for those living in Austria

"In Austria, Miles & More offers you a special credit card. You get miles for each purchase with the credit card. The Miles & More program calculates miles earned based on the distance flown and booking class. For European flights, the booking class is a flat rate. For intercontinental flights, mileage is calculated by multiplying the booking class by the distance flown." They offer a calculator so you can see how many points you could earn: https://www.miles-and-more.com/at/en/earn/airlines/mileage-calculator.html

### The best air-mile credit cards for those living in Spain:

"The American Express card is the best known and oldest to earn miles, thanks to its membership Rewards program. When making payments with this card, points are added, which can then be exchanged for miles from airlines such as Iberia, Air Europa, Emirates or Alitalia." More information is available here: https://www.americanexpress.com/es-es/

### The best air-mile credit cards for those living in Australia

ANZ Rewards Black comes out top for 2024.

180,000 bonus ANZ Reward Points (can get an $800 gift card) and $0 annual fee for the first year with the ANZ Rewards Black
Points Per Spend: 1 Velocity point on purchases of up to $5,000 per statement period and 0.5 Velocity points thereafter.
Annual Fee: $0 in the first year, then $375 after.
Ns no set minimum income required, however, there is a minimum credit limit of $15,000 on this card.

Here are some ways you can hack points onto this card: https://www.pointhacks.com.au/credit-cards/anz-rewards-black-guide/

### The best air-mile credit card solution for those living in the USA with a POOR credit score

The downside to Airline Mile cards is that they require good or excellent credit scores, meaning 690 or higher.

If you have bad credit and want to use credit card air lines you will need to rebuild your credit poor. The Credit One Bank® Platinum Visa® for Rebuilding Credit is a good credit card for people with bad credit who don't want to place a deposit on a secured card. The Credit One Platinum Visa offers a $300 credit limit, rewards, and the potential for credit-limit increases, which in time will help rebuild your score.

**PLEASE don't sign-up for any of these cards if you can't trust yourself to repay it in full monthly. This will only lead to stress for you.**

In the USA, the Chase Sapphire Preferred card offers 60,000 bonus points after spending $4,000 in the first 3 months. Points transfer 1:1 to leading airline and hotel loyalty programs. However, it comes with a $95 annual fee, and after the first year, this fee remains. Additionally, there's a higher minimum spend requirement for bonus points and limited travel redemption options compared to premium cards. It requires a good credit score.

In the UK, the Amex Preferred Rewards Gold card provides a 20,000-point bonus on £3,000 spend in the first 3 months and earns 1 point per £1 spent. Cardholders also receive two free visits per year to airport lounges. While there's no fee in the first year, there's a £140 annual fee afterward. Drawbacks include a high 59.9% representative APR interest rate if the balance isn't repaid in full and limited acceptance compared to Visa/Mastercard. It also requires a good credit score.

For Australians, the ANZ Rewards Black card offers 180,000 bonus ANZ Reward Points and $0 annual fee for the first year. It earns 1 Velocity point on purchases up to $5,000 per statement period and has no set minimum income required. However, after the first year, there's a $375 annual fee, and rewards on purchases over $5,000 per statement period are limited. Moreover, there are limited airline partnerships compared to other cards. It also requires a good credit score.

In Canada, the American Express Gold Rewards Card grants 25,000 Membership Rewards points after spending $1,500 in the first 3 months and a $100 annual travel credit. It offers flexible redemption options including travel, merchandise, and gift cards. Nevertheless, there's a $150 annual fee and limited acceptance compared to Visa/Mastercard. Additionally, it has a higher minimum spend requirement compared to some other cards. It requires a good credit score.

In Germany, the Lufthansa Miles & More Credit Card offers 50,000 award miles upon spending $3,000 within the first 90 days. Cardholders earn 2 award miles per $1 spent on ticket purchases from Miles & More integrated partners. However, it comes with an €89 annual fee and is limited to flights with Lufthansa and its partners. Additionally, it requires excellent credit.

For Austria, the Miles & More Credit Card allows users to earn miles for each purchase and redeem them for flights based on distance flown and booking class. It also offers a mileage calculator for estimating points. However, it's limited to the Miles & More program, and there may be annual fees and other charges. Furthermore, it may have limited acceptance compared to other cards. Similar to Germany, it requires a good credit score.

In Switzerland, the SWISS Miles & More Credit Card allows cardholders to earn miles for every purchase and provides priority boarding and check-in with SWISS. Additionally, it has no foreign transaction fees. Nevertheless, it's also limited to the Miles & More program and may have annual fees and other charges. Furthermore, its acceptance may be limited compared to other cards. Like the other mentioned cards, it requires a good credit score.

# Frequent Flyer Memberships

"Points" and "miles" are often used interchangeably, but they're usually two very different things. Maximise and diversify your rewards by utilising both.

A frequent-flyer program (FFP) is a loyalty program offered by an airline. They are designed to encourage airline customers to fly more to accumulate points (also called miles, kilometres, or segments) which can be redeemed for air travel or other rewards.

You can sign up with any FFP program for free. There are three major airline alliances in the world: Oneworld, SkyTeam and Star Alliance. I am with One World https://www.oneworld.com/members because the points can be accrued and used for most flights.

The best return on your points is to use them for international business or first class flights with lie-flat seats. You would need 3 times more miles compared to an economy flight, but if you paid cash, you'd pay 5 - 10 times more than the cost of the economy flight, so it really pays to use your points only for upgrades. The worst value for your miles is to buy an economy seat or worse, a gift from the airlines gift-shop.

Sign up for a family/household account to pool miles together. If you share a common address, you can claim the miles with most airlines. You can use AwardWallet to keep track of your miles. Remember that they only last for 2 years, so use them before they expire.

Delta Air Lines' SkyMiles program offers no blackout dates for award flights and the ability to earn miles through flights, credit card spending, and partners. However, it has variable award pricing, limited availability of saver-level award seats, and a miles expiration policy.

American Airlines' AAdvantage program boasts an extensive network of routes and partners. Elite status perks include complimentary upgrades, priority boarding, and waived fees. Nevertheless, it has dynamic award pricing, limited availability of saver-level award seats, and some benefits restricted to elite members.

United Airlines' MileagePlus program provides a wide range of redemption options including flights, upgrades, and merchandise. Its Star Alliance membership offers access to a global network. Yet, it has variable award pricing, limited availability of saver-level award seats, and some elite benefits restricted to higher-tier members.

Southwest Airlines' Rapid Rewards program stands out with no blackout dates or seat restrictions on award flights. Additionally, its Companion Pass program allows a designated companion to fly for free (excluding taxes and fees). However, its points value can vary depending on fare class, and it has limited international routes compared to other carriers.

British Airways' Executive Club allows Avios points to be redeemed for flights, upgrades, and partner awards. Tiered membership offers benefits like lounge access and priority check-in. Nonetheless, it has high fuel surcharges on some award flights, a distance-based award chart that may not offer good value for short-haul flights, and limited partner availability.

Emirates' Skywards program offers access to luxury experiences like first-class flights and premium lounges. Its family membership allows pooling of miles for faster rewards. However, it has high fuel surcharges on some award flights, limited availability of premium cabin award seats, and tier-based earning and benefits.

# How to get 70% off a Cruise

An average cruise can set you back $4,000. If you dream of cruising the oceans, but find the pricing too high, look at repositioning cruises. You can save as much as 70% by taking a cruise which takes the boat back to its home port.

These one-way itineraries take place during low cruise seasons when ships have to reposition themselves to locations where there's warmer weather.

To find a repositioning cruise, go to vacationstogo.com/repositioning_cruises.cfm. This simple and often overlooked booking trick is great for avoiding long flights with children and can save you so much money!

It's worth noting we don't have any affiliations with any travel service or provider. The links we suggest are chosen based on our experience of finding the best deals.

Royal Caribbean offers repositioning cruises between continents, such as transatlantic or transpacific voyages. Passengers have the opportunity to explore multiple destinations during one cruise, typically with longer itineraries and more sea days. There's potential for lower fares compared to traditional cruises due to one-way routes. However, availability is limited as repositioning cruises are seasonal and occur during specific times of the year. Additionally, some passengers may prefer shorter, port-intensive itineraries, and it may involve one-way airfare or additional travel arrangements.

Princess Cruises provides repositioning cruises spanning various regions, including Asia, Europe, and the Americas. They offer diverse itineraries with stops in different countries and regions, allowing for more onboard activities and relaxation. There's potential for lower fares compared to regular sailings. However, departure dates and availability are limited as repositioning cruises typically occur during shoulder seasons. Moreover, one-way itineraries may require additional travel arrangements.

Celebrity Cruises offers transatlantic and transpacific repositioning cruises between Europe, the Caribbean, and Alaska. They provide a modern luxury experience with upscale amenities and dining options, along with the opportunity to visit multiple destinations in one trip. However, availability is limited as repositioning cruises are seasonal and occur during specific times of the year. Additionally, higher fares for premium amenities and services may not fit all budgets, and there may be additional costs associated with one-way travel.

Holland America offers transatlantic and transpacific repositioning cruises, including itineraries between Europe, the Caribbean, and Alaska.

# Relaxing at the Airport

The best way to relax at the airport is in a lounge where they provide free food, drinks, comfortable chairs, luxurious amenities (many have showers) and, if you're lucky, a peaceful ambience. If you're there for a longer time, look for Airport Cubicles, sleep pods which charge by the hour.

You can use your FFP Card (Frequent Flyer Memberships) to get into select lounges for free. Check your eligibility before you pay.

If you're travelling a lot, I'd recommend investing in a Priority Pass for the airport.

It includes 850-plus airport lounges around the world. The cost is $99 for the year and $27 per lounge visit or you can pay $399 for the year all inclusive.

If you need a lounge for a one-off day, you can get a Day Pass. Buy it online for a discount, it always works out cheaper than buying at the airport. Use www.LoungePass.com.

Lounges are also great if you're travelling with kids, as they're normally free for kids and will definitely cost you less than snacks for your little ones. The rule is that kids should be seen and not heard, so consider this before taking an overly excited child who wants to run around, or you might be asked to leave even after you've paid.

Priority Pass offers access to a large network of airport lounges worldwide, with various membership levels available. Some plans include free visits, but there's an annual membership fee and an additional fee for guest visits. Moreover, it's limited to participating lounges.

Credit cards provide complimentary lounge access as a card benefit, along with additional travel perks. There's no need for a separate membership, but premium cards often come with high annual fees. Additionally, lounge access is limited to specific lounges and may require minimum spending or qualifications.

Airline status grants lounge access based on frequent flyer status, available to elite members of airline loyalty programs. However, it requires achieving and maintaining elite status and is limited to specific airlines and alliances.

Day passes offer flexibility to purchase access only when needed, with no annual commitment. However, they can be expensive for frequent travelers, and availability may be limited depending on lounge capacity and policies.

Membership programs provide consistent lounge access with annual membership, along with loyalty benefits with the airline. Access to additional perks depends on the program, but there's an annual membership fee and it's limited to lounges operated by the airline or its partners.

Subscription services offer pay-per-visit access with no annual commitment and access to a variety of lounges. However, the per-visit fee may add up for frequent travelers, availability may be limited in some airports, and there may be additional fees for certain features or lounges.

# How to spend money

Bank ATM fees vary from $2.50 per transaction to as high as $5 or more, depending on the ATM and the country. You can completely skip those fees by paying with card and using a card which can hold multiple currencies.

Budget travel hacking begins with a strategy to spend without fees. Your individual strategy depends on the country you legally reside in as to what cards are available. Happily there are some fin-tech solutions which can save you thousands on those pesky ATM withdrawal fees and are widely available globally. Here are a selection of cards you can pre-charge with currency for Great Britain:

### N26

N26 is a 12-year-old digital bank. I have been using them for over 6 years. The key advantage is fee-free card transactions abroad. They have a very elegant app, where you can check your timeline for all transactions listed in real time or manage your in-app security anywhere. The card you receive is a Mastercard so you can use it everywhere. If you lose the card, you don't have to call anyone, just open the app and swipe 'lock card'. It puts your purchases into a graph automatically so you can see what you spend on. You can open an account from abroad entirely online, all you need is your passport and a camera n26.com

### Revolut

Revolut is a multi-currency account that allows you to hold and exchange 29 currencies and spend fee-free abroad. It's a UK based neobank, but accepts customers from all over the world.

### Wise debit card

If you're going to be in one place for a long time, the Wise debit card is like having your travel money on a card – it lets you spend money at the real exchange rate.

### Monzo

**Monzo** is good if your UK based. They offer a fee-free UK account. Fee-free international money transfers and fee-free spending abroad.

### The downside

The cards above are debit cards, meaning you need to have money in those accounts to spend it. This comes with one big downside: safety. Credit card issuers' have "zero liability" meaning you're not liable for unauthorised charges. All the cards listed above do provide cover for unauthorised charges but times vary greatly in how quickly you'd get your money back if it were stolen.

The best option is to check in your country to see which credit cards are the best for travelling and set up monthly payments to repay the whole amount so you don't pay unnecessary interest. In the USA, Schwab regularly ranks at the top for travel credit cards. Credit cards are always the safer option when abroad simply because you get your money back faster if its stolen and if you're renting cars, most will give you free insurance when you book the car rental using the card, saving you money.

### Always withdraw money; never exchange.

Money exchanges, whether they be on the streets or in the airports will NEVER give you a good exchange rate. Do not bring bundles of cash. Instead, withdraw local currency from the ATM as needed and try to use only free ATMs. Many in airports charge you a fee to withdraw cash. Look for bigger ATMs attached to banks to avoid this.

### Recap

- Take cash from local, non-charging ATMs for the best rates.

- Never change at airport exchange desks unless you absolutely have to, then just change just enough to be able get to a bank ATM.

- Bring a spare credit card for emergencies.

- Split cash in various places on your person (pockets, shoes) and in your luggage. It's never sensible to keep your cash or cards all in one place.

- In higher risk areas, use a money belt under your clothes or put $50 in your shoe or bra.


### Revolut
Revolut is a multi-currency account that allows you to hold and exchange 29 currencies and spend fee-free abroad. It's a UK based neobank, but accepts customers from all over the world.

### Wise debit card
If you're going to be in one place for a long time the Wise debit card is like having your travel money on a card – it lets you spend money at the real exchange rate.

### Monzo
**Monzo** is good if your UK based. They offer a fee-free UK account. Fee-free international money transfers and fee-free spending abroad.

### The downside

The cards above are debit cards, meaning you need to have money in those accounts to spend it. This comes with one big downside: safety. Credit card issuers' have "zero liability" meaning you're not liable for unauthorised charges. All of the cards listed above do provide cover for unauthorised charges but times vary greatly in how quickly you'd get your money back if it were stolen.

The best option is to check in your country to see which credit cards are the best for travelling and set up monthly payments to repay the whole amount so you don't pay unnecessary interest. In the USA, Schwab[1] regularly ranks at the top for travel credit cards. Credit cards are always the safer option when abroad simply because you get your money back faster if its stolen and if you're renting cars, most will give you free insurance when you book the car rental using the card, saving you money.

**Always withdraw money; never exchange.**

Money exchanges whether they be on the streets or in the airports will NEVER give you a good exchange rate. Do not bring bundles of cash. Instead withdraw local currency from the ATM as needed and try to use only free ATM's. Many in airports charge you a fee to withdraw cash. Look for bigger ATM's attached to banks to avoid this.

Recap

- Take cash from local, non-charging ATMs for the best rates.
- Never change at airport exchange desks unless you absolutely have to, then just change just enough to be able get to a bank ATM.
- Bring a spare credit card for emergencies.
- Split cash in various places on your person (pockets, shoes) and in your luggage. Its never sensible to keep your cash or cards all in one place.
- In higher risk areas, use a money belt under your clothes or put $50 in your shoe or bra.

---

[1] Charles Schwab High Yield Checking accounts refund every single ATM fee worldwide, require no minimum balance and have no monthly fee.

# How NOT to be ripped off

"One of the great things about travel is that you find out how many good, kind people ther e are."
— Edith Wharton

The quote above may seem ill placed in a chapter entitled how not to be ripped off, but I included it to remind you that the vast majority of people do not want to rip you off. In fact, scammers are normally limited to three situations:

1.  Around heavily visited attractions - these places are targeted purposively due to sheer footfall. Many criminals believe ripping people off is simply a numbers game.

2.  In cities or countries with low-salaries or communist ideologies. If they can't make money in the country, they seek to scam foreigners. If you have travelled to India, Morocco or Cuba you will have observed this phenomenon.

3.  When you are stuck and the person helping you know you have limited options.

Scammers know that most people will avoid confrontation. Don't feel bad about utterly ignoring someone and saying no. Here are six strategies to avoid being ripped off:

1.  **Never ever agree to pay as much as you want. Always decide on a price before.**

Whoever you're dealing with is trained to tell you, they are uninterested in money. This is a trap. If you let people do this they will ask for MUCH MORE money at the end, and because you have used there service, you will feel obliged to pay. This is a conman's trick and nothing more.

**2. Pack light**

You can move faster and easier. If you take heavy luggage, you will end up taking taxis which are comparatively very costly over time.

**3. NEVER use the airport taxi service. Plan to use public transport before you reach the airport.**

**4. Don't buy a sim card from the airport. Buy from the local supermarkets it will cost 50% less.**

**5. Eat at local restaurants serving regional food**

Food defines culture. Exploring all delights available to the palate doesn't need to cost enormous sums.

**6. Ask the locals what something should cost,** and try not to pay over that.

**7. If you find yourself with limited options.** e.g. your taxi dumps you on the side of the road because you refuse to pay more (common in India and parts of South America) don't act desperate and negotiate as if you have other options or you will be extorted.

## 8. Don't blindly rely on social media[2]

Let's say you post in a Facebook group that you want tips for travelling to The Maldives. A lot of the comments you will receive come from guides, hosts and restaurants doing their own promotion. It's estimated that 50% or more of Facebook's current monthly active users are fake. And what's worse, a recent study found Social media platforms leave 95% of reported fake accounts up. These accounts are the digital versions of the men who hang around the Grand Palace in Bangkok telling tourists its closed, to divert you to shops where they will receive a commission for bringing you.

It can also be the case that genuine comments come from people who have totally different interests, beliefs and yes, budgets to yours. Make your experience your own and don't believe every comment you read.

Bottom line: use caution when accepting recommendations on social media and always fact-check with your own research.

### Small tweaks on the road add up to big differences in your bank balance

### Take advantage of other hotel amenities

If you fancy a swim but you're nowhere near the ocean, try the nearest hotel with a pool. As long as you buy a drink, the hotel staff will probably grant you access.

### Fill up your mini bar for free.

Fill up your mini bar for free by storing things from the breakfast bar or grocery shop in your mini bar to give you a greater selection of drinks and food without the hefty price tag.

### Save yourself some ironing

Use the steam from the shower to get rid of wrinkles in clothing. If something is creased, leave it trapped with the steam in the bathroom overnight for even better results.

### See somewhere else for free

Opt for long stopovers, allowing you to experience another city without spending much money.

### Wear your heaviest clothes

On the plane to save weight in your pack, allowing you to bring more with you. Big coats can then be used as pillows to make your flight more comfortable.

### Don't get lost while you're away.

Find where you want to go using Google Maps, then type 'OK Maps' into the search bar to store this information for offline viewing.

---

[2] https://arstechnica.com/tech-policy/2019/12/social-media-platforms-leave-95-of-reported-fake-accounts-up-study-finds/

### Use car renting services

Share Now or Car2Go allow you to hire a car for 2 hours for $25 in a lot of European countries.

### Share Rides

Use sites like blablacar.com to find others who are driving in your direction. It can be 80% cheaper than normal transport. Just check the drivers reviews.

### Use free gym passes

Get a free gym day pass by googling the name of a local gym and free day pass.

### When asked by people providing you a service where you are from..

If there's no price list for the service you are asking for, when asked where you are from, Say you are from a lesser-known poorer country. I normally say Macedonia, and if they don't know where it is, add it's a poor country. If you say UK, USA, the majority of Europe bar the well-known poorer countries taxi drivers, tour operators etc will match the price to what they think you pay at home.

### Set-up a New Uber/ other car hailing app account for discounts

By googling you can find offers with $50 free for new users in most cities for Uber/ Lyft/ Bolt and alike. Just set up a new gmail.com email account to take advantage.

### Where and How to Make Friends

"People don't take trips, trips take people." – John Steinbeck

### Become popular at the airport

Want to become popular at the airport? Pack a power bar with multiple outlets and just see how many friends you can make. It's amazing how many people forget their chargers, or who packed them in the luggage that they checked in.

### Stay in Hostels

First of all, Hostels don't have to be shared dorms, and they cater to a much wider demographic than is assumed. Hostels are a better environment for meeting people than hotels, and more importantly, they tended to open up excursion opportunities that further opened up that opportunity.

### Or take up a hobby

If hostels are a definite no-no for you; find an interest. Take up a hobby where you will meet people. I've dived for years and the nature of diving is you're always paired up with a dive buddy. I met a lot of interesting people that way.

# Small tweaks on the road add up to big differences in your bank balance

**Take advantage of other hotel's amenities**

If you fancy a swim but you're nowhere near the ocean, try the nearest hotel with a pool. As long as you buy a drink, the hotel staff will likely grant you access.

**Fill up your mini bar for free.**

Fill up your mini bar for free by storing things from the breakfast bar or grocery shop in your mini bar to give you a greater selection of drinks and food without the hefty price tag.

**Save yourself some ironing**

Use the steam from the shower to get rid of wrinkles in clothing. If something is creased, leave it trapped with the steam in the bathroom overnight for even better results.

**See somewhere else for free**

Opt for long stopovers, allowing you to experience another city without spending much money.

**Wear your heaviest clothes**

on the plane to save weight in your pack, allowing you to bring more with you. Big coats can then be used as pillows to make your flight more comfortable.

**Don't get lost while you're away.**

Find where you want to go using Google Maps, then type 'OK Maps' into the search bar to store this information for offline viewing.

**Use car renting services**

Share Now or Car2Go allow you to hire a car for 2 hours for $25 in a lot of Europe.

**Share Rides**

Use sites like blablacar.com to find others who are driving in your direction. It can be 80% cheaper than normal transport. Just check the drivers reviews.

**Use free gym passes**

Get a free gym day pass by googling the name of a local gym and free day pass.

**When asked by people providing you a service where you are from..**

If there's no price list for the service you are asking for, when asked where you are from, Say you are from a lesser-known poorer country. I normally say Macedonia, and if they don't know where it is, add it's a poor country. If you say UK, USA, the majority of Europe bar the well-known poorer countries taxi drivers, tour operators etc will match the price to what they think you pay at home.

**Set-up a New Uber/ other car hailing app account for discounts**

By googling you can find offers with $50 free for new users in most cities for Uber/ Lyft/ Bolt and alike. Just set up a new gmail.com email account to take advantage.

# Where and How to Make Friends

"People don't take trips, trips take people." – John Steinbeck

**Become popular at the airport**

Want to become popular at the airport? Pack a power bar with multiple outlets and just see how many friends you can make. It's amazing how many people forget their chargers, or who packed them in the luggage that they checked in.

**Stay in Hostels**

First of all, Hostels don't have to be shared dorms, and they cater to a much wider demographic than is assumed. Hostels are a better environment for meeting people than hotels, and more importantly they tended to open up excursion opportunities that further opened up that opportunity.

**Or take up a hobby**

If hostels are a definite no-no for you; find an interest. Take up a hobby where you will meet people. I've dived for years and the nature of diving is you're always paired up with a dive buddy. I met a lot of interesting people that way.

# When unpleasantries come your way...

We all have our good and bad days travelling, and on a bad day you can feel like just taking a flight home. Here are some ways to overcome common travel problems:

**Anxiety when flying**

It has been over 40 years since a plane has been brought down by turbulence. Repeat that number to yourself: 40 years! Planes are built to withstand lighting strikes, extreme storms and ultimately can adjust course to get out of their way. Landing and take-off are when the most accidents happen, but you have statistically three times the chance of winning a huge jackpot lottery, then you do of dying in a plane crash.

If you feel afraid on the flight, focus on your breathing saying the word 'smooth' over and over until the flight is smooth. Always check the airline safety record on airlinerating.com I was surprised to learn Ryanair and Easyjet as much less safe than Wizz Air according to those ratings because they sell similarly priced flights. If there is extreme turbulence, I feel much better knowing I'm in a 7 star safety plane.

Supplements can really help relieve the symptoms of anxiety. Here are the best. I've taken all of these and never have problems, but please consult a medical doctor if you are on any other medications.

Supplement: Magnesium Glycinate

Benefits: Tons of clinical data say it helps relax muscles and promote calmness.

Cons: May cause gastrointestinal discomfort in some individuals.

Supplement: CBD oil (Cannabidiol)

Benefits: May help reduce anxiety and promote relaxation.

Cons: Legality and regulations may vary by region.

Supplement: Valerian Root

Benefits: Herbal remedy for anxiety and sleep.

Cons: May cause drowsiness and dizziness.

Supplement: Chamomile
Benefits: Herbal tea with calming properties.
Cons: May cause allergic reactions in some individuals.

**Wanting to sleep instead of seeing new places**

This is a common problem. Just relax, there's little point doing fun things when you feel tired. Factor in jet-lag to your travel plans. When you're rested and alert you'll enjoy your new temporary home much more. Many people hate the first week of a long-trip because of jet-lag and often blame this on their first destination, but its rarely true. Ask travellers who 'hate' a particular place and you will see that very often they either had jet-lag or an unpleasant journey there.

**Going over budget**

Come back from a trip to a monster credit card bill? Hopefully, this guide has prevented you from returning to an unwanted bill. Of course, there are costs that can creep up and this is a reminder about how to prevent them making their way on to your credit card bill:

- To and from the airport. Solution: leave adequate time and take the cheapest method - book before.

- Baggage. Solution: take hand luggage and post things you might need to yourself.

- Eating out. Solution: go to cheap eats places and suggest those to friends.

- Parking. Solution: use apps to find free parking

- Tipping. Solution Leave a modest tip and tell the server you will write them a nice review.

- Souvenirs. Solution: fridge magnets only.

- Giving to the poor. (This one still gets me, but if you're giving away $10 a day - it adds up) Solution: volunteer your time instead and recognise that in tourist destinations many beggars are run by organised crime gangs.

**Price v Comfort**

I love traveling. I don't love struggling. I like decent accommodation, being able to eat properly and see places and enjoy. I am never in the mood for low-cost airlines or crappy transfers, so here's what I do to save money.

- Avoid organised tours unless you are going to a place where safety is a real issue. They are expensive and constrain your wanderlust to typical things. I only recommend them in Algeria, Iran and Papua New Guinea - where language and gender views pose serious problems all cured by a reputable tour organiser.

- Eat what the locals do.

- Cook in your Airbnb/ hostel where restaurants are expensive.

- Shop at local markets.

- Spend time choosing your flight, and check the operator on arilineratings.com

- Mix up hostels and Airbnbs. Hostels for meeting people, Airbnb for relaxing and feeling 'at home'.

## Eat Hot Meals While You're Exploring

This is one hack that saves my family thousands a year. Using a thermos allows you to eat hot food while enjoying the sights. Here's a guide on how to do it effectively along with some recipes:

- **Choose the Right Thermos**: Look for thermoses with double-wall insulation and a wide mouth for easy filling and cleaning.
- **Preheat the Thermos**: Fill the thermos with boiling water and let it sit for a few minutes before pouring out the water and adding your hot food. This will help to maintain the temperature of your meal for longer.
- **Choose the right food**: soups, stews, pasta dishes, or even oatmeal for breakfast. Anything crispy will go soggy in the thermos.

Now, here are some food ideas that work well for packing in a thermos:

- **Hotdogs:** Just cook the dogs, pack buns and ketchup etc and you have a meal for four or more. This is great at outdoor markets with kids and can save you $20 + a day.
- **Chicken Congee:** A chicken porridge.
- **Vegetable Soup**: A hearty vegetable soup with beans or lentils is a satisfying and nutritious option. Make a big batch at home and portion it into the thermos for a warm and comforting meal on the go.
- **Chili**: Cook up a batch of your favorite chili recipe and pack it in the thermos. It's flavorful, filling, and perfect for chilly days.
- **Pasta with Tomato Sauce**: Cook your favorite pasta and toss it with a rich tomato sauce. This dish reheats well and tastes delicious straight from the thermos.
- **Curry**: Prepare a flavorful curry with vegetables, tofu, chicken, or meat of your choice. Serve it with rice or naan bread for a complete meal.
- **Oatmeal**: For breakfast on the go, make a batch of oatmeal with your favorite toppings such as nuts, fruits, and honey. It will stay warm and keep you full until lunchtime.

### Not knowing where free toilets are

Use Toilet Finder - https://play.google.com/store/apps/details?id=com.bto.toilet&hl=en

### Your Airbnb is awful

Airbnb customer service is notoriously bad. Help yourself out. Try to sort things out with the host, but if you can't, take photos of everything e.g bed, bathroom, mess, doors, contact them within 24 hours. Tell them you had to leave and pay for new accommodation. Ask politely for a full refund including booking fees. With photographic evidence and your new accommodation receipt, they can't refuse.

### The airline loses your bag

Go to the Luggage desk before leaving the airport and report the bag missing. Hopefully you've headed the advice to put an AirTag in your checked bag and you can show them where to find your bag. Most airlines will give you an overnight bag, ask where you're staying and return the bag to you within three days. It's extremely rare for Airlines to lose your bag due to technological innovation, but if that happens you should submit an insurance claim after the three days is up, including receipts for everything you had to buy in the interim.

### Your travel companion lets you down

Whether it's a breakup or a friend cancelling, it sucks and can ramp up costs. The easiest solution to finding a new travel companion is to go to a well-reviewed hostel and find someone you want to travel with. You should spend at least three days getting to know this person before you suggest travelling together. Finding someone in person is always better than finding someone online, because you can get a better idea of whether you will have a smooth journey together. Travel can make or break friendships.

### Culture shock

I had one of the strongest culture shocks while spending 6 months in Japan. It was overwhelming how much I had to prepare when I went outside of the door (googling words and sentences what to use, where to go, which station and train line to use, what is this food called in Japanese and how does its look etc.). I was so tired constantly but in the end I just let go and went with my extremely bad Japanese. If you feel culture shocked its because your brain is referencing your surroundings to what you know. Stop comparing, have Google translate downloaded and relax.

### Your Car rental insurance is crazy expensive

I always use carrentals.com and book with a credit card. Most credit cards will give you free insurance for the car, so you don't need to pay the extra. Some unsavoury companies will bump the price up when you arrive. Ask to speak to a manager. If this doesn't resolve, it google "consumer ombudsman for NAME OF COUNTRY." and seek an immediate full refund on the balance difference you paid. It is illegal in most countries to alter the price of a rental car when the person arrives to pickup a pre-arranged car.

### A note on Car Rental Insurance

Always always always rent a car with a credit card that has rental vehicle coverage built into the card and is automatically applied when you rent a car. Then there's no need to buy additional rental insurance (check with your card on the coverage they protect some exclude collision coverage). Do yourself a favour when you step up to the desk to rent the car tell the agent you're already covered and won't be buying anything today. They work on commission and you'll save time and your patience avoiding the upselling.

### You're sick

First off ALWAYS, purchase travel insurance. Including emergency transport up to $500k even to back home, which is usually less than $10 additional. I use https://www.comparethemarket.com/travel-insurance/ to find the best days. If I am sick I normally check into a hotel with room service and ride it out.

**Make a Medication Travel Kit**

Take travel sized medications with you:

- Antidiarrheal medication (for example, bismuth subsalicylate, loperamide)

- Medicine for pain or fever (such as acetaminophen, aspirin, or ibuprofen)

- Throat Lozenges

**Save yourself from most travel related hassles**

- Do not make jokes with immigration and customs staff. A misunderstanding can lead to HUGE fines.

- Book the most direct flight you can find nonstop if possible.

- Carry a US$50 bill for emergency cash. I have entered a country and all ATM and credit card systems were down. US$ can be exchanged nearly anywhere in the world and is useful in extreme situations, but where possible don't exchange, as you will lose money.

- Check, and recheck, required visas and such BEFORE the day of your trip. Some countries, for instance, require a ticket out of the country in order to enter. Others, like the US and Australia, require electronic authorisation in advance.

- Airport security is asinine and inconsistent around the world. Keep this in mind when connecting flights. Always leave at least 2 hours for international connections or international to domestic. In Stansted for example, they force you to buy one of their plastic bags, and remove your liquids from your own plastic bag…. just to make money from you. And this adds to the time it will take to get through security, so lines are long.

- Wiki travel is perfect to use for a lay of the land.

- Expensive luggage rarely lasts longer than cheap luggage, in my experience. Fancy leather bags are toast with air travel.

**Food**

- When it comes to food, eat in local restaurants, not tourist-geared joints. Any place with the menu in three or more languages is going to be overpriced.

- Take a spork - a knife, spoon and fork all in one.

**Water Bottle**

Take a water bottle with a filter. We love these ones from Water to Go.

Empty it before airport security and separate the bottle and filter as some airport people will try and claim it has liquids…

**Bug Sprays**

If you're heading somewhere tropical spray your clothes with Permethrin before you travel.  It lasts 40 washes and saves space in your bag. A 'Bite Away' zapper can be used after the bite to totally erase it. It cuts down on the itching and erases the bite from your skin.

**Order free mini's**

Don't buy those expensive travel sized toiletries, order travel sized freebies online. This gives you the opportunity to try brands you've never used before, and who knows, you might even find your new favourite soap.

**Take a waterproof bag**

If you're travelling alone you can swim without worrying about your phone, wallet and passport laying on the beach.

You can also use it as a source of entertainment on those ultra budget flights.

**Make a private entertainment centre anywhere**

Always take an eye-mask, earplugs, a scarf and a kindle reader - so you can sleep and entertain yourself anywhere!

**The best Travel Gadgets**

**The door alarm**

If you're nervous and staying in private rooms or airbnbs take a door alarm. For those times when you just don't feel safe, it can help you fall asleep. You can get tiny ones for less than $10 from Online Retailers: https://www.Online Retailers.com/Travel-door-alarm/s?k=Travel+door+alarm

**Smart Blanket**

Online Retailers sells a 6 in 1 heating blanket that is very useful for cold plane or bus trips. Its great if you have poor circulation as it becomes a detachable Foot Warmer: Online Retailers http://amzn.to/2hTYIOP I paid $49.00.

**The coat that becomes a tent**

https://www.adiff.com/products/tent-jacket. This is great if you're going to be doing a lot of camping.

**Clever Tank Top with Secret Pockets**

Keep your valuables safe in this top. Perfect for all climates. https://www.Online Retailers.com/Clever-Travel-Companion-Unisex-secret/dp/B00O94PXLE on Online Retailers for $39.90

**Optical Camera Lens for Smartphones and Tablets**

Leave your bulky camera at home. Turn your device into a high-performance camera. Buy on Online Retailers for $9.95

**Travel-sized Wireless Router with USB Media Storage**

Convert any wired network to a wireless network. Buy on Online Retailers for $17.99

**Buy a Scrubba Bag to wash your clothes on the go**

Or a cheaper imitable. You can wash your clothes on the go.

# Hacks for Families

### Rent an Airbnb apartment so you can cook

Apartments are much better for families, as you have all the amenities you'd have at home. They are normally cheaper per person too. We are the first travel guide publisher to include Airbnb's in our recommendations if you think any of these need updating you can email me at philgtang@gmail.com

### Shop at local markets

Eat seasonal products and local products. Get closer to the local market and observe the prices and the offer. What you can find more easily, will be the cheapest.

### Take Free Tours

Download free podcast tours of the destination you are visiting. The podcast will tell you where to start, where to go, and what to look for. Often you can find multiple podcast tours of the same place. Listen to all of them if you like, each one will tell you a little something new.

### Pack Extra Ear Phones

If you go on a museum tour, they often have audio guides. Instead of having to rent one for each person, take some extra earphones. Most audio tour devices have a place to plug in a second set.

### Buy Souvenirs Ahead of Time

If you are buying souvenirs somewhere touristy, you are paying a premium price. By ordering the same exact products online, you can save a lot of money.

### Use Cheap Transportation

Do as the locals do, including weekly passes.

### Carry Reusable Water Bottles

Spending money on water and other beverages can quickly add up. Instead of paying for drinks, take some refillable water bottles.

### Combine Attractions

Many major cities offer ticket bundles where one price gets you into 5 or 6 popular attractions. You will need to plan ahead of time to decide what things you plan to do on vacation and see if they are selling these activities together.

### Pack Snacks

Granola bars, apples, baby carrots, bananas, cheese crackers, juice boxes, pretzels, fruit snacks, apple sauce, grapes, and veggie chips.

**Stick to Carry-On Bags**

Do not pay to check a large bag. Even a small child can pull a carry-on.

**Visit free art galleries and museums**

Just google the name + free days.

**Eat Street Food**

There's a lot of unnecessary fear around this. You can watch the food prepared. Go for the stands that have a steady queue.

**Travel Gadgets for Families**

**Dropcam**

Are what-if scenarios playing out in your head? Then you need Dropcam.

'Dropcam HD Internet Wi-Fi Video Monitoring Cameras help you watch what you love from anywhere. In less than a minute, you'll have it setup and securely streaming video to you over your home Wi-Fi. Watch what you love while away with Dropcam HD.'

Approximate Price: $139

**Kelty-Child-Carrier**

Voted as one of the best hiking essentials if you're traveling with kids and can carry a child up to 18kg.

**Jetkids Bedbox**

No more giving up your own personal space on the plane with this suitcase that becomes a bed.

# How to Believe Something You Don't Believe

"Our deepest fear is not that we are inadequate. Our deepest fear is that we are powerful beyond measure." Marianne Williamson.

To embark on a luxurious trip to Great Britain on a budget requires more than just the tips in this book and financial planning; it demands a shift in mindset. It require you believing in abundance, in your ability to have anything you really want. While it may seem daunting, especially when faced with harsh realities of the cost of living crisis, etc, **fostering a belief in abundance is truly life-changing.**

The common advice is to "act as if" or "feel as if." I wholeheartedly concur, yet the challenge arises when one's circumstances appear far from prosperous. You're juggling multiple jobs, drowning in debt, and attempting to conjure the feeling of opulence? How is this even possible?

I understand this struggle intimately. I grew up poor in London. I was a kid from a run-down council estate where gang violence sent nine of my closest friends to prison. I went to an average state school. At 19 I went to one of England's elite universities to study Law. Out of 2,000 students, it was just me who didn't come from a background of privilege. Talk about a fish out of water?

I didn't just feel poor; I was. My clothes had holes, I couldn't afford a laptop or even books (even on a scholarship) and don't even get me started on culture and etiquette. It felt like I was playing a game without knowing the rules. I was about to quit and then my dad said this : "You are better than everyone here because you earned you spot. You've weathered losses that would break others." It was a lie, a big fat one, that would hurt me later, but boy, did it get me through law school.

I graduated top of my class, secured a prestigious job, and even launched my own successful business. Yet, despite my newfound wealth and the errant belief that I was "better", I still felt like the kid from the council estate with holes in my shoes.

Life gives you what you believe. I lost most of my money investing in a start-up, and of course, I found a strange comfort in my familiar poverty. **This sparked an introspective journey: How could I believe in abundance and success when my own mind seemed to be comfortable in poverty? How could I believe something I didn't believe?**

First, I recognized that abundance comes in many forms. I replaced 'money' with 'abundance.' Somehow, this just felt way less stressful than the word 'money.' I don't know how it feels for you, but try it out.

I was pretty horrified to release my core belief was I was somehow better off poor but when I finally did, I embarked on the journey to transform my relationship with abundance. Since undertaking this journey in 2016. I've accomplished significant milestones: purchasing a home in Vienna, pursuing my passion for writing travel guides, getting married, having two children, and embracing abundance. **These are the exact steps I took to believe…**

## Affirmations

Affirmations are positive statements that challenge self-sabotaging and negative thoughts. Repeating these affirmations make most people feel like "this is a load of bull". That's why you have to find a belief that is believable and specific to the desired outcome you are going for. Was it true that I was better than everyone at the University because I came from poverty? No. It most definitely wasn't, but believing it gave me the confidence I needed to succeed (and fuelled my ego).

- **Find your believable affirmation**: You could start with "I'm in the process of taking lots of luxury vacations every year". If you add "I'm in the process" it makes it way more believable. In the beginning, I just repeated to myself: 'I can have everything and anything I desire.'
- **Consistency in Writing:** It's crucial to write down affirmations daily, preferably in the morning and before bed, to strengthen the new belief. Merely placing them somewhere isn't enough; research suggests that when we're constantly exposed to something, we tune it out. By physically writing out the affirmations, you engage muscle memory, imprinting them more deeply.

## Visualization

Used widely in sports psychology and personal development for its effectiveness in enhancing performance and fostering belief in one's abilities. "If you go there in the mind, you're go there in the body."

- **Detailed Imagery:** The more detailed your visualization, the more effective it will be. Imagine the sights, sounds, and feelings associated with your desired belief or outcome. You might imagine, the hot sun on your back, the air skirting over your skin in that aircon'ed bar.
- **Know it works**: A study published in Psychosomatic Medicine investigated the effects of pre-surgery visualization on surgical outcomes. Patients who practiced guided imagery and visualization before undergoing surgery experienced shorter hospital stays, fewer postoperative complications, and faster recovery times compared to those who didn't engage in visualization exercises. This research shows that mental rehearsal can positively impact surgical outcomes and recovery processes. If it can affect surgery outcomes, it can affect your vacation!
- **Visualise your rich person problems**: My first job out of university was risk assessment. I was promoted again and again because I could identify the risks of any endeavor within 15 seconds. My brain still works like that. I take my 3-year-old swimming, and before we've even gotten in the pool, I've identified 14 threats and a flat surface to deliver CPR to her… It's a human trait to worry so why not use your ability to worry to your advantage? Imagine all the "problems" you'll have when you're abundant. Your cocktail on a tropical beach might be too cold. You might forget to tax-deduct all the donations you made to charities. You might tip someone really well and find them hugging you desperately. Don't take this too far; you don't want to manifest actual problems, but it definitely redirects your mind to believe you are rich.

**Mo' Money Mo' Problems isn't true**

Contrary to the popular notion that "more money, more problems," recent studies suggest otherwise. Achieving a certain level of financial comfort alleviates many concerns. Research indicates that individuals who feel financially secure tend to experience higher levels of overall life satisfaction and lower levels of stress. This comfort allows for greater flexibility in decision-making, reduces anxiety about meeting basic needs, and provides a sense of stability for the future. While excessive wealth does not necessarily equate to happiness, having enough resources to cover necessities and pursue meaningful experiences significantly enhance your quality of life.

**Behavioral Experiments**

Behavioral experiments involve acting as if you already hold the new belief. This "fake it till you make it" approach can gradually shift your internal beliefs to align with your actions.

- **Dress the Part:** In London we say "If you look good, you feel good." Consider upgrading your look. This doesn't mean splurging on designer brands; it's about being smart and feeling good in what you wear. Think of it as costume design for the movie of your life where you're the wealthy protagonist. Clean, well-fitted, and confident clothes can change your self-perception and how others perceive you.
- **Focus on Abundance:** Redirect your attention towards abundance rather than scarcity. Instead of dwelling on what you lack, consciously focus on the abundance that surrounds you, such as the beauty of nature, the support of loved ones, or the opportunities to travel. When you see a beautiful car, say to yourself, someone else has that beautiful car, I can have one too, thanks for showing me, it's possible.
- **Create an Abundance Journal:** Keep a journal dedicated to recording moments of abundance, gratitude, and success in your life. Regularly write down your achievements, blessings, and things you're thankful for.
- **Steal beliefs**: Once my friend who is never sick said, "No bacteria could ever conquer me," I decided to adopt the same mindset and my stomach issues, especially while traveling in India, disappeared. If you hear someone say "money always comes so easy to me" don't be jealous, just start affirming that for yourself.
- **Help people:** When we give to others of compliments, time, praise, money, it is always returned to us and can let our minds know, we have enough to share.
- **Spend a day being aware of your thoughts:** Identify and challenge any limiting beliefs you have about money, such as "money is hard to come by" or "I'll never be wealthy." Replace these beliefs with thoughts, such as "I am capable of creating wealth" or "I attract abundance into my life effortlessly." The prefrontal cortex produces our thoughts. It is 40% of our entire brain. This region, located at the front of the brain is not producing stone cold facts. It's pulling information from life experience and things around us to generate thoughts.

Trying to believe something you don't yet believe is about making a genuine effort to adopt a new belief, and it feels very challenging at first. Dismissing the importance of financial abundance overlooks the practical realities of navigating the world we live in and the opportunities it presents. Set your intention to believe it is right for you to be abundant and keep looking for evidence that it is true - and gradually you will believe you are entitled to all the abundance life has to offer. You do!

# How I got hooked on luxury on a budget travelling

"We're on holiday" is what my dad used to say, justifying our accumulation of debt that eventually led to losing our home and possessions when I was 11. We transitioned from the suburban tranquility of Hemel Hempstead to a dilapidated council estate in inner-city London, near my dad's new job as a refuge collector, a euphemism for a dustbin man. I watched my dad go through a nervous breakdown while losing touch with all my school friends.

My dad reveled in striding up to hotel lobby desks without a care, repeatedly booking overpriced holidays on credit cards. The reality hit hard—we couldn't afford any of them. Eventually, my dad had no option but to declare bankruptcy. When my mum discovered the extent of our debt, our family unit disintegrated—a succinct, albeit painful, summary of events that steered me towards my life's passion: budget travel without compromising on enjoyment, safety, or comfort.

At 22, I embarked on full-time travel, writing the inaugural Super Cheap Insider guide for friends visiting Norway, a venture I accomplished on less than $250 over a month.. I understand firsthand the suffocating burden of debt and how the flippant notion of "we're on vacation" fails to absolve financial responsibility; in fact, it contradicts the essence of travel—freedom.

Many skeptics deemed my dream of LUXURY budget travel unattainable. I hope this guide proves otherwise, showcasing insider hacks that render budget travel luxurious.

And if my tale of hardship brought you down, I apologize. My dad has since remarried and happily works as a chef at a prestigious hotel in London—the kind he used to take us to!

# A final word...

There's a simple system you can use to think about budget travel. In life, we can choose two of the following: cheap, fast, or quality. So if you want it cheap and fast, you will get lower quality service. Fast-food is the perfect example. The system holds true for purchasing anything while traveling. I always choose cheap and quality, except at times when I am really limited on time. Normally, you can make small tweaks to make this work for you. Ultimately, you must make choices about what's most important to you and heed your heart's desires.

**'Your heart is the most powerful muscle in your body. Do what it says.' Jen Sincero**

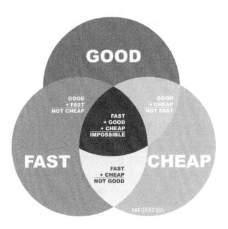

**If you've found this book useful, please select five stars, it would mean genuinely make my day to see I've helped you.**

## Copyright

Published in Great Britain in 202 by Super Cheap Insider Guides LTD.

Copyright © 2023 Super Cheap Insider Guides LTD.

The right of Phil G A Tang to be identified as the Author of the Work has been asserted in accordance with the Copyright, Designs and Patents Act 1988.

All rights reserved.

Made in the USA
Monee, IL
29 September 2024

66809086R00144